Muriel Fitzsimmons
Cortland Fitzsimmons

COOKING
FOR
ABSOLUTE BEGINNERS

Formerly titled

"You Can Cook If You Can Read"

Dover Publications, Inc., New York

Published in Canada by General Publishing Company, Ltd., 30 Lesmill Road, Don Mills, Toronto, Ontario.

Published in the United Kingdom by Constable and Company, Ltd., 10 Orange Street, London WC 2.

This Dover edition, first published in 1976, is an unabridged and unaltered republication of the work originally published by The Viking Press in 1946 under the title *You Can Cook if You Can Read*.

International Standard Book Number: 0-486-23311-1
Library of Congress Catalog Card Number: 75-35405

Manufactured in the United States of America
Dover Publications, Inc.
180 Varick Street
New York, N.Y. 10014

WE DEDICATE THIS BOOK
*to Sally Gallishaw, because she challenged
our statement; to Harold and Jo, who kept us
encouraged; and to the countless number of
good cooks who have, down through the ages,
contributed to the lore of cookery*

CONVERSION TABLES FOR FOREIGN EQUIVALENTS

DRY INGREDIENTS

Ounces		Grams	Grams		Ounces	Pounds		Kilograms	Kilograms		Pounds
1	=	28.35	1	=	0.035	1	=	0.454	1	=	2.205
2		56.70	2		0.07	2		0.91	2		4.41
3		85.05	3		0.11	3		1.36	3		6.61
4		113.40	4		0.14	4		1.81	4		8.82
5		141.75	5		0.18	5		2.27	5		11.02
6		170.10	6		0.21	6		2.72	6		13.23
7		198.45	7		0.25	7		3.18	7		15.43
8		226.80	8		0.28	8		3.63	8		17.64
9		255.15	9		0.32	9		4.08	9		19.84
10		283.50	10		0.35	10		4.54	10		22.05
11		311.85	11		0.39	11		4.99	11		24.26
12		340.20	12		0.42	12		5.44	12		26.46
13		368.55	13		0.46	13		5.90	13		28.67
14		396.90	14		0.49	14		6.35	14		30.87
15		425.25	15		0.53	15		6.81	15		33.08
16		453.60	16		0.57						

LIQUID INGREDIENTS

Liquid Ounces		Milliliters	Milliliters		Liquid Ounces	Quarts		Liters	Liters		Quarts
1	=	29.573	1	=	0.034	1	=	0.946	1	=	1.057
2		59.15	2		0.07	2		1.89	2		2.11
3		88.72	3		0.10	3		2.84	3		3.17
4		118.30	4		0.14	4		3.79	4		4.23
5		147.87	5		0.17	5		4.73	5		5.28
6		177.44	6		0.20	6		5.68	6		6.34
7		207.02	7		0.24	7		6.62	7		7.40
8		236.59	8		0.27	8		7.57	8		8.45
9		266.16	9		0.30	9		8.52	9		9.51
10		295.73	10		0.33	10		9.47	10		10.57

Gallons (American)		Liters	Liters		Gallons (American)
1	=	3.785	1	=	0.264
2		7.57	2		0.53
3		11.36	3		0.79
4		15.14	4		1.06
5		18.93	5		1.32
6		22.71	6		1.59
7		26.50	7		1.85
8		30.28	8		2.11
9		34.07	9		2.38
10		37.86	10		2.74

NOTE

THIS book was written for the beginner who is really interested in learning to cook. We have tried to present the facts and material in a progressive form. We realize that the order of the material does not conform to the usual pattern of presentation in most standard cookbooks. There is, we think, method in our listing of the various foods and their preparation. We do not believe that the inexperienced cook will want to follow a menu schedule at first. We have had fun writing the book and hope that you may derive pleasure and benefit from the use of it.

M & C F

CONTENTS

ix

COOKING
FOR
ABSOLUTE BEGINNERS

CHAPTER I

PREPARING TO BE A COOK

T H E R E is no mystery about cooking. It is true that to prepare
and serve good food properly is an art which satisfies the inner
man and gives pride and pleasure to the cook. But it is not an art
which demands a special talent. It is a skill which you can learn.
All you need to become a good cook is proper education, training,
and good everyday common sense. There is really no such thing
as a natural cook. They all have had to learn. The process may
have been painless and the training absorbed unconsciously; but,
rest assured, every good cook has been exposed to cooking education of some sort, if only days in the kitchen watching mother
make cakes and pies.

It is true that some people take to cooking more readily than
others, but that is true of everything. If you are interested in good
food, if you enjoy the preparation of food, then you can be a good
cook.

This book is not an inclusive cookbook, but a guidebook for
beginners. Its aim is to give you those few simple rules which will
make cooking easy for anyone who wants to learn. It assumes that
you know absolutely nothing about cooking. It gives you all the
terms that may confuse you, explains what they mean as you meet
them in a recipe. The authors' intention is to explain everything
about cooking and the kitchen so that, equipped with a good can
opener, a pair of eyes, common sense, and adequate supplies, you
will be able to prepare as tasty a meal as anybody's mother ever
put before a favorite son.

Before you do any actual cooking, read the book through. Especially familiarize yourself with the section Definitions and Use-

ful Information (page 5). You will want to refer to it now and
again as you practice cooking.

One thing more than any other will contribute to your ease and
comfort in the kitchen. Start immediately to form the habit of
keeping your kitchen clean—that is, cleared—free of debris, rubbish, soiled pots, pans, and dishes. Clean up! Wash up as you
work. It is a matter of habit. Start right now and you won't want
to work any other way.

Decide on a spot in your kitchen which you will use for the
preparation of foods. Keep that spot clear of clutter. Have another
place in the kitchen for soiled dishes and utensils. Don't get into
the habit of throwing everything into the sink. You may want to
use it for something else. Rinse! Stack! Wash up as you work!
There are always a few odd minutes as you cook to take care of the
soiled utensils.

Plan your cooking job. Assemble the materials you are going
to need. Place them in your preparation area to be easily available when you need them. It is a nuisance when your hands are
covered with flour or grease to have to open the refrigerator for an
egg or a cupboard for something you have forgotten. (Your nose
will probably start to itch when your hands are fully occupied, but
we seem to have no control over that situation.) Keep a waste-
basket under your sink for papers and rubbish. If your garbage
can is outside your kitchen, have a plate or bowl handy and put all
refuse material into it until it can be transferred to the can.

Rinse used dishes and utensils and wash them. Do you know
what rinsing means? In case you don't, this is a sample of the way
we plan to educate you.

R I N S E.—To rinse means to clean or clear off all excess starch
(cooked rice or paste), dirt, or grease, by the application of water,
hot or cold. Rinse egg and milk dishes in cold water first.

Washing up and keeping clean as you work takes but a few minutes, keeps your sink free for legitimate uses, and gives your kitchen

a workmanlike appearance. It is a good habit and pays big dividends in satisfaction. All dishes, pots, and pans must be washed eventually, so why not get rid of them as you finish with them? It makes the after-meal chores less distasteful. It is a good habit and looks professional.

DEFINITIONS AND USEFUL INFORMATION

A C I D U L A T E D W A T E R.—This is ordinary water to which vinegar, lemon juice, or some other acid has been added. The acid helps to keep foods white. A tablespoon of acid per quart of water is the usual proportion.

A U G R A T I N.—Au gratin literally means "with bread crumbs." But it has come to be associated with cheese dishes so that now it usually refers to a baked casserole dish in which the food, usually moistened with a cream sauce, is covered with grated cheese or buttered crumbs, or both, and baked or broiled until the top is brown.

B A K E.—To bake means to cook in the oven so that the dish is exposed to heat on all sides. Have the oven at the temperature given in the recipe before putting in the dish you are cooking. When only one dish is being baked, the exact center of the oven is usually the best place.

B A S T E.—To baste means to bathe or moisten the article you are cooking with the fat and juice in which it is being cooked, or sometimes additional liquid is used.

B E A T.—To beat means to stir with a brisk, over-and-under or rotary motion. Doughs and batters can be beaten with a large spoon, preferably perforated. For beating eggs, see E G G S, B E A T- I N G. The principle of beating is to incorporate air into the mixture.

BLEACH A SUGAR BAG.—The printing on the bag is done with dye or ink which is soluble in soap. Soak the bag in cool water, cover well with kitchen soap, and rub the printed surface. Most of the printing will wash out. Soak the bag again in rich suds, wash in warm water, then boil for about 10 minutes.

BOIL.—When a liquid has reached a quick bubbling stage, it is said to be boiling. At sea level water boils at 212°.

To bring to the boil means to heat a liquid until the state of boiling has been reached.

To boil food means to cook in boiling water.

A full rolling boil means that the liquid is boiling so rapidly that the bubbles cannot be smoothed down by stirring with a spoon.

To boil over means that the contents of the pot creep up as the mixture boils until it spills over. Coffee and such starches as beans, rice, macaroni, noodles, etc., cause the water to foam while boiling, hence are most likely to boil over.

To boil dry refers to the pot in which liquid is boiling. When the liquid boils so long that it all evaporates, the pot has boiled dry. When this happens the food in the pot will burn unless caught in time, and the pot is likely to be ruined.

BRAISE.—Braising is a method of cooking in water. It differs from stewing and simmering in that very little water is used, and the food is first seared in hot fat. Use a heavy kettle or a Dutch oven and cover tightly.

BREAD.—To bread means to coat or cover the food with bread crumbs. To make the crumbs stick, the food is dipped first in egg beaten with a little milk, then into fine bread crumbs. Three-fourths cup of crumbs will coat 4 chops, 4 croquettes, or 1 pound of filleted fish. Use 1 egg, 1 tablespoon of milk, and a little seasoning to ¾ cup of crumbs.

BREAD CRUMBS, BUTTERED.—See CRUMBS, BUTTERED.

BREAD CRUMBS, HOW TO MAKE.—Dry stale bread in the oven. When it is completely dry, roll with a rolling pin on a sheet of waxed paper. Pick up the paper, pour the crumbs into a fine sieve, and sift. Use the fine crumbs for breading and the coarse ones which stick in the strainer for soufflés or other dishes in which the crumbs are mixed with the other ingredients.

BROIL.—To broil means to cook with the surface of the food directly exposed to the fire, with no pan between. In gas or electric ovens there is a broiling rack under the heating element upon which the food is laid.

CHOCOLATE, HOW TO MELT.—Put a large piece of waxed paper in the top of a double boiler, then put the chocolate in the paper. Melt over hot water, lift out the paper, use the chocolate— and have no messy pot to clean.

CHOP.—To chop means to cut in very small pieces, either with a knife on a board or in a chopping bowl with a chopper.

CLARIFY.—Such liquids as coffee and clear soups should be sparkling and transparent. To remove all sediment from them, or clarify them, egg white is added to make the solid matter coagulate. For coffee, 1 teaspoon of egg white per cup is mixed with the coffee grounds and a little cold water before the grounds are put in the boiling water. This applies only to boiled coffee.

To clarify soup stock, use the white and crushed shell of 1 egg for 1 quart of stock. Beat the egg white lightly with 2 teaspoons of cold water. Add to the stock and bring to a boil. Boil at least 2 minutes, remove from the fire, and let stand for half an hour. Strain through a double thickness of cheesecloth.

COAT A SPOON.—Custards and like mixtures thickened with egg yolk are said to be done when they "coat a spoon." This means that when you dip a spoon into the mixture then let the liquid run back into the pan, the spoon will not come out clean but will be coated with custard.

C O O K I N G F A T S.—See F A T S, C O O K I N G.

C O R E.—The core of a fruit is the hard center surrounded by seeds as in an apple. To core means to remove the core. It is easiest done with a hollow punch known as a corer.

C R A C K E R   C R U M B S.—Dry soda crackers in the oven to make sure they are crisp, then roll and sift as for B R E A D C R U M B S. Cracker crumbs may be used to coat food before frying. Follow the method under B R E A D.

C R E A M.—To cream, referring to butter or fat, means to work or press with a flat knife or a spoon until it is soft and creamy.

C R O U T O N S.—Croutons are small cubes of stale bread which have been browned with butter. You can butter the bread before cutting in cubes and then brown it under the broiler, or cube the bread, melt butter in a skillet and brown the bread in the butter. This is a good way to use up leftover buttered toast.

C R U M B L E.—To crumble means to break or crush into small pieces with the fingertips.

C R U M B S,   B U T T E R E D.—Buttered crumbs are made by melting fat, preferably butter, in a skillet, then putting crumbs in the hot fat. Mix thoroughly until all the crumbs are covered with fat. The ratio of crumbs to butter is 4 to 1. If the recipe calls for ½ cup of buttered crumbs, use 2 tablespoons of fat and ½ cup of crumbs. In other words, use 4 times as much crumbs as fat.

C U T   I N.—To cut in, said of shortening, means to combine with flour by using 2 knives and actually cutting the fat into the flour until the fat has been reduced to fine particles. A pastry blender will hasten the work.

D A S H.—A dash is an unspecified small amount of liquid. When it is water, a dash means about 2 tablespoonfuls. Sometimes it is used of dry ingredients, in which case it means a pinch.

DEEP-FAT FRYING.—This method of frying, known also as French frying, means to cook in a large kettle full of fat, deep enough to float the food.

DEVILED FOOD.—Deviled food is food finely chopped and highly spiced.

DICE.—To dice means to cut into ¼-inch cubes or smaller.

DRAW.—To draw, referring to poultry, means to cut open and draw out the entrails. All are discarded except the gizzard, liver, and heart.

DREDGE.—To dredge means to cover or coat with a dry material, usually seasoned flour, although some foods are dredged with sugar. An easy way to dredge meat is to put the flour, salt, and pepper in a paper bag, add the meat, and shake vigorously until the pieces of meat are coated.

DRESSED.—Referring to poultry, dressed means with the feathers plucked, but the head, feet, and entrails not yet removed.

DRIPPINGS.—The fats which cook out of beef, veal, pork, lamb, mutton, or poultry are called drippings.

DUST.—To dust means to coat lightly with flour or sugar, as contrasted with dredge, which means to coat thoroughly.

EGGS, BEATING.—Eggs are beaten either whole, meaning yolks and whites together, or yolks and whites separately. Eggs give better volume if they are allowed to warm to room temperature before beating. Use an egg beater.

To beat whole eggs lightly means to beat just until the white and yolk are mixed.

To beat whole eggs well means to beat until the whites and yolks are thoroughly mixed and the mixture is foamy.

To beat egg yolks. Egg yolks are sometimes beaten lightly, but more often "until thick and lemon colored." That means to beat thoroughly until the egg yolks thicken and their color changes to a lighter yellow.

To beat egg whites foamy means to beat only slightly until large bubbles are formed.

To beat egg whites stiff but not dry means to beat until peaks stand up when you remove the beater, but the white mass still glistens with moisture. Be sure there is no speck of yolk in the whites before you start, or the whites will not beat properly. Also, egg whites will not beat if the egg is too fresh—something that won't bother you unless you keep your own chickens.

EGGS, HOW TO OPEN.—*To open a raw egg,* first crack the shell across the center with a sharp rap with the back of a knife or by tapping it on the edge of a skillet or pan. Be gentle but firm when cracking an egg shell, as it is always best not to break the yolk. Once the shell is cracked, hold the egg in the fingers of both hands. Insert both thumbs in the crack and pry the shell apart. Since eggs are slippery and elusive, have something at hand to catch the egg in case it tries to escape. It is wise to break each egg separately into a saucer to see whether it is good. Unfortunately you cannot always judge the quality of an egg by its shell or the price you paid for it. If the white is thick so the yolk stands up firmly above it, the egg is fresh. The staler the egg, the more watery it will be. In a really stale egg the yolk and white will both look runny and will be hard to separate.

To open a soft-boiled egg, crack the shell near one end with a sharp blow of a knife. The egg is easier to handle if you slice off one end above where the yolk is.

EGGS, HOW TO SEPARATE.—Have 2 bowls ready before you start. Crack the egg shell and pry open as described above, but up-end one half of the shell and keep the yolk in that half, letting the white drip over the edge of the shell and into the bowl. Transfer the yolk to the other half, letting the rest of the white slip into the bowl. Continue transferring the yolk from half-shell to half-shell until the yolk is free of white. Put the yolk in the second bowl.

Eggs separate more easily when cold, so when you wish to beat white and yolk separately, do your separating when you take the eggs out of the refrigerator, then let them warm to room temperature before beating.

EGG WHITES, LEFTOVER.—Place in a tightly covered jar just big enough to hold the amount you have, and keep in the refrigerator.

EGG YOLKS, LEFTOVER.—If the yolks are not broken, put them in a deep dish and cover them with cold water, then store in the refrigerator. Or drop them into boiling water and simmer until firm and mealy. Use them for garnishing or for sandwiches. If the yolks are broken, store as for leftover egg whites.

EVAPORATED MILK, WHIPPING.—The main thing is to have the evaporated milk thoroughly chilled before you try to whip it. With an automatic refrigerator your problem is simple —pour the milk into a tray, let it freeze to a heavy mush, then whip. If you do not have an automatic refrigerator, put a can of milk in a kettle, cover with water, and boil for 5 minutes. Chill in the refrigerator and whip. You can do several cans at once and keep them until you need them.

If you want to use whipped evaporated milk to top desserts, it's better to use the gelatin method. Soak ¼ teaspoon of gelatin in 1 tablespoon of cold water. Then scald ½ cup of the milk in the top of a double boiler, add the gelatin, and stir until dissolved. Pour into a bowl, chill, then whip. Fold in sugar and vanilla to taste.

FATS, COOKING.—Cooking fats are those fats suitable for searing or frying. They include butter, margarine, vegetable oils and shortenings, lard, and the drippings from beef, lamb, veal, pork, or fowl. Bacon fat is useful and adds flavor to many foods. Keep it in a container in the refrigerator. Butter browns easily and has to be watched, lest it burn, hence it is not good for foods which have to be cooked at high temperature or for a long time. For frying meats, therefore, and for all French frying, vegetable shortenings or lard are best.

FATS, SHORTENING.—Fats for shortening are butter and margarine, vegetable shortenings, or lard. Meat drippings are not used, with the exception of chicken fat occasionally. Shortening is fat used in baked goods to make them tender.

FLOUR.—To flour nuts and raisins for a cake means to dredge with flour.

FLOUR, BROWNED.—To brown flour, heat it in a hot ungreased skillet over medium heat. Stir often to keep it from burning.

FOLD IN.—To fold in means to incorporate one mixture into another by lifting the bottom one and folding it over the top one. Insert the spoon vertically through the food, lift up the bottom, bring it up, and fold over. Repeat until the two parts are mixed. Do not overdo and do not stir. The point is to keep the air in the two mixtures. Fold in is usually used of egg whites.

FRY.—To fry means to cook in a skillet with a little hot fat. Usually the fat is added; bacon and sausage provide their own fat as they start to cook. Variations in the method of frying are deep-fat, or French frying, and sautéing.

GARLIC, RUB WITH.—To rub with garlic means to peel and bruise a clove of garlic, then, with the garlic held firmly in the fingers, rub it over the surface of the bowl and discard the clove.

GRATE.—To grate means to rub on a grater.

GREASE.—To grease a pan or dish means to rub the inside surface with butter, lard, oil, or other suitable shortening. Don't use a strong-flavored fat for a dish in which a delicate-flavored food is to be cooked.

GRIND OR CHOP STICKY FRUITS.—When you try to chop sticky fruits or put them through a food grinder, you can make things easier for yourself by heating the grinder or the scissors in boiling water until it is thoroughly hot.

HEAPING.—Used of measurements, generally teaspoon or tablespoon, heaping means as much as can be piled on the spoon, usually twice as much as a level spoonful.

HULL.—To hull means to pull the stems off fruits and berries. Hold the berry in your left hand and pull off the stem with your right, or you can buy a little tweezerlike gadget called a huller.

JELLY TEST.—To tell when jelly is done, dip a spoon into the boiling juice and let the juice run off the edge of the spoon, slightly tilted. If the liquid runs off in two separate streams, the jelly is not done. Keep testing until the last few drops run off the spoon in a solid sheet instead of two streams.

Or you can put a little jelly in a saucer and cool it quickly. Be sure to take your kettle off the fire while you wait for the sample to cool. If jelly forms in the saucer, the jelly is ready.

With a candy thermometer the reading for jelly is 220° at sea level, less at higher altitudes.

KNEAD.—To knead dough means to work or press with the hands until it is a smooth, pliable mass. See page 286 for complete directions.

LARD.—To lard means to insert thin slivers of fat salt pork or bacon into dry, solid meat or fish. Slits may be cut with a sharp pointed knife and the slivers inserted. Meat or fish may also be larded by covering with salt pork or bacon.

LEMON JUICE.—Squeeze the lemon with a lemon squeezer and strain through a fine sieve or a piece of cheesecloth. One lemon will yield 3 or 4 tablespoons of juice.

L E V E L.—Used of measurements, level means filled just to the level of the top rim. In measuring dry ingredients, fill the cup or spoon generously and level off with a knife.

M A R I N A T E.—To marinate means to soak in oil and acid. The simplest and easiest way is to soak in good French dressing, either your own or a prepared dressing bought at the market.

M A S H.—To mash means to break down to a mushy consistency by using a round wooden potato masher, a wire one, or if you have neither, a clean warmed milk bottle will do the trick.

M I L K, S C A L D E D.—See S C A L D.

M I N C E.—To mince means to cut into very small pieces. You can mince garlic, chives, celery, slices of onion—in fact all small quantities of foods—with a sharp knife on your cutting board by slicing first and then chopping with your knife. For larger quantities a chopping bowl and chopper are handier.

O N I O N   J U I C E.—If you don't have a special onion squeezer, cut the onion in half and scrape the cut edge with the edge of a spoon or fine grater to extract the juice. Or grate 1 medium onion into a piece of cheesecloth and then squeeze through the cloth. This will yield about 2 tablespoons of onion juice.

O R A N G E   J U I C E.—Squeeze the orange with an orange squeezer. Strain through a fine sieve or a piece of cheesecloth and measure if the juice is to be used in cooking. An average orange will yield about ½ cup of juice.

P A N - B R O I L.—To pan-broil means to cook in a sizzling hot skillet with no added fat except in the case of very lean meats such as chopped beef.

P A R B O I L.—To parboil means to cook partially in boiling water for a specified time. Unless boiling water is specified in the recipe, start in cold water and cook for the period indicated after the water has come to the boil.

P E E L, P A R E.—To peel or to pare means to remove the outer skin of a fruit or vegetable. It is best done with a sharp knife, thus sacrificing as little of the food as possible.

Soft, thin-skinned fruits and vegetables such as apricots, peaches, tomatoes, and green peppers can be peeled more easily if you will plunge them into boiling water for a minute, then immediately into cold water. The skins.will slip off in your fingers. Or hold them in a flame for a second or two with a long-tined fork. The skin will blister and peel off. The second method is more suitable for tomatoes and peppers than for fruit.

P I N C H.—A pinch is used of dry ingredients and means approximately the amount you can pinch between your thumb and index finger. If that method doesn't seem sanitary to you, toss in a few grains. The term pinch was in use long before shakers were invented.

P L U C K.—To pluck, referring to poultry, means to pull out the feathers.

P O A C H.—Poaching is cooking in liquid which is kept just below the boiling point. It is really simmering. Eggs are the food most often poached. Fish also may be poached. Poaching is applied only to foods which cook quickly. Long simmering is called braising or stewing. The liquid for poaching may be water, wine, milk, or stock.

P O T R O A S T.—To pot roast is the same thing as to braise.

P U R É E.—To purée means to press through a coarse sieve or a food mill.

R E N D E R.—See T R Y O U T.

R I C E.—To rice means to put through a ricer, a kind of coarse strainer with a platen to force the food through.

R I N S E.—To rinse means to clean or clear off all excess starch (cooked rice or paste), dirt, or grease, by the application of water, hot or cold. Rinse egg and milk dishes in cold water first.

R O A S T.—To roast means to cook by dry heat, usually in an oven. It is much the same as baking, but roasting is usually used of meats. Roast meats are baked uncovered.

R O U N D E D.—Used of measurements, usually a tablespoon. In measuring dry ingredients, let the tablespoonful remain rounded instead of leveling it off. A rounded tablespoonful is about 2 level tablespoonfuls.

S A U T É.—To sauté means to cook or brown in a pan or skillet, using very little fat. Strictly speaking, sauté means to fry lightly in butter, but we have come to use the word to describe frying lightly in any fat.

S C A L D.—To scald means to pour boiling water over—except when it refers to milk. *To scald milk* means to heat it *slowly* until small beads or bubbles appear around the edge of the pan. It may be done over a low flame, but is safest in a double boiler.

S C A L L O P E D.—A scalloped dish is one cooked in the oven and moistened with milk, white sauce, or other liquid. As a rule it is topped with buttered crumbs.

S C A N T.—Used of measurements, scant means a little less than a full level cupful, spoonful, etc.

S C O R E.—To score means to cut with crossed or parallel lines the surface fat or skin of foods.

S C R A P E.—To scrape, referring to vegetables, means to remove the outer skin by scraping the surface with a sharp knife held perpendicular to the skin.

S E A R.—To sear means to seal with heat. It generally refers to meat, and the principle is that by exposing the outside surface to intense heat, the juices are sealed into the inside so they are not lost during cooking. It is done by placing in a very hot pan for 10 or 15 minutes, by frying in hot fat, and sometimes by plunging into boiling water.

S E A S O N E D   F L O U R.—Flour to which salt and pepper have been added. It is used to dredge meats before frying or roasting. You will season to taste as you gain experience. Try 1 teaspoon of salt per cup of flour to start with.

S E A S O N   T O   T A S T E.—To season to taste means to add as much seasoning—salt and pepper—as you personally like. In case of doubt, season too little rather than too much. It's easier to add more seasoning than to take it away.

S I M M E R.—To simmer means to cook just under the boiling point, so the liquid looks as though it might boil any minute but doesn't. Only an occasional bubble floats to the top.

S K I M.—To remove with a spoon, a flat skimmer, or other methods material which floats to the top of a liquid. Cream, for instance, floats to the top of milk and is skimmed off.

To skim fat from soup, drop a few ice cubes in the soup. The fat will congeal around them. Lift out the cubes, slip off the hardened fat, and return the cubes to the soup until all the fat has been removed.

Or drop a few lettuce leaves into the soup. The leaves will absorb much of the fat. Or lay a piece of blotting paper over the fat on top of the soup and blot up like ink. Or, best of all, let the soup cool, remove the hard crust of fat, and reheat.

S O U R   M I L K.—When you need sour milk and have none on hand, add 2 teaspoons of vinegar or lemon juice to 1 cup of sweet milk and stir over low heat a minute or two until the milk curdles.

S T E A M.—To steam means to cook in the vapor from boiling water, but the food is not immersed in the water. It rests either in a perforated rack just above the level of the water, in the case of vegetables and meats; or in a container surrounded by water, as in the case of steamed puddings. A double boiler is in essence a steamer.

S T E E P.—To steep means to steam or heat in liquid which has been brought to the boil but is not allowed to boil after the article to be steeped is put into it. Tea or herbs are steeped to the color and flavor desired.

S T E W.—To stew means to cook in a small amount of water or liquid. Usually the food is brought to the boil and then allowed to simmer.

A stew is a combination of foods which have been stewed together, usually meat and vegetables.

S T O C K.—Liquid in which meat, fish, poultry, or vegetables has been cooked.

S W E E T E N T O T A S T E.—To sweeten to taste means to add as much sugar or syrup as you prefer. There is no set rule as tastes vary.

T E S T W I T H A F O R K.—When the tines of a fork will pierce the cooking food without resistance, the food is done.

T O A S T.—To toast means to cook or brown lightly over, under, or in front of direct heat.

T O A S T, M E L B A.—Cut stale bread in ¼-inch slices. Put the slices on a cookie sheet and dry slowly in a slow oven (200°). It will take a couple of hours. If you like Melba toast brown, increase the heat for the last 15 minutes. Remember that dry food burns easily.

T O S S A S A L A D.—To toss a salad means to lift the leaves or combination of vegetables from the bottom of the bowl and turn over lightly. It is not a mixing movement. It is a lifting from the bottom and dropping gently back into the bowl. Use a wooden spoon and fork.

TRY OUT OR RENDER.—To try out or render means to cook or fry the fat out of salt pork, bacon, suet, or any other form of uncooked fat. This is done slowly so as not to burn the fat or grease. Some people recommend the top of a double boiler as the safest way to try out.

WARM THROUGH.—To warm through means to heat either by frying, steaming, or in the oven, until the food is hot or warm inside as well as out.

MISCELLANEOUS HINTS

1. Never use a damp towel or a wet dish cloth when handling hot kitchen utensils.

2. If you can't buy an oven broiler you can improvise one by buying a shallow baking pan which will hold a cake cooler. Use the cooler for a rack.

3. A mashed avocado added to three or four cups of prepared or packaged soups gives the soup added flavor.

4. A lid placed over a pan in which eggs are frying will help to cook the yolks lightly or well done without the bother of turning them in the pan.

5. A woman who does her own work will appreciate a powder box and a bottle of hand lotion in her kitchen cabinet for that last-minute refresher before serving dinner.

6. Don't plan a meal which requires two items to be cooked in the oven at different temperatures if both dishes must be ready at the same time.

7. Lamb or mutton may be rubbed with a clove of garlic to take away that "lamby" odor.

8. Two powdered gingersnaps per cup of liquid makes a good thickening for pot roast gravy.

9. To remove the odor of fish from cooking utensils, wash with soapy water and rinse. Then fill the utensil with water, add 2 tablespoons of washing soda, and bring to the boil. Rinse again. Wash again with soap and water. Rinse and air.

10. Rub a piece of dry hard bread or a very dry roll with garlic. Crumble the bread or roll and add to a mixed salad.

11. To flavor stews or creamed sauces and soups with garlic, peel a clove of garlic, pierce it with a toothpick, and cook it in the mixture. The garlic may be easily removed by lifting out by the toothpick.

12. Boiled beets may be peeled or skinned easily by immersing in cold water. Rub the skin with the fingers. It will slough off.

13. Mushrooms, oyster plant, and parsnips will not discolor if dropped into acidulated water immediately after peeling.

14. A little lemon juice sprinkled over freshly cut fruit will generally keep it from discoloring.

15. If you are unfortunate enough to burn or scorch food while cooking, your pots become a problem to clean. Empty the contents from the pot or pan, place it in cold water at once, and allow it to cool in the cold water. If you use enamel pans, allow them to cool somewhat before putting them in cold water. Then add cold water to the pan and let it stand for about an hour. Unless you have done a very severe job of burning your food, the pan will clean up nicely by rubbing the burned area with a dish cloth. Salt and baking soda help in obstinate cases. Watch a once-scorched pan. Food is likely to catch or start burning quicker than in other utensils.

16. To prevent tears while peeling onions, try to breathe through your mouth. A crust of bread held between the teeth will sometimes help. Some people like to peel onions under water. No matter how you do it, keep your hands away from your eyes as much as possible.

17. To separate lettuce leaves. Cut out the hard core of a head of lettuce. Hold the lettuce under the cold water spigot and allow

the water to run into the hole left by the removed core. The water will loosen the leaves and allow them to be separated easily without breaking.

MEASUREMENTS AND EQUIVALENTS

As you explore cooking you will find good recipes and bad. You will come across references to can numbers, ounces, gills, "size of a walnut," "size of an egg," and so forth. Here are some of the measurements you are likely to meet as your cooking progresses, with their more familiar equivalents.

CAN SIZES

All canned goods have an identifying name or number on the can. The net weight also should appear somewhere on the label. The different sizes of cans contain the following number of cups:

Size of Can	Average Weight (Ounces)	Average Cups
½ flat	7	¾
Buffet	8	1
No. 1 flat	9–10	1
Picnic	10	1¼
No. 1 (eastern)	11	1⅓
No. 300	12	1¾
No. 1 tall	15½–16	2
No. 303	15½–16	2
No. 2	20	2½
No. 2½	28	3½
No. 3	33	4
No. 10	106	13
Juice	12	1½
Juice	·46	5¾

EQUIVALENT MEASURES

3 teaspoons	= 1 tablespoon
1 rounded tablespoon	= 2 level tablespoons
4 tablespoons	= ¼ cup
5⅓ tablespoons	= ⅓ cup
16 tablespoons	= 1 cup
1 small teacup	= 6 tablespoons
2 cups	= 1 pint or 1 pound
4 cups	= 1 quart
4 quarts	= 1 gallon
8 quarts	= 1 peck
4 pecks	= 1 bushel
1 pound	= 16 ounces

LIQUID MEASURES

60 drops	= 1 teaspoon
1 tablespoon	= ½ ounce
8 tablespoons	= 1 gill
1 gill	= ¼ pint (½ cup)
1 ounce	= 2 tablespoons
1 wine glass	= 2 ounces (¼ cup)
1 small teacup	= ½ cup

TABLE OF WEIGHTS AND MEASURES

Food	Weight	Measure
Fats and shortenings		
Butter	1 ounce	2 tablespoons
	2 ounces	¼ cup
	¼ pound	½ cup
	1 pound	2 cups
Lard	1 pound	2 cups
Margarine	1 pound	2 cups

Food	Weight	Measure
Vegetable shortenings	1 pound	2⅓ cups
Flour	1 ounce	4 tablespoons
White	1 pound	4 cups
Whole-wheat	1 pound	3½ cups
Cake	1 pound	4½ cups
Sugar	1 ounce	2 tablespoons
Brown	1 pound	2⅔ cups
Confectioners'	1 pound	3½ cups
Granulated	1 pound	2 cups
Powdered	1 pound	2½ cups
Corn meal	5⅓ ounces	1 cup
	1 pound	3 cups
Rice	1 pound	2 cups
Bread crumbs, dry	2 ounces	1 cup
Salt	1⅓ ounces	2 tablespoons
Oatmeal	1 pound	2¾ cups

APPROXIMATE KITCHEN MEASURES

Pinch	= ¹⁄₁₆ teaspoon
Size of walnut	= ½ ounce or 1 tablespoon
Size of egg	= ¼ cup or 2 ounces
1 saltspoon	= ¼ teaspoon
2 teaspoons	= 1 dessert spoon
3 teaspoons	= 1 tablespoon
1 tablespoon	= ½ ounce
1 scant cup	= 1 level cup less 1 tablespoon
1 heaping cup	= 1 level cup plus 3 tablespoons

TABLE OF PROPORTIONS

Bread dough: 1 cup liquid to 3 cups flour
Muffins: 1 cup liquid to 2 cups flour
Batters: 1 cup liquid to 1 cup flour

Baking soda: 1 teaspoon to 1 pint sour milk
1 teaspoon to 1 cup molasses

Salt: ¼ teaspoon to 4 cups custard
½ teaspoon to 4 cups water
¾ teaspoon to 1 cup white sauce

Pepper: ⅛ teaspoon to 1 cup white sauce

MISCELLANEOUS EQUIVALENTS

	Approximate Measure
1 cup shelled almonds or walnuts	¼ pound
4 cups shelled almonds or walnuts	1 pound
1 pound nuts in shell	½ pound shelled
1 cup shelled pecans	⅓ pound
5 cups ground coffee	1 pound
1 cup dry tea leaves	2 ounces
1 square chocolate	1 ounce
1 square chocolate, grated	3 tablespoons
1 ounce chocolate	¼ cup of cocoa
2 cups chopped meat, packed	1 pound
1 cup cleaned currants	6 ounces
1 cup stemmed raisins	6 ounces
2 cups dry beans	1 pound
4 cups dry cocoa	1 pound
¼ pound cheese	¾ cup grated
1 pound salt	2⅜ cups
1 envelope unflavored gelatine	1 tablespoon

CHAPTER II

THE FIRST NECESSITY

THE FIRST necessity for good cooking is adequate heat. You can't cook at all without heat of some kind.

Your heating equipment depends upon your environment. You may do very well in an apartment but find yourself completely baffled when you take a summer cottage and find yourself faced with an oil stove with a detachable oven, or that mystery of mysteries to most city cooks, the wood stove. You may be living in a mountain cabin, a trailer, or on a boat and find yourself forced to cook with gasoline or a spirit stove (alcohol).

No matter what your heating medium is, it supplies the energy to cook your food.

GAS

Gas heat is generally accepted as the quickest heat and is probably the most common. If you are a stranger to a gas stove, have a man come in from the local gas company to test it for you. If it is a modern range, fully equipped with gadgets, the gas man will explain the stove or range to you, light and adjust the pilots. Pilot lights are automatic attachments for burners and ovens which remain lighted at all times. With a pilot you don't have to worry about matches. You simply turn on the oven cock or the burner handles, and the burners will ignite from the pilot.

If you have never met a gas range and the one you have is not a modern wonder, there is no trick about getting heat. You strike a match, hold it over the burner, turn the handle, and presto, you have fire. Don't ever turn on the burners and forget to light them, particularly in the oven. If you should turn on the oven burner and your match goes out before the burner is lighted, turn off the burner until you get another match.

All heat must be controlled by you, and you alone. When the burner is on full force you have your hottest fire. Reduce the flame by turning the cock or handle toward the "shut" or "off" position until you are getting the amount of heat you need.

ELECTRIC RANGES

The modern electric range is quick, efficient, and clean. Most ranges have the knobs or dials well marked to indicate the degrees of heat it is possible to use. All you do to get heat is turn the knob. Don't put your hand on a burner or element to see if it is getting hot. You may get a bad burn. If you are not sure that you have turned the proper burner knob, hold your hand about four inches above the burner. You will be able to feel the heat radiations almost as soon as the knob is turned.

ELECTRIC COOKERS

These are modern contraptions which look like an overgrown roasting pan, which in truth they are. They come equipped with a book of instructions for their operation, which you should follow carefully. They plug into an ordinary light socket.

GAS AND ELECTRIC PLATES

These are small units ranging from one burner to three. With gas you use a tube to a connection in the wall or floor. It is always wise to turn off the gas at the main connection when the plate is not in use. Electric plates plug into light sockets.

OIL STOVES

There are oil ranges with built-in ovens; and there are one-, two-, and three-burner models with detachable ovens. Cooking by oil is likely to be slow as it takes time to reach the maximum heat. In some parts of the country people have converted their old ranges into oil stoves by having heating units installed in the firebox.

Oil burners vary. There are two common types: the long cylinder with a short wick which gives a low blue flame; and the shorter, thicker chimney type which has an inner casing, an asbestos wick, and is so built that the flame creeps up between the inner and outer cylinders until it reaches the cooking surface of the pot or pan.

To light an oil burner, turn on the oil until the wick becomes saturated with the oil. In the wick type of stove there is a spreader which is lifted away from the wick. In the chimney type the chimney is tilted away from the wick when lighting. It takes some time for the flame to circle the wick.

W A R N I N G.—When using all types of oil stoves, do not allow liquids to boil over. It is bad for the burners and dangerous, as it sends a flame several feet into the air. If the flame doesn't start a fire in your kitchen, it will make a mess of your pots and pans. Because of this danger, *never* hang anything over the oil stove to dry.

DETACHABLE OVENS

These ovens are light and are made in varying sizes to fit one, two, and sometimes three burners of gas, electric, or oil flat-top stoves. They are efficient and very useful.

WOOD STOVES

There's nothing comparable to the smell of a thin curl of wood smoke coming from a kitchen chimney, but city cooks see no romance in the smoke of a wood stove because it fills the kitchen instead of the chimney and gets in their eyes, not to mention what it does to their pots and pans.

The first thing to do when approaching a wood stove is to inspect the drafts or dampers. The chimney damper is in the black pipe which connects the stove to the main house chimney. It usually has a bright wirelike handle. When the handle is parallel to the side of the pipe, the damper or draft is open. When the handle is crosswise, the draft is closed.

There is also a little gadget in the stove close to the chimney or pipe outlet which controls the draft from the stove to the pipe. On some stoves the control of this damper is near the pipe outlet and is marked "open" or "closed." On other models the control is at the front of the stove, usually at the right of the two front lids, hidden under the overlap of the stove top. This type is pulled in or out to control the damper. To determine just how these dampers work, take the stove lids off so that you can see the damper itself near the pipe opening. Light a piece of paper and drop it through one of the open lids to get a better view of the damper. Work the gadget so you will know what is what.

As soon as you have solved the mystery of the dampers, you are ready to start a fire. Have your grate or firebox clean. The firebox is the open space under the two end lids. Put in crumpled paper, several sheets of newspaper—enough to start your kindling.

Scatter kindling (thin slivers of wood or twigs) over the paper. Use enough so that they will be able to ignite the slightly larger pieces of wood which you will place over them. Do not overstuff your firebox but put in enough paper to light the kindling, enough kindling to ignite the wood, and enough wood to take care of the heavier pieces which will be added when the fire is burning.

Do not use kerosene, gasoline, or alcohol to start your fire! It is a dangerous thing to do, and unnecessary. When your fire is laid, drop a match onto the crumpled paper, close the lids, be sure the drafts are open, and let it burn. In the door under the firebox you will find a slit draft. Open the slide when starting a fire; close it when the fire is burning well. Empty the ash pan at least once a day. If you have a garden, sprinkle the ashes around your rose bushes— they like it.

When the kindling and light wood have caught and are burning merrily, add your stove wood, heavy pieces. Fill your kettle and put it on so that you'll have hot water when you want it. It sounds warm and friendly as it sings.

Remember this about a wood stove: you must feed it. Get the habit of putting a stick in every once in a while. When your fire is burning briskly you can close the chimney damper and the pipe damper and keep your heat in the stove where you want it.

To reduce cooking heat on a wood or coal stove, close all dampers and pull the utensil away from the firebox area.

COAL STOVES

In a coal stove the preparation of your fire is the same as in the wood stove. When the heavy wood is burning and a bed of wood embers has formed, cover the burning wood with coal. Keep the drafts or dampers open for a little while until the gases from the coal have burned off, then close them to keep the heat in the stove.

GASOLINE OR SPIRIT STOVES

If you are faced with one of these stoves, get in touch with someone who is familiar with the particular stove or follow carefully the instructions given for its proper operation. Do not experiment unless you like to get into trouble. These stoves can be dangerous unless properly handled. Be wise! Be safe!

OVEN HEAT

If your stove is modern and equipped with a heat regulator, have the regulator checked by the utility company at least once a year. Then you have nothing to worry about. If it is not, buy an oven thermometer. If you can't get an oven thermometer you will have to use your judgment. Remember that the heat of your fire controls the temperature of your oven. A very hot fire will give you a very hot oven, and vice versa. Long before modern equipment and oven thermometers, cooks did all right by using white paper and common sense. They simply put a piece of paper in the oven. If it browned immediately, they knew they had a very hot oven. This is the way to use the paper test.

If paper browns in 30 seconds, the oven is Very Hot, 500°–550°.[1]

If paper browns in 2–4 minutes, the oven is Hot, 400°–450°.

If paper browns in 5–8 minutes, the oven is Medium, 350°–400°.

If paper browns after 10 minutes, the oven is Slow, 250°–300°.

OUTDOOR FIRES

You may have to cook on an outdoor fire sometime. If possible, build a hollow square with bricks or stone with the opening facing the general direction of the wind. Cover the top with a large flat stone or a piece of sheet iron if you can get it.

If you can't cover your firebox, put a couple of crotched sticks outside your firebox, planting them firmly in the ground. Put a stick or pole in the crotch and hang your pots or kettle on the stick so they will swing over the fire.

Building an outdoor fire is similar to building a fire in a stove. Start with an adequate amount of dry paper and leaves, thin strips of bark, wood, or twigs, then heavier wood. Best results will be had if you build your fire tepee fashion with twigs and wood laid toward the center.

We mentioned "boiling over" when talking about oil stoves but did not stop to explain the term.

TO BOIL.—When a liquid has reached a quick bubbling stage, it is boiling. At sea level water boils at 212°.

If you live in the mountains or on high plateau country, you should know that with each 1000-foot rise in altitude, because of a decrease in atmospheric pressure, water boils at approximately 2° less. If you live at 2400 feet, then, your water boils at about 207°. At 5000 feet it boils at about 202°. The higher you go, the less heat

[1] All cooking temperatures in this book are given in degrees Fahrenheit.

you have when your water is boiling. Therefore, in high altitudes it is necessary to remember that boiling time is longer.

TO BRING TO THE BOIL means to heat a liquid until the state of boiling has been reached.

TO BOIL FOOD means to cook in boiling water.

FULL ROLLING BOIL. When liquid is boiling so rapidly that its bubbles cannot be smoothed down by stirring with a spoon, the liquid is at full rolling boil.

BOIL OVER. Certain foods, particularly starches such as beans, rice, macaroni, noodles, etc., foam while boiling. The foam creeps up the inside of the pot and finally spills over.

There are ways of preventing food from boiling over. First, do not completely cover with the pot lid. This permits some air to enter the cooking utensil. It can be done by adjusting the lid on a slant or by inserting a spoon. Be wary of the spoon; it will get hot. Second, once the liquid has reached the boiling stage, it will continue to boil on reduced heat. Third, if you will rub the inside, upper surface of pot or pan with cooking oil or shortening, the hazards of boiling over will be greatly reduced. Try to prevent boiling over. It makes a mess of your pots and stove.

BOIL DRY. When the liquid in which food is cooking boils away or evaporates or is absorbed by the article being cooked, it is said to have boiled dry. When this happens, unless caught in time, the food will burn and your pot or pan is likely to be ruined.

To prevent boiling dry, first use an adequate amount of water or liquid and reduce your heat after the water starts to boil. Once the water and the food are boiling, the food will continue to cook on a reduced flame. You gain nothing by using extra heat to keep the pot boiling furiously. Heat enough to maintain the boil is good cooking economy. You will find that certain foods boil dry faster than others, so form the habit of watching your cooking.

If you see that the water or liquid is boiling away, add more.

If you are fortunate enough to have special waterless cooking utensils, follow the instructions which come with them. Do exactly as you are told. The instructions are the result of careful tests made for your benefit. If you use a pressure cooker, be very particular to understand and follow the instructions. Check or have the pressure gauge examined at least once a year. Your local heating company will be glad to test the pressure cooker for you. It is one of the services most of them are glad to render. Recent surveys show that at least 40 per cent of the gauges do become clogged. This is no criticism of the manufacturer; it is directed toward you. The manufacturer gave you a perfect working article which can, after use, become defective. Check it!

CHAPTER III

THE TOOLS OF YOUR TRADE

A GOOD artisan needs good tools. Here is the list of those you should have to make cooking fun. The list may seem long if you are just beginning to cook, but you will find that you will need all the things recommended here and more which will be mentioned later.

APPLE CORER	You may want to bake some apples or stuff a potato.
ANCHOR OPENER	Very handy to pry lids from glass jars. Much better than using the point of one of your good knives.
ASBESTOS PADS	Necessary for oil and gas stoves for some forms of cooking.
BOTTLE OPENER	Many fruit juices come in capped bottles.
BOWL, LARGE MIXING	
BOWLS, 5 OR 6 GLASS OR POTTERY	Buy a nest of five or six—you never seem to have enough—and use them all the time for mixing, beating, and the storing of food.
CAKE TESTER	Usually a wire gadget with a loop end. Grandma probably used a splint out of her broom.
CAKE TURNER	For pancakes, eggs, anything else you want to turn over.

CAN OPENER	Who can cook without one? The wall type is a good investment.
COFFEEPOT OR MAKER	Get the coffee maker which appeals to you. Buy a small pot for 1 or 2 cups. Never try to make a small amount of coffee in a large pot.
COLANDER	For washing and draining cooked or raw foods.
COOKIE SHEETS, 2	Good for cookies, biscuits, etc. Fine to put under a pie or casserole that might possibly boil over and soil your oven.
CORKSCREW	
COVERED CASSEROLE	You will find many uses for this dish. Try several sizes of the French pottery ones.
CUPS, MEASURING, 2 SETS	Buy 2 nests of measuring cups, one for liquids and one for dry ingredients.
CUPS, CUSTARD	Even if you don't like custard, the cups will be useful for individual desserts, shirred eggs, popovers, etc.
DISH CLOTHS	A cook's best friend.
DISHES	We assume you have these. If not, you'd better get some right away.
DOUBLE BOILERS, 1-QUART AND 2-QUART	For cream sauces, slow-cooked cereal, custards, and dishes that should be cooked just under the boiling point. A double boiler comes in 2 sections, the bottom one for the water, the top one for the food. Usu-

DOUBLE BOILERS, *cont.*	ally the water in the bottom section is kept boiling, but a few recipes specify a lower heat.
DOVER EGG BEATER	For eggs, cream, etc.
DUTCH OVEN	Good for pot roasts, stews, fried or smothered chicken, rabbit, etc. Get a fairly large cast-iron one.
EGG TIMER	For soft-boiled eggs.
FLOUR SIFTER	You'll use it eventually. You may want to try biscuits, dumplings, or a cake.
FOLEY FOOD MILL	This will be easier on your hands and arm than an ordinary sieve when you want to pulp some fruit or make a purée.
FOOD GRINDER	
FORKS, 3	1 large fork with a long, heavy set of tines for lifting heavy meats. 1 long handled fork for turning fried foods. 1 smaller fork for light work and testing.
FRYING PANS OR SKILLETS, 3	Buy cast-iron ones with covers to fit. 1 small for one or two eggs, 1 medium, and 1 large which can be used as a griddle for pancakes, etc.
FUNNELS, 2	1 medium for general use. 1 small for filling salt and pepper shakers.

GRATER	For shredding foods for salads. The flat-wire safety type is preferable to the punctured metal varieties. The wire grater is efficient, keeps your fingers and knuckles whole and your food free from gore.
KETTLES, ENAMEL OR ALUMINUM	For stewing. It's nice to have several sizes, 4-quart, 8-quart, and 12-quart.
KNIFE SHARPENER	There are several on the market designed to keep an edge on your blade.
KNIVES, 4	Buy good steel knives—they should be the best obtainable. 2 paring knives. 1 heavy kitchen knife. 1 carving knife.
LADLE OR DIPPER	Very useful for serving soups and broths or dishing up stews.
LEMON SQUEEZER	The round glass cone type is efficient and practical.
MEAT GRINDER (OR FOOD CHOPPER)	Very useful and quite necessary.
MOLDS, 2	1 circular or ring mold for salads and rings. 1 pudding mold.
MUFFIN TINS	These have many uses other than for muffins.
PANS	1 large roasting pan big enough to hold a turkey. 4 cake pans, 2 8-inch and 2 9-inch.

PANS, *cont.*   2 pie pans. Don't think you can't make pastry, you can.
1 square 8- or 10-inch baking pan.
1 bread pan for meat loaf, etc.
1 oven broiler. If they don't have them in stock, buy a cake-cooling rack and a pan that will hold it.

PAPER TOWELS   Good for so many things.

PASTRY BLENDER   This is a most useful gadget. It is much easier and simpler than "cutting in" shortening with two knives.

PASTRY SET   Takes the heartache and horror out of pastry making. It consists of a canvas cloth which is rubbed with flour and used for a rolling surface for pastry and a white stockinet cover for your rolling pin. It is well worth the investment.

POT HOLDERS   Have several. They can be the most elusive things in a kitchen. We think they crawl out of sight when they are most needed.

POTATO MASHER   The round wooden type or the strong bent wire type are good. If you are hard put to it, a milk bottle can be used. We don't advise it except as a necessity, as bottles sometimes crack. If you ever use a milk bottle, heat it with hot water before using it.

RACK, ROASTING   Very useful for all meats and fowl.

RICER   For potatoes and puréed foods.

ROLLING PIN	Fine for crumbling crackers, rolling out pastry. It is no longer considered an implement of domestic warfare.
SAUCEPANS, 3	Buy small, medium, and large pans of enamel, aluminum, or steel, with covers.
SCOOPS	2 small ones will be useful for flour and sugar.
SHEARS, KITCHEN	You'll be amazed how useful kitchen shears can be. Get a pair that will open bottle caps.
SPATULA	You'll find a number of uses for this. Fine for omelets, cakes, etc. It is flexible and gets under things. Many cooks prefer it to the regular cake turner. Both have their uses.
SPOONS, 7	At least 3 mixing or tablespoons. 1 nest of measuring spoons. 1 long-handled wooden spoon. 1 large basting spoon. 1 strainer spoon, either wood or metal.
STORAGE CONTAINERS	Either tin or glass for sugar, flour, coffee, tea, and other things.
STRAINERS, 3	1 large wire strainer for vegetables, rice, etc. 1 small strainer for fruit juices. 1 tea strainer unless you like the leaves in your tea.
TEAKETTLE	For boiling water.

TEAPOT	China or earthenware is best.
TEA TOWELS	Because we must wash and wipe dishes.
TOOTHPICKS	They make excellent small skewers.
WASTEBASKET	
WAXED PAPER	

After you start to cook and find it fun, you will probably become a gadget collector. You will find yourself drawn to hardware and housewares departments. There are hundreds of fascinating kitchen gadgets on the market. Most of them are very good and do the job for which they were designed. The five-and-ten-cent stores do all right by a gadget lover. Let yourself go some day. Gadgets may not make you a better cook, but they may help you present your food in a more attractive manner.

FIRST AID IN THE KITCHEN

Your kitchen is your workshop, and accidents are bound to happen in workshops. Therefore it is wise to have on hand some simple first-aid remedies.

Cuts and burns are the chief kitchen casualties, so keep in your kitchen a tube of vaseline or prepared burn ointment. Boiling water, steam, and hot utensils can give you bad burns. If you burn yourself, apply the vaseline or ointment at once. If you take care of a burn immediately you will save yourself trouble and pain.

These are some of the things you can do to avoid burns:

1. Always have pot holders and use them when you pick up any pan which has been exposed to heat.

2. Never use a damp towel or a wet dish cloth when handling hot utensils. The steam will burn you, perhaps making you drop the pot or pan and you may get a fat burn or scald on your feet or legs.

3. Be careful of hot fat. Water will make it spatter, and so will certain foods. Always use a long-handled fork or spoon when working with it.

4. Remember that metal handles on pots and pans get very hot, so use your holder.

5. Be careful when removing lids from boiling, baking, or roasting foods. The steam generated under the cover can burn you badly. Always lift such lids away from you and on a slant, never toward your face.

6. When pouring hot or boiling foods into a colander or strainer, be careful of the steam.

7. If you have a kettle or pot without a handle and want to empty it of its hot contents, take it by the edges. Use both hands with two pot holders. Never take the pot by one hand and pour. You are likely to burn your hand, drop the pot, spoil the food, and wish you hadn't.

8. Remember that all parts of a hot oven will burn you. Use a holder on all things exposed to oven heat.

If you forget these simple warnings or have an accident, use the vaseline or burn ointment. If you should get a really bad burn over a large area, cover the burned surface to keep the air out and call a doctor immediately.

You will probably cut yourself once in a while. The best of cooks do. Have a disinfectant of some kind handy and keep a box of prepared bandages near by. They are useful, neat, and sanitary.

APPETIZING SERVICE

One hears talk about plain and fancy cooking. All cooking can be both. There is nothing particularly fancy about a lamb chop, peas, and a boiled potato. As a matter of fact, it may be considered very plain cooking. The meal, however, can be served attractively. First, the plates on which lamb is to be served should be hot. A lamb chop on a cold plate with a white ring of solid grease around it is not an appetizing sight. On your hot plate arrange the chop and put the serving of peas on one side of the chop. Place your boiled potato on the other side. A little melted butter and a dash of chopped parsley scattered over the potato will make the plate attractive.

Much good food has been and is being served in unappetizing ways. Don't you do it. Give a little time and thought to the arrangement of your food after it is cooked and you will enjoy the results.

SUPPLIES

This is merely a basic list of supplies to keep on hand. Follow your own inclinations when selecting staple canned goods as a back log or an emergency shelf. With the items we list, you can, if necessary, get a good meal ready with very little trouble. You will need:

BACON	Useful in many dishes.
BAKING POWDER	
BICARBONATE OF SODA or BAKING SODA	Good for so many things: baking, burns, etc.
BOUILLON CUBES	To be used in sauces, gravies, etc., or for a quick cup of something hot.
BREAD	
BUTTER	
CHEESE	Have your favorite for snacks, also grated cheese in a sprinkler container for flavoring many dishes. If you have to prepare lunches, cheese in glass jars is useful.
COCOA	
CHOCOLATE, COOKING OR BAKING	

COFFEE	Buy your favorite brand and have it ground for your particular type of coffee maker.
CORNSTARCH	Used for thickening puddings, sauces, etc.
CREAM OF TARTAR	Buy a small can to be used in baking.
EGGS	Buy Grade A for eating, Grade B for cooking.
FISH, CANNED	For quick meals or supper dishes: Crab Lobster Salmon Shrimp Tuna
FLAVORING EXTRACTS	Buy small bottles at first. Almond Lemon Maple Vanilla
FLOUR	Buy an enriched all-purpose flour.
FRUITS, CANNED	For quick desserts or salads: Applesauce Apricots Fruit salad Peaches, whole or sliced Pears Pineapple, slices, chunks, or crushed Plums
GELATIN	1 each of standard flavors for quick desserts.

GELATIN, *cont.*

1 package of plain, unflavored for salads and molded desserts.
1 package of prepared aspic.

HERBS, DRIED

There are small herb chests on the market which are a good investment. In any case, be sure to have on hand:
Bay leaf
Garlic, a bulb or a few cloves at a time
Parsley, fresh or dehydrated
Sage
Thyme
Fresh herbs are delicious and are easily grown. Chives and parsley and many of the common herbs do well in pots. If you have a garden, grow your own, use them fresh, and dry them for the winter.

LARD

For frying and shortening.

LEMONS

Buy 3 or 4 at a time.

MARGARINE

Can be used as a substitute for butter in recipes.

MEATS, CANNED

There are a number of good canned meats of pork, veal, and beef products. They can be used for the base of a meal, can be served with eggs for breakfast, and make good sandwiches.

MILK

Buy fresh milk by the quart.

MILK, CANNED

Evaporated milk can be whipped when kept very cold and is a substi-

MILK, CANNED, cont.	tute for whipped cream. Sweetened condensed milk can be used for making some very good desserts.
OIL	Olive oil for salads and French dressing. Peanut or other cooking oil for shortening and frying, or for French dressing.
ONIONS	For themselves and for flavoring.
POTATOES	Buy 5 to 10 pounds at a time.
RAISINS	For cakes, puddings, etc.
SOUPS, CANNED	Bouillon Celery Consommé Mushroom Pea Tomato
SOUPS, PACKAGED	In addition to the canned soups, there are now a number of packaged soups, easy to prepare and really excellent. Basically they are good and can be doctored a little if you like to experiment.
SUGAR	It is wise to have on hand: Brown Cubed Granulated Powdered Confectioners'
SEASONINGS	There's more to seasoning than just salt and pepper. We'll talk about it later. You will find the following very useful:

SEASONINGS, *cont.*	Celery salt
	Chile powder
	Curry powder
	Garlic salt
	Kitchen bouquet
	Mustard, both the dry English and the prepared
	Onion salt
	Pepper
	Poultry seasoning
	Salt, table
	Worcestershire sauce
SPICES	Allspice
	Cinnamon
	Cloves, whole and powdered
	Ginger
	Mace
	Nutmeg
TEA	You know the brand or kind you like.
TOMATO SAUCE	Adds zest to certain dishes.
VEGETABLES, CANNED	Beets
	Baked Beans
	Carrots
	Corn
	Peas
	String beans
	Tomatoes
VEGETABLE SHORTENING	Buy any good brand.
VINEGAR, CIDER AND WINE	Pint or quart bottle to give a zip to salads.

CHAPTER IV

LET'S COOK A BREAKFAST

T H E R E are aromas even more tantalizing than the smell of wood smoke—for instance the aroma of coffee and breakfast bacon. But first comes the breakfast fruit.

FRESH FRUITS

Fresh fruits are seasonal, you know, and the best fruit is the one which is in season. Be gentle in all your handling of fruits—they are fragile. All fruits and berries should be washed before being used to remove dirt and grit, of course, and also any harmful spray which may have been used on them. Store fruits in a cool, dry place, not the refrigerator, and spread them out so they do not touch. Never pile soft fruits or berries. Chill fruits in the refrigerator only just before serving—except bananas, which should never be chilled. Apples and pears and other fruits which turn dark when cut and exposed to air may be dipped in lemon, orange, grapefruit, or pineapple juice to prevent discoloration.

APRICOTS AND PEACHES

Apricots and peaches are usually served peeled, with sugar or cream and sugar.

T O P E E L means to remove the outer skin of a fruit or vegetable. It is best done with a sharp knife, thus sacrificing as little of the food as possible.

To peel apricots and peaches more easily, plunge them in boiling water for half a minute, then immediately into cold water to keep the fruit from softening. The skins will then slip off easily. Tomatoes and peppers can be skinned in the same way.

BANANAS

Serve whole or sliced with sugar, or try them with honey and a sprinkling of nuts. Bananas are good baked or broiled, after brushing with honey; or sprinkle with brown sugar and a little lemon juice.

T O B A K E means to cook in the oven so that the dish is exposed to heat on all sides. Have the oven at the temperature given before putting in the dish. When only one dish is being baked, the exact center of the oven is usually the best place.

T O B R O I L means to cook with the surface of the food directly exposed to the fire, with no pan between. In a gas or electric oven there is a broiling rack under the heating element upon which the food is laid.

BAKED BANANAS

Peel bananas and leave whole or split in half lengthwise. Bake in a moderate over (375° F.) until soft—about 15 minutes.

BROILED BANANAS

Peel the bananas and split lengthwise. Place them in a shallow pan and broil 3 inches from the flame until lightly browned.

BERRIES

Sort over the berries and remove any soft ones. If you are using them the same day, wash them gently in a sieve or colander, and hull.

T O H U L L means to pull the stems off fruits and berries. Hold the berry in your left hand and pull off the stem with your right, or you can buy a little tweezerlike gadget called a huller.

If the berries are to be kept overnight, sort them and store them in the refrigerator, but do not wash or hull until the next day.

Put the berries in a large serving bowl or individual dishes, as preferred. If you like them with the juice drawn out, sprinkle with sugar and let stand. Otherwise serve plain and add sugar and cream at the table.

RIPE FIGS

Remove the skin of the figs and slice them. Add sugar and a dash of lemon or lime juice.

GRAPEFRUIT

Cut the grapefruit in half, across the fruit, not lengthwise through the stem end. Take a sharp knife and cut out the core, which will take care of the seeds. Then cut the pulp away from the skin—you can buy a specially curved grapefruit knife for this —and sprinkle with sugar if you like it.

BROILED GRAPEFRUIT

Sometime try adding a tablespoon of honey to each half and broil it 3 inches from the flame until the honey is melted and the surface lightly browned. Broiled grapefruit makes an excellent first course or dessert.

MELONS

When melons are chilled in the refrigerator, their odor is likely to permeate other foods. It is advisable, therefore, to chill them by using ice or ice cubes. Cut open the melon, remove the seeds, and fill with ice at least half an hour before time to serve.

ORANGES

Peel the orange and either divide it into sections or slice across the grain in thin slices. This is a good variation from the popular orange juice.

FRUIT JUICES

Orange and grapefruit juice should be squeezed as near to the time of serving as possible. If it must be stored, put it in a tightly covered vessel and store in the refrigerator until ready to serve. Besides the fresh citrus juices, you can buy many delicious canned juices. And don't forget tomato juice.

STEWED FRUITS

Many people like stewed fruits in the morning, and they are good for supper desserts too. Too long cooking or too much sugar destroys the natural fruit flavor.

TO STEW means to cook in a small amount of water or liquid. Usually the food is brought to the boil and then allowed to simmer.

TO SIMMER means to cook just under the boiling point, so the liquid looks as though it might boil any minute but doesn't. Only an occasional bubble floats to the top.

STEWED FRESH FRUITS

Most fresh fruits can be stewed with or without their skins. Wash the fruit and place in a saucepan. Add just enough water to cushion the fruit on the bottom of the pan. Do not cover the fruit with water—the fruit makes its own juice. Cover the saucepan and bring the fruit to a boil, then simmer until the fruit is tender. The length of time depends upon whether the fruit is hard or soft.

Sweeten to taste with sugar or a colorless corn syrup after the fruit is stewed. Or, if preferred, a soft, tender fruit can be stewed with the sugar. If you want the fruit to hold its shape, boil the sugar and water together first to make a syrup, then add the fruit and finish cooking. Hard fruits such as apples and winter pears should be cooked tender before the sugar is added. Cook a moment more until the sugar is dissolved, then remove from the heat. Cool covered.

TO SWEETEN TO TASTE means to add as much sugar as you prefer. There is no set rule, as tastes vary.

You will find that fresh plums, nectarines, and rhubarb require more sugar than most fruits.

STEWED RHUBARB

Wash 1 pound of rhubarb. Do not peel. It is the peeling which gives stewed rhubarb a pink color. Cut the stalks into 1-inch pieces and add very little water—not more than ¼ cup. Measure the rhubarb. It usually requires half as much sugar as fruit. Add the sugar before cooking. Since sugar burns easily, the safest and easiest way to cook rhubarb is to put it in the top of a double boiler, over boiling water, and let it cook until tender. It is really delicious prepared in this way, and the pieces remain whole.

APPLESAUCE

5 or 6 medium apples
1 cup sugar
1 cup water
Nutmeg or cinnamon if
          desired

METHOD I: Pare the apples, core, and slice into a saucepan. Add the water and simmer until the apples are tender and mushy. Add the sugar and a sprinkling of nutmeg or cinnamon. Cook until the sugar is melted and remove from the heat.

METHOD II: The apples may be quartered, cored, sliced, and cooked with the skins on. Put through a colander or food mill. Add sugar and cook until the sugar is melted. Remove from the heat.

TO PARE means the same thing as "to peel."

TO CORE means to take out the center seed core. It is easiest done with a hollow punch known as a corer.

STEWED DRIED FRUITS

You can buy dried apples, apricots, figs, nectarines, and peaches. To stew any of them, wash the fruit first and cover with water. Let soak overnight. Do not soak or cook the fruits in a tin or aluminum pan. Use glass or enamel instead.

In the morning, transfer the fruit and water to a saucepan. Dried fruits are best cooked very slowly until tender. Test by piercing with a fork. If the tines pierce the fruit easily, it is done.

Most dried fruits require very little sugar. If you have a sweet tooth, add 2 to 4 tablespoons of sugar per pound of fruit, just before the cooking is completed. Or colorless corn syrup may be used instead of sugar.

BREAKFAST CEREALS

The next item on the breakfast menu is cereal. You probably know all the trade names of prepared dry cereals. Everyone has his favorites among the many on the market today. These dry cereals are generally served simply with milk or cream, with or without sugar. Try them also with fresh fruit over them. Honey makes a pleasant change from sugar. Try it some morning. And if you like raisins, add some to your dry cereal.

COOKED CEREALS

If you prefer a cooked cereal, you now know enough about cooking to follow the recipe on the package. Most instructions tell you to add the specified quantity of cereal to boiling salted water. The instructions are very clear. Follow them exactly. It is best to add the cereal slowly, stirring constantly until all the cereal has been added.

Cereal is one of the foods that will boil over. If you find that it creeps up the pot faster than you can stir it down, reduce your heat until all the cereal has been added. The quick-cooking brands take about 5 minutes of boiling. Keep stirring because cereal has a tendency to stick to the bottom of the pot and will burn if your fire is too hot. You can reduce your heat and let it simmer until you are ready to use it, or after it is cooked you can transfer it to a double boiler to keep it hot.

Have you been washing up as you worked? If you prepared grapefruit or squeezed orange juice, you have used your cutting board, have put the fruit skins either in the garbage can or in a bowl ready to be transferred to that receptacle. Now rinse off the board and stand it up to dry. Clean and wipe the knife, wash the juicer and strainer, and put them away. If you let things scatter and clutter up your kitchen, it will soon look li¹ e the tail end of a hurricane.

COFFEE

Now for that most important of breakfast items, coffee. Coffees vary greatly in flavor. Try different brands until you find the one you enjoy.

DRIP COFFEE

Drip coffee is made by pouring hot boiling water over ground coffee. Buy fresh coffee ground for drip. Keep your coffee in the refrigerator.

To get the best flavor, use a china or glass pot, not a metal one. With a china pot you will need filter papers for the bottom of the coffee chamber. Use one paper at a time.

Use 1 heaping tablespoon of coffee for each cup you want to make of average strength coffee. For instance, if you want 4 cups of coffee, put 4 heaping tablespoons of ground coffee in the coffee chamber. Pour 4 cups of boiling water over the grounds and allow it to drip. Use a coffee cup for measuring instead of a measuring cup.

CAUTION: Remove the grounds as soon as the coffee is brewed.

Drip coffee should never be boiled, and the problem is to keep it hot while the water is dripping. Before you start the coffee, pour boiling water into the pot and let the china heat through. Be sure, of course, to throw out the water before you pour the water in the top part. Also, you can put the pot on an asbestos mat over a very low fire while the dripping goes on.

Just a suggestion—sometimes a pinch of salt added to the ground coffee seems to improve the flavor.

C A U T I O N: Always see that your coffee is ground for the method of coffee maker you use.

H E A P I N G or R O U N D E D T A B L E S P O O N means to have the material well rounded over the edges of the spoon. Equals 2 level tablespoons.

L E V E L T A B L E S P O O N means exactly what it says—to have the ingredients level with the top of the bowl of the spoon.

A P I N C H in cooking means approximately the amount of grain or powder that can be confined between the tips of the thumb and index finger. If it doesn't seem sanitary to you, toss in a few grains. The term pinch was in use long before shakers were invented.

BOILED COFFEE

Buy a coarsely ground coffee intended for open pots. Measure the required number of cups of cold water into the pot. Add 1 heaping tablespoon of ground coffee for each cup and 1 extra spoonful for the pot. It's a nice old custom and takes up some slack in case you have miscounted. Add a pinch of salt, but don't overdo the pinch. It means just a few grains.

Put your pot over the fire. It will take about 15 minutes for it to reach the boiling point. Better form the habit now of watching the pot. They say, "A watched pot never boils," but in the case of boiled coffee, a watched pot never boils over. Do *not* rub the upper rim of the pot with grease when making coffee. You wouldn't like the coffee. Watch the pot instead.

When the water starts to creep up the sides, take a spoon and stir well. Let the water come to a full rolling boil and allow it to boil vigorously for about 1 minute, longer if you like a strong coffee. Reduce the heat and add a dash of cold water to settle the grounds. As soon as the dregs have settled, strain the coffee into a heated coffeepot.

Another way to insure clear coffee is to mix egg white and a little water with the coffee grounds before adding the rest of the water. About a teaspoon of egg white for each cup of coffee is enough. Your grandmother probably stirred in a handful of crushed egg shells instead of egg white, but this method is chancier because it depends on how much egg white clings to the shells.

A DASH in cooking means a small amount. When it is water, about 2 tablespoons.

BOILED COFFEE—BAG METHOD

Coffee for large groups and parties is often a problem to the average hostess because of the size of the family coffee maker. The easiest and simplest way to surmount the difficulty is to make boiled coffee by the bag method.

Make a bag out of clean, soft, porous cloth or use a bleached sugar bag.

TO BLEACH A SUGAR BAG. The printing on the bag is done with dye or ink which is soluble in soap. Soak the bag in cool water, cover well with kitchen soap, and rub the printed surface. Most of the printing will wash out. Soak the bag again in rich suds, wash in warm water, and then boil for about 10 minutes.

You will need a large kettle or pot. Be sure the pot is clean and free from cooking odors. It is best to wash it well with good hot soapsuds, rinse thoroughly, and allow to air for several hours before you are going to use it.

If you want to make a gallon of coffee, you will need 4 quarts of water, or 16 cups. After you have measured the water into the kettle, measure your coffee into the bag, 1 heaping tablespoon for each cup of coffee. Tie the bag securely and float it in the water.

Put the kettle over medium heat and bring the water to the boil. Allow the water to boil for 5 minutes. Remove the bag, add a pinch of salt, and keep the coffee hot until served.

PERCOLATOR COFFEE

Buy fresh coffee ground for percolators. Keep unused coffee in the refrigerator.

Measure the required number of cups of water into the percolator. Place 1 heaping tablespoonful of coffee per cup in the basket and add a pinch of salt. An extra spoonful for the pot is not necessary unless you like very strong coffee. Adjust the spreader over the coffee, fasten down the lid, and apply heat. After the water starts to bubble and gurgle up the tube and pops against the glass dome, it is perking. Allow it to perk for 6 minutes and then remove from the heat. Remove the coffee grounds.

DOUBLE-DECK OR SILEX COFFEE

Buy fresh coffee ground for Silex. Store in refrigerator. There are several varieties of double-deck coffee makers which make excellent coffee. Read the instructions which come with your particular maker so you will know how to put it together and operate it. Measure the required cups of water in the bottom container. Adjust the top and be sure to put in the filter, or the glass rod if it is that type. Add a heaping tablespoon of coffee per cup of water and a pinch of salt. Put the maker over the heat. The pressure generated in the lower chamber will force the water up the glass rod or tube onto the coffee in the upper chamber. It is well to stir the water and coffee in the upper chamber. Allow the water to bubble in the chamber for about 2 minutes and then lower the heat or remove the maker from the heat. This depends on the brand of maker. Most of them must be removed from the heat. The water will return to the lower chamber, and your coffee is made. Remove the top and serve.

AFTER-DINNER COFFEE

Use your favorite method of making coffee, but use 2 heaping or 4 level tablespoons of ground coffee for each measuring cup of water. When done, pour into a preheated coffeepot and serve in demitasse cups. Most people prefer after-dinner coffee black, but offer both cream and sugar.

PREPARED OR INSTANT COFFEES

There are several good brands on the market. They are excellent for a quick cup of coffee, for picnics or camping trips. The package gives explicit instructions. Do exactly as it says.

TEA

Although tea is usually associated with afternoons in this country, some people prefer it for breakfast.

Tea is best when made in a china, glass, or earthenware pot. For really good tea one should have 2 teapots, one for the steeping and one for service after the tea has steeped. Heat them both with boiling water before putting in the tea leaves.

After pot number one has been heated, pour off the water and put into the pot 1 teaspoon of tea per cup desired. Pour the required amount of boiling water over the tea leaves.

It is claimed that the teapot should be taken to the kettle, never the kettle to the pot. Use freshly boiled water for tea. Water boiled too long gets tired. After the water has been poured on the leaves, allow the tea to steep from 3 to 5 minutes in a warm place.

TO STEEP means to steam or heat in liquid which has been boiled, but is now removed from the heat. Tea or herbs are always steeped to the color and flavor desired.

When the tea is steeped in pot number one, empty pot number two. Strain the liquid from pot one into pot two. This will give you a fresh cup of tea without any bitter flavor.

Tea is often made by putting the tea leaves in a pot, pouring the boiling water over the leaves, and serving from the original pot. Use a little less tea for the one-pot method.

EGGS

You are going to meet eggs often from now on, and in many places other than on the breakfast menu. Although there are several kinds of eggs, in cooking we are concerned only with hens' eggs. They usually come in three sizes—small, medium, and large. The medium egg is average-sized and will meet the requirements of all recipes.

Eggs for direct eating, fried, scrambled, in omelets, or boiled, should be Grade A fresh. Eggs for general cooking, that is eggs used in batters, sauces, puddings, etc., can be Grade B.

HOW TO OPEN AN EGG

An egg when opened has two parts, the white and the yolk. You of course know that, but the parts are often used separately in cooking.

To open an egg, crack the shell. This may be done by a sharp rap with the back of a knife, by tapping it on the edge of a skillet or pan, or by giving it a quick rap on any hard surface. Be gentle but firm when cracking an egg shell, as it is always best not to break the yolk. Once the shell is cracked or opened, hold the egg in the fingers of both hands, insert the thumbs in the crack, and pry the shell apart. Since eggs are slippery and elusive, have something at hand to catch the egg in case it tries to escape.

It is wise when opening eggs to break each one separately into a saucer because unfortunately you cannot always judge an egg according to its shell or the price you paid for it.

HOW TO TELL A FRESH EGG

If the egg you have broken into a saucer is a good fresh one, the egg white will be thick so the yolk stands up firmly above the white. The staler the egg, the more watery it will be. In a really stale egg the yolk and white will both look runny and they will be hard to separate.

THE CARE OF EGGS

Always keep your eggs in the refrigerator in a covered dish or pan. They deteriorate much more rapidly in warm air than in cold. And if possible, find a grocer who keeps his eggs in the refrigerator too. All the grading and government inspection in the world cannot guarantee fresh eggs to the purchaser as long as grocers and householders keep them in the open air.

If the shells are dirty, wipe them with a clean dry cloth or rub stubborn spots lightly with a brush. Never wash them—unless just before you use them—because washing makes the shells more porous, hence the egg deteriorates faster.

Extra egg yolks can be stored in the refrigerator for use later on if you cover them with a little cold water to keep them from drying out. This refers to unbroken yolks only. Once they are broken, you can put them in a tightly covered container.

Egg whites can also be kept in a covered dish in the refrigerator.

RULES FOR COOKING EGGS

The first rule in cooking eggs by any method is *always use low heat*. A high temperature toughens the white and cooks it through before the yolk is cooked. High heat—or even cooking too long at simmering temperature—will produce the unpleasant greenish color sometimes seen in hard-cooked eggs.

Second, remove the egg from the cooking utensil and serve it at once, the moment it has been cooked to the desired degree. Eggs will go on cooking after the heating element has been turned off, simply from the heat already in them.

When you plan to cook eggs in the shell, remove them from the refrigerator and let them stand at room temperature for a while before you put them in the water. This will make the shells less likely to crack.

FRIED EGGS—SUNNY SIDE UP

Fried eggs are eggs cooked in fat in a skillet or frying pan. Your choice of cooking fat will depend upon your preference. Some people like the delicate flavor of eggs fried in butter; others the stronger flavor of meat drippings—beef fat, bacon fat, chicken fat, or sausage drippings.

COOKING FATS or GREASE are fats used for frying or searing and include the following:

Butter.

Margarine can be used as a substitute for butter in most cooking.

Shortening is any clean, sweet fat or oil and is used for frying, in pastries, doughs, or batters. Shortening can be butter, margarine, vegetable oils, lard, or prepared vegetable shortening.

Drippings are the fats that come from beef, lamb, veal, pork, or fowl when it is cooking. Bacon fat, if kept in a container in the refrigerator, is useful and adds flavor to many foods.

METHOD: Put your pan over medium heat and in it put 1 teaspoon of fat for each egg to be fried, or enough fat to cover the bottom of the pan with an oily film.

While the fat is melting, break the eggs—1 or 2 per person—into a saucer, one at a time. When the fat is heated through, reduce the heat and slide the eggs into the pan. Cook slowly until the whites are white and firm, which will take 3 to 5 minutes. If humps and bubbles appear in the whites, your fire is too hot.

When the eggs are done, remove at once and season with salt and pepper.

TO SEASON or SEASON TO TASTE means to add as much salt and pepper as you personally like. In case of doubt, season too little rather than too much. It is easier to add more seasoning than to take it away.

FRIED EGGS—OVER LIGHTLY

Fry the eggs as for Fried Eggs—Sunny Side Up. When the white has cooked enough to be firm, turn the egg over with a pancake turner or a spatula in order to cook the yolk lightly.

If you have trouble turning the eggs in the pan without breaking the yolks, here is an easy way to get the "over lightly" effect. Cover the skillet with a lid. The heat held in the pan will film the yolk and save you a lot of trouble. But be careful not to leave the lid on too long or the yolk will cook solid. Egg fanciers are fussy about their eggs, and the "over lightly" school does not like the yolks well done.

POINTER: This is for your washing-up program. Raw egg is susceptible to heat, and hot water will simply cook the egg onto the dish. Rinse egg dishes in cold water before washing with hot.

FRIED EGGS—WELL DONE

Fry the eggs as for Fried Eggs—Sunny Side Up. Then, to have them well done, turn them over in the pan with the pancake turner or spatula and cook until the yolk is hard and firm. Or put a lid on the pan and keep it on until the yolks become hard.

FRIED EGGS—BASTED

TO BASTE means to bathe or moisten the article cooking with the fat and juices in which it is being cooked, or sometimes additional liquid is used.

To baste eggs use 1 tablespoon of fat per egg or each 2 eggs. Prepare as for Fried Eggs—Sunny Side Up. When the white begins to cook, lift the fat in a tablespoon and pour it over the yolk until the latter becomes filmed and the white is firm. Season and serve.

SOFT-COOKED EGGS

Soft-cooked and hard-cooked eggs, as well as boiled eggs, are cooked in their shells.

The white of a soft-cooked egg is tender and evenly coagulated; the yolk either liquid or partly firm, depending on how long it was cooked.

Whichever of the following two methods you use, be sure you have enough water to cover the eggs completely. And do not let the water boil once the eggs have been put into it.

METHOD I: Put the water in a saucepan and bring it to the boil. Carefully lower the eggs into the water with a spoon. Then reduce the heat so that the water simmers but does not boil while the eggs are cooking.

For a soft egg, simmer 3–5 minutes.

For a medium egg, simmer 6–8 minutes.

METHOD II: Put the eggs in a saucepan, preferably resting on a rack. Cover the eggs completely with cold water and place the pan over low heat. Slowly bring the water to a boil, then reduce the heat so the water simmers but does not boil. Keep the water simmering until the eggs have reached the desired firmness, as follows:

For a soft egg, simmer no more than 2 minutes. If you like your eggs really soft, you may prefer to take them out as soon as the water reaches the boiling point.

For a medium egg, simmer 3–5 minutes.

HARD-COOKED EGGS

Follow either Method I or Method II for soft-cooked eggs, but simmer longer. If you use Method I, simmer 15 to 20 minutes. With Method II, simmer 12 to 15 minutes. If you stir the eggs around once or twice while they cook, it will help keep the yolk in the middle.

CODDLED EGGS

Coddled eggs are the most delicate of the soft-cooked eggs, and the easiest to do once you get the hang of it. In this method of cooking, the only heat applied is the heat from boiling water, so the amount of water is important.

First choose a straight-sided vessel which will keep the eggs well covered when the correct amount of water is poured over them. Then measure ⅓ quart of water for each egg to be cooked—but for cooking a single egg 2 cups are safer. Boil the water and pour it over the eggs. Let them stand uncovered in the hot water for about 8 minutes. With this method both white and yolk will be cooked to the same consistency.

Experiment a little with coddled eggs until you find exactly the consistency you prefer. Taking the eggs out earlier than 8 minutes will give you a softer egg, but the yolk will not be cooked through. More water per egg will make a firmer egg; less water a softer one.

SOFT-BOILED EGGS

Soft-cooking or coddling are the methods recommended by modern nutritionists, but the soft-boiled egg has a long and honorable history and many people still prefer it. Here is how you do it:

Drop the eggs gently into boiling water and keep the water boiling while the eggs are cooking. From 3 to 3½ minutes is the time which produces an egg to meet the average taste, but some hold out for 4 minutes. Remove the egg *instantly* when the cooking time is up or you will have a hard-boiled egg.

SERVING BOILED EGGS

Have an egg cup hot and ready. Crack the shell with a sharp blow of a knife, pull apart, and scoop out with a spoon. Add butter, salt, and pepper, and serve at once. If you have several people to serve, it will be better to serve the eggs whole and let them open their own. The eggs are likely to get cold if you try to open them all in the kitchen.

The British people like to eat their eggs straight from the shell. They are very adroit at snipping off the end, adding their seasoning bit by bit, and scooping out the egg with a small spoon.

POACHED EGGS

P O A C H I N G is cooking in liquid which is kept just below the boiling point. The liquid may be water, wine, milk, or stock.

Put your liquid into a skillet and heat it just under the boiling point. You can buy shallow rings to hold the egg in shape while it is poaching. These rings are placed in the hot liquid. Break the eggs into a saucer one at a time and then transfer them to the hot water or pour them into the cups of the ring which is immersed in the water.

Expert cooks sometimes use a fancier method. They put a quart of water in a deep saucepan and add a little vinegar. When it boils, they stir it into a whirlpool, drop an egg into the hollow center of the whirlpool, and remove the pan from the fire. The egg poaches before the water stops whirling, which gives it a nice rounded shape. A disadvantage is that you can cook only 1 egg at a time.

When poaching eggs allow them to remain in the water, kept just under the boiling point, until the whites are firm and the yolk is glazed. Poached eggs are used on hash, some vegetables, and because no grease is used they are good for invalids.

BAKED EGGS

To bake eggs a small dish or pan is necessary. Grease the dish or pan.

T O G R E A S E means to rub the inside surface of the dish or pan with butter, lard, oil, or other suitable shortening.

Break the eggs into a saucer one at a time, then transfer them to the greased dish, season, and place in a slow oven (300°). For soft-baked eggs allow 6–10 minutes. For hard-baked, allow 15–20 minutes. Ovens vary. Watch the eggs. It may take more than 10 minutes to soft-bake them in your oven.

SHIRRED EGGS

Shirred eggs are fancy baked eggs. Use small dishes, ramekins or custard cups. If you want to do several eggs, you can press your muffin tins into service. Grease the containers and put in a layer of buttered crumbs. Crumbs may be mixed with butter, or small pieces of butter may be dropped over the crumbs. Pour the eggs over the crumbs, being careful not to break the yolks. Season the eggs, cover with more crumbs, and bake in a slow oven (300°) until the eggs are set and the crumbs brown. It takes from 15 to 20 minutes.

A tablespoon of cream may be used instead of crumbs, or cream may be added to the crumbs before adding the eggs.

SCRAMBLED EGGS

Allow 2 eggs per person. Break the eggs into a bowl, add seasoning and 2 tablespoons of whole milk or cream for each egg. Beat this mixture lightly.

T O   B E A T   L I G H T L Y means to beat until ingredients are just mixed.

Use about 1 teaspoon of butter per egg. Melt the butter in a skillet but do not let it brown. Pour the egg mixture into the pan and stir, lifting the cooked egg from the bottom of the pan. Repeat the lifting process until the eggs begin to solidify. If you or your family like hard scrambled eggs, cook a little longer. Remember that eggs continue to cook from the heat generated. When they are done to suit your taste, remove from fire and pan at once. When you have served the eggs, fill the pan with cold water until you are ready to wash it.

SCRAMBLED EGGS—DOUBLE-BOILER METHOD

Eggs may be scrambled in the top of a double boiler over water maintained just below the boiling point. Butter to grease the cooking chamber is optional.

Follow the recipe for scrambled eggs. When the mixture is ready, transfer to the top of the double boiler. The eggs will cook at the edges and bottom first. Stir the cooked part into the mixture and continue cooking until the eggs are the texture you like. Remove the eggs from the pan. Soak the pan in cold water. It will be easier to clean.

PAN-SCRAMBLED EGGS

Allow 2 eggs per person and 1 teaspoon of butter per egg. Melt the butter in a skillet. Break the eggs into a bowl and season. Pour the eggs into the butter. When the whites begin to solidify, break the yolks with a fork and with a stirring motion mix the whites and yolks together. Cook to suit your taste. Some people like them creamy, some prefer them solid. Remove from the fire and serve at once.

PLAIN OMELET I

Allow 2 eggs per person. Break the eggs into a bowl and add 1 tablespoon of milk or cream per egg. Add seasoning and beat well.

TO BEAT WELL means to beat until ingredients are thoroughly mixed and the liquid is foamy.

Put about 1 teaspoon of butter per egg in a skillet. When the butter is filmed over the bottom of the pan, pour in the egg mixture. As the egg begins to cook, prick the bottom with a fork or spatula and lift up so the uncooked egg can run through to the bottom of the pan. Use the spatula to loosen the mixture from the sides of the pan. Do not stir. Cook slowly. When the egg is beginning to set firmly, fold one half over the other section and press the top down gently. Use your spatula or pancake turner for this operation. Serve at once.

PLAIN OMELET II

Allow 2 eggs per person. Separate the yolks from the whites.

TO SEPARATE AN EGG means to separate the yolk from the white. Have 2 bowls ready before you start. Crack the egg shell and open. Up-end the egg and allow the excess white to drop into one of the bowls. Transfer the yolk to the empty half of the shell, allowing the remainder of the white to slip into the bowl. Continue this transfer of yolk from half-shell to half-shell until the yolk is free of white. Put the yolk in the second bowl.

When the eggs have been separated, add 1 tablespoon of milk or cream per egg to the yolks. Use your Dover egg beater and beat the whites until they are stiff but not dry.

TO BEAT EGG WHITES STIFF BUT NOT DRY means to beat until sharp peaks form when the beater is lifted from mixture, but the mass still glistens with moisture.

Beat the yolks and milk and add seasoning. Put about 1 teaspoonful of butter per egg in your skillet, and melt it. Fold the egg white into the yolk mixture.

TO FOLD IN means to blend two mixtures by lifting the bottom mixture and folding it over the top. Insert the spoon vertically through the food, lift up the bottom, bring it up, and fold over. Repeat the operation until the mixture of the two parts is complete. Do not overdo and do not stir. The point is to keep the air in the two mixtures.

Pour the folded mixture into the skillet and cook until the mixture begins to set. Lift half of the omelet and fold over, allowing a little more cooking to heat the middle. The omelet should puff up and be foamy.

It is possible to do all sorts of things with omelets. Chopped chives, parsley, onion, ham, bacon, mushrooms, or jelly may be added to the bottom half of the omelet before the top is turned over and put in place. Try it sometime. It makes a good luncheon or supper dish.

ECONOMY OMELET

PREPARATION TIME: about 15 minutes
COOKING TIME: about 10 minutes

2 slices white bread	½ teaspoon salt
5 eggs	½ teaspoon baking powder
⅓ cup milk	2 tablespoons shortening
Pepper	

METHOD: Cut the crusts from the bread and crumble it.

TO CRUMBLE means to break into small pieces.

Add the milk to the crumbled bread. Separate the eggs and add the salt and baking powder to the yolks with a little pepper. Beat the whites stiff but not dry. Beat the yolks until well mixed. Add the yolk mixture to the crumb mixture, mix, then fold in the beaten whites. Heat the fat in the skillet and pour in the egg mixture. Allow to cook slowly and brown on the bottom. Lift the edges with a spatula to inspect the degree of brownness of the bottom. When the bottom is a nice golden brown put your pan under the broiler for a few minutes to cook the top part of the omelet. Watch it while it is in the broiler. Don't let it brown; you are cooking the upper surface only. When it is firm remove from the broiler, cut in half, and fold over. About 10 minutes in the oven at 300° may be used instead of the broiler. It takes longer but does not need the careful watching.

A filling of creamed chicken, mushrooms, or other mixtures may be added to this omelet before it is folded over.

You will be proud of this omelet. It will be light and fluffy and will stand up stiff and strong, yet still be tender.

BREAKFAST MEATS

You should now be able to handle eggs whenever you meet them in any recipe. Now for those inseparable companions of the breakfast egg—bacon, ham, and sausage.

OVEN-COOKED BACON

COOKING TIME: about 15 minutes

For this method you will need an oven-broiler.

Allow 2 or 3 strips per person. Lay the strips of bacon on the broiler rack and put the pan on the top shelf of an oven at medium heat (350°). That's all there is to it. Look at it once in a while to be sure it doesn't cook too much. In about 15 minutes the bacon will be flat, crisp, and free from excess fat, which drips into the pan under the rack.

This fat is clear, and is good to be saved and used for other foods.

FRIED BACON

COOKING TIME: about 5 minutes

Allow 2 or 3 strips per person.

TO FRY means, strictly speaking, to cook in a skillet with a little hot fat. But with foods which have fat in them, such as bacon and sausage, no fat is added to the pan.

DEEP-FAT FRYING means cooking in fat deep enough to float the food.

Lay the bacon—2 or 3 strips per person—flat in the bottom of the skillet. Put the skillet over a medium flame and keep turning the bacon with your long fork. If you don't it will curl and assume weird shapes. Drain off the excess fat as you cook, or the bacon may be grease-sodden. When the bacon is brown and crisp, remove from pan and drain on brown paper or a paper towel. The whole process will take about 5 minutes.

BROILED BACON

COOKING TIME: about 5 minutes

If you are using a gas or electric broiler, place the bacon in the broiling pan and put it under the heat, at least 4 inches below the element or flame at medium heat. Turn several times to insure even cooking. You will have to pay attention to it while cooking, for it will cook quite rapidly and may burn.

If you are broiling over wood or coal embers, put the bacon on a grid or open grill and place over the coals, turning often to equalize the cooking.

FRIED SAUSAGE

COOKING TIME: at least 20 minutes

You might like sausage or ham with your eggs for a change. Allow about ¼ pound of sausage per person. If you buy link sausage, prick the skin with a fork and place the sausages in the skillet. Add enough water to cover the bottom of the pan and put over medium heat. The water will soon cook away, leaving the sausage to fry in its own fat. Turn often until the sausage is evenly browned on all sides. Rather overcook than undercook all pork products.

If you buy bulk sausage, shape the meat into flat cakes in your hands. Cook in the same manner as above, using the small amount of water to start.

No seasoning has been suggested because sausage meat is usually very highly seasoned.

FRIED HAM

Grease the bottom of your skillet lightly, put in the ham, and cook it slowly so that it browns lightly but does not become leathery. Tenderized and boiled ham is delicious if just warmed through. It needs no special cooking.

TO WARM THROUGH means to heat either by frying, steaming, or in the oven until the food is hot or warm inside as well as out.

TOAST

The last item on a breakfast list is toast.

TO TOAST means to cook or brown lightly over, under, or in front of direct heat.

If you have an automatic toaster you need not worry. You just put the bread in and let the mechanical gadget do the work and worrying. If you toast in a gas or electric range, you toast in the broiling compartment. Place your bread on the broiling tray and have your oven at maximum heat. Watch the toast; it burns easily. For good, even, well-browned slices, it is advisable to turn the bread once or twice.

If you toast over coals, use a grid or broiling rack. Watch the bread and turn often.

To toast over an open gas burner or over a coal-oil burner, buy a gadget especially made for the job. There are several types.

A good cook seldom burns the toast. Make up your mind right now that when you are doing toast you cannot do anything else. If you forget the toast or try to do something else, a cloud of smoke will tell you that the bread has burned. When toast is nicely browned, butter and serve at once.

FRENCH TOAST

PREPARATION TIME: about 5 minutes
COOKING TIME: about 10 minutes

4 slices bread	⅔ cup milk
1 egg	⅛ teaspoon salt

If you want to make more than 4 slices, figure an additional egg for each 4 slices and increase the other ingredients accordingly. That is, 12 slices of bread would take 3 eggs, 2 cups of milk, and nearly ½ teaspoonful of salt.

METHOD: Put about 1 teaspoon of fat in your skillet, just enough to film the bottom of the pan. Heat.

Break the eggs or egg into a soup plate or shallow dish, add the milk and salt, and beat with a fork until well mixed. Dip a slice of bread into the egg-milk mixture, transfer at once to the skillet, and sauté, turning often.

TO SAUTÉ means to cook or brown in a pan or skillet using very little fat. Strictly speaking, sauté means to fry lightly in butter, but we have come to use the word to describe lightly frying in any fat.

Keep turning the bread until it is a light golden brown on both sides. Serve hot with powdered sugar, syrup, jelly, jam, or honey.

You are now able to get as good a breakfast as the seasoned cook and are, we hope, anxious to try something else.

CHAPTER V

HOW TO HAVE A MEAL ALL READY ON TIME

M A N Y new cooks and some cooks with experience find it difficult to gauge their cooking so that all parts of a meal are ready at a specified time. It is a question of planning, of timing, of organization and knowledge. Mathematics enter into it too.

We will be as helpful as we can by giving cooking time for foods, and we will try to give you a general idea of how long it takes to prepare the food for cooking. It is the preparation of foods, particularly vegetables, which is the stumbling block. Therefore allow plenty of time to take care of the unexpected interruptions which occur in a normal household. Telephone calls, visitors, children, neighbors, minor accidents, all deserve consideration.

Meat, unless it is to be broiled or fried, requires the longest cooking time. Roasts, pot roasts, braised dishes, casserole dishes, and other concoctions requiring long cooking periods should be prepared first.

Let us suppose you are going to have a pot roast.

Check the recipe (page 110). It doesn't seem to help much at the first glance because it says the cooking time is from 3 to 5 hours. The reason for the range in time is the fact that some cuts of meat are tougher than others and need longer cooking to become tender. At least you will know the probable maximum time it will take for your meat to cook. Don't forget, however, that if you plan to have pot roast at 6 o'clock, it may take 5 hours for it to cook. If it should take 5 hours, will your dinner be ready at 6? It won't if you start to prepare your meat at 1 o'clock. You will probably be 15 or 20 minutes late.

Always when preparing a meal add to the cooking time the time needed for preparation. This is important and must not be forgotten.

The assembling of all the materials you will need takes time. Have them ready for use in your preparation area. The fat in which the meat is to be seared must be hot. That can be heating while you wipe, season, and dredge the meat. If you are going to add a clove of minced garlic to the fat, that must be prepared. Allow about 2 minutes. You are going to add 1 sliced onion when the cooking starts, that must be peeled and sliced. It takes approximately 3 minutes to peel and slice an onion. When you become expert you will do it in a much shorter time. Allow the maximum time until you do become experienced. The meat must be seared on all sides. The preparations will probably take from 20–30 minutes. That time must be added to your cooking time if the roast is to be ready at 6 o'clock as planned.

If you find that the meat is tender sooner than you expected, it will do no harm to turn the fire out for an hour or so.

You do want to have dinner ready at 6, however, because you hope to leave the house at 7 to keep an appointment.

The directions with the pot-roast recipe say to add the vegetables about an hour before the meat is to be served. What about those vegetables? It also says to cook the potatoes separately. Perhaps you like mashed potatoes with pot-roast gravy. What about them?

You must add to the pot roast 1 cup each diced onion, celery, and carrots, and the turnips. Did you forget that the gravy must be made? It is easy to forget that fact, which would mean that the dinner would not be ready until 6:10. All right, then; you plan to add the vegetables at 10 minutes of 5 to allow enough time. When must you start preparing the vegetables? You know you want to allow an hour's cooking time. To that cooking time add the preparation time.

It takes about 5 minutes to peel and slice or dice a cup of onions.

It takes at least 5 minutes to peel and dice a cup of carrots. That is 10 minutes now.

It will take another 5 minutes to peel the white turnips. That is 15 minutes.

It will take about 10 minutes to wash, clean, and dice the celery.

Twenty-five minutes will be required to prepare the vegetables which are to go into the pot with the roast. You decided to add the vegetables at 10 minutes of 5. In order to have them ready at that time you must start preparing them at 4:25—and that allows for no interruptions. There may be 3 telephone calls and 2 people at the front door and a neighbor who wants to borrow an egg. Or, if you have children in the house, little Willie may take that time to skin his knee and Gwendolyn to fall into the fish pool. There goes the whole schedule, and the dinner is going to be late.

So allow an extra 15 minutes to take care of possible interruptions. It won't hurt the dinner if it is ready 15 minutes before serving time. Just remember to start earlier. A pot-roast dinner won't spoil by being kept warm. As a matter of fact, it gives extra time for the blending of all flavors.

And don't forget those mashed potatoes. You are going to be busy the last few minutes. Mashed potatoes should be hot, and there is the gravy to be made and coffee or tea to think about.

Potatoes will boil in about 45 minutes. It will take about 5 minutes to drain, mash, add butter and hot milk, and beat to an appetizing fluffiness.

When the vegetables are in the pot the potatoes can be peeled. It will probably take 15 minutes to prepare them. While the potatoes are cooking, you can prepare your flour and water for the gravy. Set the table if you haven't already done so and make the coffee or have the kettle boiling for the tea.

At a quarter of 6 remove the meat and vegetables from the pot. Keep them warm. Add the flour and water thickening to the gravy in the pot and stir often while cooking to avoid lumps.

Drain the potatoes. Put some milk on to heat. Stir the gravy while you are at the stove with the milk. Mash the potatoes and add a lump of butter and seasoning. Stir the gravy, bring back the milk, add to the potatoes, and beat vigorously with a large spoon.

Put some of the gravy over the meat and vegetables. Put other gravy in a serving dish. Dish up the potatoes and give a sigh of satisfaction. The dinner is ready as the town clock strikes 6.

For a few minutes at the very end you may have wished for two extra pairs of hands. You may be a little hot and bothered, your face may be a bit flushed. Perhaps you keep a powder puff tucked away somewhere in the kitchen and can take that refreshing dab of powder before calling the family to dinner.

If you don't keep a powder box and hand lotion in the kitchen, do it now. It's nice to have it handy.

Now try a dinner with broiled meat. Suppose you are having broiled steak, a green salad, baked potatoes, fresh peas, and coffee.

The baked potato will require the longest cooking time. It takes 40–60 minutes to bake a potato in a 400° oven.

The greens for the salad will have to be washed and crisped. The salad dressing will have to be made unless you like one of the prepared salad dressings.

The peas will have to be shelled and cooked and the steak broiled.

It takes about 10 minutes to separate and wash a head of lettuce, shake it free from water, wrap it in a towel, and place it in the refrigerator for crisping.

It takes 5 minutes to wash the potatoes to be baked. Don't forget to prick the potatoes with the tines of a fork to prevent an explosion.

Dinner is to be at 7. At a quarter of 6 wash the potatoes and prepare them for the oven. Turn the oven on and set it at 400°, or if you don't have a thermometer you want a hot oven.

Wash the lettuce, shake it and put it in the refrigerator.

Put the potatoes in the oven.

Shell the peas. It takes about 15 minutes to shell a pound of peas; but if you have 2 pounds, it will probably take less than 30 minutes. While the peas are being shelled, put the kettle on so that you will have boiling water when you need it.

The potatoes will be done on time because for the last 20 minutes of cooking the oven will be turned to broil, very hot (550°). It will take the steak about 20 minutes for medium done if it is 1 inch thick.

Wash the peas and at 25 minutes of 7 put them in a pot with 1 cup boiling water and some salt. Put over heat and cook. Put your steak in the broiler. Turn the indicator to broil or increase the heat.

Arrange the lettuce leaves on plates or prepare your salad in a bowl.

After 10 minutes of broiling, turn the steak.

Make the coffee.

Mince a little parsley to sprinkle over the steak.

At 5 minutes of 7 the peas should be done. Drain. Add a lump of butter and a sprinkling of pepper and keep them covered to keep hot.

Put the dressing on the salad and toss lightly in the bowl or sprinkle the dressing over the leaves arranged on plates.

Take the potatoes from the oven. Make an incision with a sharp knife and put in a wedge of butter.

Take the steak from the broiler and put on a hot platter. Rub with a pat of butter and sprinkle with minced parsley.

Take up the peas. The dinner is ready and on time.

Different cooks work in different ways. You will have to organize your work and your time, making the proper allowances for the time required for the precooking preparation. It takes experience and practice. Just remember that it is not a criminal offense to have the food ready a few minutes before the stated time —that is, if you have the facilities for keeping it hot.

Always start with the item that needs the longest cooking time and add to the cooking time the preparation time and the end time —making gravy, for instance.

Don't plan a meal which is bound to cause you trouble. If the meal is cooked on top of the stove, then you may, if you care to, make biscuits or bake a hot dessert. But don't try to bake biscuits while steak is broiling. Don't try to have 2 oven-cooked dishes which must be ready at the same time but require different cooking temperatures. If you have 2 ovens, do anything you like!

It is simple to pan-fry chicken and bake hot biscuits at the same time because the chicken is cooking on the top of the stove, which leaves the oven free for the biscuits at the proper temperature.

Broiled chicken and biscuits are good when served together and can be managed by broiling the chicken for ¾ of the required time at broiling temperature. And then finish cooking on a pan in the oven while the biscuits are baking. There are ways to get around most cooking problems, but it takes time and experience to discover the dodges to do it. It is the sum of organization, calculation, and experience that makes it possible for cooks to have a complete meal ready on time.

CHAPTER VI

SEASONING

B E F O R E you do any more cooking, consider seasoning. Not just the use of pepper and salt, but the wealth of herbs, spices, and condiments available. If "variety's the very spice of life," then herbs and spices are the infinite variety of cooking.

If you are interested in subtle flavors, cultivate the *moderate* use of herbs and spices in your cooking. What you want to achieve is a suggestion of a flavor or a delicate mixture of provoking flavors. You don't want the flavor of thyme, tarragon, garlic, or any other herb or spice to predominate. Some wag once said, "There is no such thing as a little garlic." In a sense the statement is true because the flavor is so distinctive. There is definitely such a thing as too much garlic.

Always use too little rather than too much. Even a pinch of herb or spice will make a difference in the flavor of any dish you prepare. Use smaller quantities of dry and powdered herbs than the fresh ones.

HERBS

If you have a house in the country, grow your own herbs. They are easy to grow, and you will find it a real pleasure to be able to gather your herbs from an herb bed, preferably near your kitchen door.

If you live in an apartment you can grow most herbs in pots on your windowsill. Chives, parsley, mint, rosemary, chervil, sage, and many others will stand box or pot culture.

If you do not grow herbs, buy a good herb chest. Buy leaves

rather than powdered herbs and crush them as you use them. If you grow your own herbs, pick off the green leaves and discard the stems, which are apt to be tough and are often bitter.

Here are some things you should know about herbs:

Sweet herbs are the leaves, seeds, or roots of plants which are used in cooking because of their aroma and flavor. Some of them are bay, celery, chives, dill, mint, nasturtium, parsley, rosemary, sage, savory, and thyme. These are only a few of the many herbs used in cooking.

Salad herbs are those plants or vegetables used to season salads. Onion, garlic, celery, and chives are all salad herbs. Many of the sweet herbs can be used in salads to give them a different and distinct flavor.

Fine herbs—or *fines herbes* in French—are really a combination of several herbs used to flavor certain dishes. In combination they are generally parsley, chervil, and chives. Other combinations include parsley with thyme, basil, or burnet added.

If you see the term *simpling herbs,* do not worry about it. Simpling herbs are used for medicine.

Bouquets of herbs are bunches of green herbs tied together and cooked with food and removed before serving. Or dried herbs put in a cheesecloth bag, cooked in the food and discarded. Or the herbs specified in the bouquet may be minced if green, or powdered if dry, and cooked directly in the food.

Experiment with herbs in your cooking. Refer to the following list as you cook, try your own combinations; but remember to use the herbs with a light hand always.

BASIL: ¼–½ teaspoon (more if desired) for 4 servings. Use in:

Appetizers such as	tomato juice
	cream cheese for stuffing celery
	seafood cocktails
	hot cheese dishes

Soups, particularly	spinach
	tomato
Eggs	creamed or in casserole dishes
Salad	any salad
Fish	particularly stews or chowders
Meat	lamb
	liver
	pork
	beef stew
Vegetables	string beans
	tomatoes
	boiled potatoes
	beets
	carrots
	peas
Sauces	tomato
Desserts	Fruit desserts

BAY LEAF: A part of a leaf is usually enough for from 4 to 8 servings. Use in:

Soups	any
Fish	stew or chowders
	boiled fish
Meats	beef stew
	pot roast
	kidneys
	tongue
Poultry or rabbit	fricasseed
Vegetables	tomatoes
Sauce	tomato

c h i v e s: 1 tablespoon, chopped (more if desired) for 4 servings. Use in:

Appetizers such as	cottage cheese combinations
	sour cream fillings
Soups	cream of potato
	cream of pea
	cream of carrot
Egg dishes such as	omelets and soufflés
Salads	any green or vegetable
Fish	stews or chowders
Meats	chopped meat
	pork
	steak
Poultry	creamed chicken or turkey
Vegetables	carrots
	peas
	spinach or chard
	tomatoes
Sauces	any creamed sauce

m a r j o r a m: ½–1 teaspoon for 4 servings. Use in:

Appetizers such as	cream cheese, tomato juice
Soups	any
Eggs	casserole or creamed
Salads	green
	chicken
	rabbit
Fish	sauces
	butter

Meat	chopped meat
	lamb
	roast pork
	steak
Poultry	in stuffing
Vegetables	carrots
	peas
	tomatoes
	spinach
	potatoes
	string beans

M I N T: A few sprigs, or 1 teaspoon, chopped, or follow directions on package of dehydrated mint. Use in:

Appetizers such as	fruit cup
	fruit juices
	cream cheese
	cottage cheese
Soup	split pea or
	fresh pea
Salad	fruit
Fish	as a garnish
Meat	lamb or
	mutton
Vegetables	carrots
	peas
	cabbage
	potatoes
	spinach
Beverages	mint tea
	lemonade
	fruit ades

Desserts   in fruit cups and
                        melon desserts

PARSLEY: 1 tablespoon, chopped, for 4 servings. Use in:

Appetizers   as a garnish and in
                        cream or cottage cheese

Soups   chopped fine in creamed soups

Eggs   as a garnish or chopped in
                        scrambled eggs or in omelets

Fish   good in all sauces and in stews and
                        chowders and as a garnish

Meat   as a garnish and in stews, in casserole
                        dishes and chopped on steak

Poultry   as a garnish or in stuffing or in
                        fricassee

Sauces   good in all creamed sauces

ROSEMARY: ½ teaspoon dry or powdered, or 1 sprig of fresh for 4 servings. Use in:

Soups   beef
                        vegetable

Meat   lamb stew
                        ragouts
                        with pork, steak
                        veal dishes
                        pot roasts

Poultry   chicken

Vegetables   peas
                        baked beans

Desserts   in fruit cups

Breads   chopped in baking powder biscuits

S A G E: ¼ teaspoon for 4 servings. Use in:

Appetizers such as	cottage cheese, just a little
Salads	cream or cottage cheese
Fish	boiled fish, a little
Meat	pork or veal
Vegetables	onions
	tomatoes
	string beans
Breads	baking powder biscuits as meat dish topping
	biscuit used for chicken shortcake
	bread stuffings, for chicken and small roasts
	Use more sage for turkey dressing

S A V O R Y: ½ teaspoon or a sprig for 4 servings. Use in:

Appetizers	tomato juice
Soups	beef broth
	lentil soup
Salads	cottage cheese or cream cheese
Meats	lamb
	veal
	roast beef
Poultry	chicken or rabbit fricassee
Vegetables	string beans
	beets
	carrots
	peas
Sauces	good in gravies
Bread stuffing	for fowl and turkey and small roasts

TARRAGON: ¼–½ teaspoon for 4 servings. Use in:

Appetizers such as	tomato juice
	fish cocktails
Soups	chicken
	chowders
Eggs	any recipe
Salads	fish
	green
Fish	stews
	chowders
Meat	roast beef
	pot roast
Poultry	chicken
	turkey
Vegetables	lima beans
	baked potato
	onions
Sauces	drawn butter
	tartar

SPICES

Most recipes give definite amounts for spices. It is wise to follow instructions carefully. The common spices are allspice, ground clove, whole cloves, ground cinnamon, cinnamon sticks, ginger, mace, and nutmeg. (Nutmeg is preferably freshly ground. Buy the nuts and a grater; it is worth the trouble.)

CONDIMENTS

Condiments include all the salts, beginning with table salt, and then the combinations, onion-celery, garlic and hickory.

If you want really good pepper, buy a peppermill. Get a good one, for they last a lifetime. Buy whole pepper or peppercorns and grind the fresh pepper into or over your food.

Mustard, horse-radish, and all the vinegars—cider, white, wine, malt, etc.—are also condiments.

Then there is the long list of prepared table sauces, beginning with the popular tomato catsup and chili sauce and going on down the list through the various steak and meat sauces. Don't omit the Worcestershire sauce, and for a treat keep a bottle of chutney on hand. A tablespoon of chutney added to a French salad dressing gives it an unexpected zip.

CHAPTER VII

MEATS

WHAT TO BUY

M E A T is divided into two types, the tender cuts such as steaks, chops, prime rib cuts, and tenderloin; and the tougher parts—the neck, shoulders, rump, legs, etc. The tougher cuts are full of flavor, but they do require longer cooking to make them tender.

Be on good terms with your butcher and take his word for the quality of the meat you buy. All meat is graded and stamped when inspected. Do not be afraid of the purple stamp marks—the dye used is harmless vegetable coloring. Cut it off, however, if you will feel happier about it. When your butcher sells you a piece of meat and assures you it is good, tell him about it if he was right. We all enjoy appreciation. If he was wrong, tell him about that too; but be nice about it. Consideration will pay you dividends.

Do not be afraid of streaks of fat that run through steaks and roasts. The fat makes the meat tender and juicy.

What to buy and how much to allow for average servings is one of the most vexing problems a cook must handle. When you buy meat which is composed of meat, bone, and fat, allow ½ to ¾ pound per person for a serving. If you buy in large quantities the ratio diminishes somewhat. A 15-pound ham, for instance, will serve 30 to 40 people.

The following list gives the quantities for *average* servings. If you are catering to lusty appetites and expect to give second helpings, allow more meat per person.

Allow ½ to ¾ pound per person, ¾ pound for the extra bone-heavy cuts, of the following:

Beef	standing roasts
	rolled roasts
	pot roasts
	short ribs (¾ pound)
	corned beef with or without bone
	steaks—porterhouse
	T-bone
	sirloin
Ham	fresh
	corned
	smoked
Lamb	legs
	shoulder with bone or boned and rolled
	breast (¾ pound)
Veal	all cuts
Pork	loin
	shoulders
	butts
	legs, part or whole
	spareribs (¾ pound)
Chicken	
Turkey	
Rabbit	
Chops	lamb
	pork
	veal

Allow 1 medium-thick chop per person. For more lusty appetites, allow 2 chops per person.

Allow ¼ to ⅓ pound per person per serving when buying boneless meat such as:

Veal cutlet	Sausage
Filet mignon	Liver
Other boneless cuts of steak	Kidneys
Round steak	Sweetbreads
Ground round steak	Tripe
Hamburger	Brains
Stew meat—beef, lamb, veal	Flank steak
Sliced ham ½ to 1 inch thick	

If you are cooking for two you are faced with another problem —what to do about roasts. A small roast doesn't taste like much of anything. It is better to buy more than you need. You will find recipes here which will make your roast truly delicious when it returns to the table for a second meal.

FROZEN MEATS

The servings of frozen meats are the same as those for fresh— ½ pound per person of meat, fat, and bone; ¼ per person of all lean meat.

Frozen foods are excellent. If you use them, be sure to follow carefully the cooking instructions on each package. Instructions vary, so read each package.

COOKING OF MEATS

Meat can be boiled or simmered, roasted, fried, broiled, pan-broiled, braised, or stewed. Always be sure your meat is clean— wipe large cuts if necessary.

Frying—cooking in fat—is one of the easiest ways of preparing meat, though the least recommended because fried meats are less digestible than those cooked in other ways. But if you like fried meat, or have no equipment to do anything else, here is the way to do it:

FRIED MEAT

COOKING TIME:

Steaks or lamb chops	rare	12–15 minutes
	medium	15–20 minutes
	well done	20–25 minutes
Pork or veal	well done	25–30 minutes, longer if cuts are thick

Put about 1 tablespoon of cooking fat or oil in a skillet and heat. Put in your steak or chops and allow them to cook over a medium fire. When browned on one side turn and brown on the other side. Season the browned side. Turn several times while cooking.

Remember, pork and veal should always be well done.

PAN-BROILED MEAT

TO PAN-BROIL means to cook in a sizzling hot skillet, with no added fat except in the case of very lean meats such as chopped beef.

COOKING TIME:

Steaks or lamb chops	rare	12–15 minutes
	medium	15–20 minutes
	well done	20–25 minutes
Veal or pork	well done	25–30 minutes, longer for thick cuts

Heat your skillet until it is sizzling hot. (If a drop of water in the skillet bounces and leaps until it disappears, the pan is sizzling.) Cut a small piece of fat from the meat. Spear it on a fork and gently rub the surface of the pan or griddle. Put your steaks or chops in and after a few minutes of cooking turn and sear the other side. The fat in the meat will begin to melt and form in the pan. Drain this off as the meat cooks. Season with pepper and salt after both sides have been seared. Turn often until done.

T O   S E A R means to seal meat at the beginning of cooking. It is done by plunging the meat into boiling water or by frying in hot fat or by placing it in a very hot oven for 10 or 15 minutes.

BROILED MEAT

C O O K I N G   T I M E:

Steaks or		
lamb chops	rare	12–15 minutes
	medium	15–20 minutes
	well done	20–25 minutes
Pork chops or		
veal	well done	30–45 minutes

In gas and electric stoves, the meat is placed on the broiling grid and placed about 4 to 6 inches below the flame or heating element. There are two schools of thought about this type of broiling. Some say put the meat in a cold broiler. Others insist that the broiler be hot. There is little difference in flavor which-ever method you use. There are times when the oven has been in use and you must use a hot broiler unless you want to wait. If the broiler is already hot, the meat will cook a little quicker and therefore needs watching.

Season steaks before cooking. If you want to have a different flavor, spread a thin coating of prepared mustard over the surface of the steaks or chops just before they finish cooking.

A thin coating of French dressing also gives the steak a fine flavor.

Crumbled roquefort cheese spread over lamb chops before they go into the oven makes them different and truly delicious.

If you cook steaks or chops on a barbecue over charcoal, the grid is part of the equipment. If you cook over live coals in a kitchen range or over an open fire, you will need a broiling grill to hold the meat. When broiling over direct fire it is better to have smoldering embers rather than flames. As the fat from the meat drips onto the embers it will ignite and sometimes give you more flame and fire than you need. Turn the meat often.

Remember, pork and veal should always be well done.

When your meat is broiled, turn it onto a hot platter, sprinkle it with some freshly chopped parsley, and serve at once.

BOILED OR SIMMERED MEAT

Some meats are cooked in water or other liquid, a process known as boiling, but it is really simmering because to obtain the best results the meat should be cooked for a long time just under the boiling point.

The tougher cuts of meat are the ones most usually boiled. The boiled favorites are rump, navel, plate, ribs, and brisket cuts of beef; also fresh or smoked ox tongue. Mutton or lamb is often boiled, and usually it is served with caper sauce. And ham is the favorite of all boiled meats.

Boiled meats are usually served with horse-radish or mustard sauce.

Cooking time is usually from 2 to 6 hours, depending on the age, size, and toughness of the meat. It is always wise to allow plenty of time. Boiled meats are rather pallid and unappetizing to look at, and they can be insipid. In addition to a sauce it is wise to season them while cooking. Add an onion to the water, a piece of bay leaf, some rosemary, and a pinch of thyme.

BOILED DINNER

A boiled dinner is boiled meat with vegetables cooked in the same pot with the meat. Corned beef is the meat most often used, but fresh meat can be used as well.

The cooking time will vary from 2–5 hours, depending on what kind of meat you are using and how big a piece. Corned beef takes

from 30–40 minutes per pound. Fresh meat cooks in less time—
about 25 minutes a pound.

Besides the meat, you will need the following vegetables and
seasonings:

White turnips	Cabbage
Carrots	1 bay leaf
Potatoes	Pinch of thyme
Onions	Salt (for fresh meat only)

Pepper

Allow at least one medium-sized vegetable for each person to
be served—except for cabbage, of course. One medium-sized head
cut in quarters will be enough for any but a very large family.
Some people like beets with a boiled dinner. They must be cooked
separately.

M E T H O D: Place the meat in a large kettle and cover it with
boiling water. For a 3–4 pound piece of fresh meat, add 1 tablespoon of salt and about ⅛ teaspoon of pepper. Corned meat requires no salt.

After the meat has cooked over low heat for about 2 hours, test
with the tines of a fork.

About an hour before the meat is to be served, add the onions,
turnips, and carrots. Add the potatoes 15 minutes later. Add the
quartered cabbage 15 minutes before serving.

When the meat and vegetables are done, remove the meat to
the serving platter. A sprinkling of chopped parsley improves its
appearance.

Trim the platter with the vegetables and serve with either a
horse-radish sauce or a mustard sauce.

Do not throw away the "pot liquor"! Save it for soups. Remember that some of the fine flavor of the meat and vegetables is
in that water in which they were cooked.

If you cooked too many vegetables, don't worry about them.
These particular vegetables make a nice vegetable hash.

BOILED CORNED BEEF

COOKING TIME: 30–40 minutes per pound

Soak the corned beef in cold water for about an hour. Then place it in a kettle and cover it with cold water. Put the kettle over slow heat or a low flame. When the water comes to a boil, turn the heat down and simmer.

Cabbage and potatoes may be cooked in the same water for a corned-beef-and-cabbage dinner. Allow 45 minutes for the pota·toes and 15 minutes for the cabbage.

If the "pot liquor" is not too salty, it can be made the basis of a good soup. Do not save it, however, if it has a briny taste.

BOILED HAM

COOKING TIME: 30–40 minutes per pound

Ask your butcher about the ham you buy. If it is tenderized, it does not need much cooking. If it is a real smoked ham, it should be washed thoroughly with a brush, rinsed, and put in a kettle of boiling water almost to cover. Simmer the required amount of time. If the ham is to be served cold, allow it to cool in the water in which it was cooked. If it is to be served hot, take it out of the water and remove the skin. To remove the skin, use a sharp, pointed knife. Cut just under the skin around the outer edge. Pull the skin back or up toward the shank or bone end as you cut it away from fat. Pull it over the bone end or slit it and cut it away from the bone. Some cooks leave a small portion of the skin near the shank. Score the fat, dot with cloves, sprinkle with some brown sugar, and put in the oven long enough to brown and glaze.

Ham which is baked after boiling may be basted with wine, pineapple juice, cider, or some of the water in which it was boiled.

BOILED SMOKED TONGUE

COOKING TIME: about 4 hours

Soak the tongue overnight. If this is not possible, scrub it well, cover it with cold water, and bring it to the boil. Remove the tongue and discard the water. Rinse the tongue, return it to the kettle, and cover it with boiling water. Bring to the boil and then simmer about 4 hours. Test with a fork to determine when done.

When the tongue is done, the skin must be removed. If too hot to handle, plunge it into cold water for a minute or two, remove the skin, and trim large end. The skin of a boiled tongue peels off easily. Start removing it from the large end. Cut away the bone, fat, and gristle at the large end. In the chunk of fat and bone there are several muscles of meat. These fleshy trimmings from the large end can be ground and used as a sandwich spread. After skinning and trimming, return tongue to original cooking water to reheat.

Spinach or other greens are a nice accompaniment to tongue.

BOILED PORK

COOKING TIME: 25–30 minutes per pound

Cover the pork with boiling water, season with salt and pepper, bring to the boil, and simmer.

Fresh pork is very good boiled and is generally served with sauerkraut and boiled potatoes. Any fresh pork may be boiled. Fresh ham, spareribs, pig's feet, pig's knuckles, or pieces of shoulder are the cuts most often cooked in this manner. Pork must be well done.

Sauerkraut may be added an hour before serving time. Potatoes may be boiled in the pork water, but they are apt to be greasy and might better be boiled separately.

CORNED PORK

COOKING TIME: 30–40 minutes per pound

Corned pork is usually ham and shoulder. Soak for an hour in cold water. Drain, place in a large kettle, nearly cover with water, and simmer until tender. This may be prepared and served with vegetables as for Boiled Dinner.

ROAST MEAT

Meat cooked in a pan in the oven is a roast. A roasting thermometer is a good investment and will aid the new cook in determining the degree of "doneness" of a roast. If you use a thermometer there are two things to watch: The bulb must not rest on a bone nor in a piece of fat. Make a hole in the thickest muscle of the roast with a skewer or an ice pick. (A skewer is a long, pointed pin or peg made of either wood or metal and is used to hold meats together so they will keep their shape.)

After you have made the incision in the muscular part of the meat, insert the thermometer so that the bulb is in about the center of the thickest part. When putting the roast in the oven, turn the thermometer so that it can be read easily. Following are the thermometer readings which tell when roasts are done:

Roast beef	Rare	140°
	Medium	160°
	Well done	170°
Pork	Fresh, well done	185°
	Smoked	170°
Veal		170°
Lamb or mutton	Medium	175°
	Well done	180°

ROAST BEEF

There's nothing better than good roast beef, unless it is a thick juicy steak. For roast beef the old way is still the best way—that is, to start it in a very hot oven (500°) to sear the outside, then reduce the heat.

For prime ribs or standing rib roast or a rolled roast, the cooking time in a 500° preheated oven is:

Rare	15 minutes per pound
Medium	18 minutes per pound
Well done	20–25 minutes per pound

Wipe the meat clean and season it. Rolled roasts and sirloins should be wiped, trimmed, and dredged.

T O   D R E D G E means to coat or cover, usually with flour and seasoning. (Some articles, however, are dredged with sugar.)

To prepare the flour for dredging a 4–5 pound roast, take ¼ cup flour, 2 teaspoons salt, and ⅛ teaspoon pepper. Increase all ingredients for larger roasts. Mix the flour and seasoning and rub the mixture over the surface of the roast. Place the roast on a rack in a shallow roasting pan. Be sure the fat side is up so that the roast will baste itself.

Put the roast in the very hot oven, 500°, and let it cook rapidly for 15 minutes. It may smoke a great deal, but don't let that worry you. Open a window and get a bit of fresh air. This method of cooking does shrink the meat somewhat, but results are worth the loss.

At the end of the initial 15 minutes of searing time, reduce the heat to 375° and cook for the required time. If possible, gauge your cooking time and your dinner preparations so that the roast can stand covered for at least 10 to 20 minutes before it is served. It seems to carve and taste better.

A meal fit for the gods is roast beef and Yorkshire pudding. Don't be alarmed at the thought of the Yorkshire pudding. It is really easy to make. Here is an easy and delicious recipe. Have the pudding mixture ready when the roast is removed from the oven, and heat the oven to 400°.

YORKSHIRE PUDDING

PREPARATION TIME: about 15 minutes

COOKING TIME: about 20 minutes in a 400° oven

There are two kinds of Yorkshire Pudding—thick and thin. The thick type has a custardlike consistency; the thin kind is crispy. The ingredients and quantities are the same for both kinds; the difference lies in the method of baking.

1 cup sifted flour	1 cup milk
½ teaspoon baking powder	2 egg yolks, beaten
½ teaspoon salt	1 tablespoon melted shortening
2 egg whites, stiffly beaten	or peanut or cooking oil

METHOD: Mix the flour, baking powder, and salt together, then sift into a bowl. Add the milk, beaten egg yolks, and melted shortening.

TO BEAT EGG YOLKS: Beat until thick and lemon-colored.

Mix well. Fold in the stiffly beaten egg whites.

Up to this point the methods of preparation are the same for thick or thin pudding. For the thick kind, cover the bottom of an ovenware or glass baking dish or an 8-inch square cake pan with some drippings from your roast beef. Pour the batter into dish and bake in a 400° oven for about 20 minutes. At the end of about 10 minutes, when the pudding is well risen, baste with some more drippings. When done, it is a delicious golden brown. Cut in squares to serve. This serves 4, generously allowing for second helpings.

For the thin pudding, use 2 glass pie plates covered with beef drippings. Divide your batter in these 2 plates and bake as above.

Yorkshire pudding is good with or without roast beef. It can be made at any time. Bacon drippings give it a good flavor.

ROAST TENDERLOIN OF BEEF

COOKING TIME: 15 minutes in a very hot oven (500°); then reduce the heat to 400° and cook

Rare	20 minutes longer
Medium	30 minutes longer
Well done	40–50 minutes or more

All skin, fat, and ligaments should be trimmed away, leaving just clear meat. Wipe the meat and lard the upper surface with thin slices of fat salt pork, using toothpicks to hold the pork in place. Rub all surfaces of the meat with butter or other suitable fat. Dredge with seasoned flour. Place the tenderloin on a rack in a shallow pan and put it into a very hot oven, following the instructions given in the cooking time.

The term "lard" as used above is self-explanatory. There is another use for the term, however, one you should know.

TO LARD means to insert thin slivers of fat salt pork or bacon into dry, solid meat or fish. Slits may be cut with a sharp pointed knife and the slivers inserted. Meat or fish may also be larded by covering with salt pork or bacon, as in the above recipe.

ROAST VEAL

COOKING TIME: 25–30 minutes per pound of meat. Cook the first 15 minutes in a very hot oven (500°), then reduce the heat to 350° and cook for the allotted time or at 375° for full time per weight.

Roast veal is apt to be a rather colorless and tasteless meat unless it is doctored and spiced. Wipe and clean the roast, make slits in the flesh, and insert slivers of onion, some cloves, and cracked pieces of bay leaves. Any other herb that you fancy may be sprinkled over the roast. Sprinkle with salt and pepper, add some fat to the bottom of a covered roasting pan, and add a clove of finely minced garlic to the fat. This is one roast which it is better to cook covered. As soon as enough juice has collected in the bottom of the pan, baste the meat. If the roast isn't brown enough, take the lid off the pan for the last 30 minutes of cooking.

ROAST STUFFED VEAL

PREPARATION TIME: about 45 minutes

COOKING TIME: 25–30 minutes per pound of meat in a 375° oven

Leg, shoulder, or breast may be used. Have the veal boned at the market or a pocket made to hold the dressing. Wipe the meat.

Prepare a stuffing or dressing and put it in the pocket. When the dressing is ready, stuff it into the pocket or slit. Do not pack too solidly as it needs some room for expansion. When the cavity is filled, the dressing must be enclosed by tying, sewing, or skewering the meat over the opening which holds the dressing. Use a very large needle with a big wide eye and heavy sewing cotton or a thin white cord. Thread the needle and sew the meat together over the opening, using long loose stitches. You can buy small skewers which you can use as pins, or if you prefer, you can use white cord to tie the meat together securely. The main trick is to keep the dressing in the pocket or sack.

Prepare the meat for roasting as described under Roast Veal.

STUFFING FOR MEAT, POULTRY, AND FISH

This is a basic recipe for stuffing for all meats, fish, and fowl.

The following quantities will be adequate for a roasting chicken, a duck, a medium-sized fish, or the average piece of veal, pork, or lamb. For turkey and large roasts increase the proportions of all ingredients, remembering that it is best not to overpack the stuffing.

12 slices bread, white or brown	1 pinch powdered sage
1 medium onion	1 pinch powdered thyme
4 stalks celery	1 scant teaspoon salt
1 teaspoon poultry seasoning	⅛ teaspoon pepper

N O T E: 2 tablespoons melted shortening may be added for veal roasts.

M E T H O D: Toast the bread brown but do not burn. Cut or crumble into small bits or cubes and place in a large bowl. Wash and clean the celery stalks, cut into strips, then cut crosswise, producing small cubes. To do this, cut the stalk into 4 long pieces, place them on your cutting board, and cross cut them. It saves time and is efficient.

Add the diced celery to the bread. Peel and grate the onion over the bowl. The flat wire type of grater is the most satisfactory one to use. (The best way to minimize onion tears is to breathe through the mouth while doing the preparation.)

Add all the seasoning and mix either with a spoon or the hands. Note that the only liquid is from the grated onion and moisture which may have adhered to the celery after washing. Neither is shortening added to the dressing because the dry dressing will absorb fat and liquid from the meat during the process of cooking.

When the ingredients are well mixed, put them into the opening and seal as suggested above.

VARIATIONS:

Instead of bread, one of the following may be used:

2 cups crumbled corn bread	2 cups mashed potatoes
1 cup uncooked quick-cooking oatmeal	2 cups mashed sweet potatoes
	1 cup mashed chestnuts

ADDITIONS:

To the basic recipe you may add:

For Roast Chicken	½ cup partly chopped oysters with a little liquid, or
	½ cup chestnuts diced, plus a diced apple
For Roast Turkey	Increase the basic recipe 2 or 3 times, depending on the size of the bird, and add variations under Chicken, doubled or trebled
For Roast Duck or Goose	1 cup diced raw apple and the grated rind of 1 orange
For Roast Meats	3 medium carrots, grated
	1 clove minced garlic

TO MINCE means to cut into very small pieces. You can mince garlic, chives, celery, slices of onion—in fact all small quantities—with a sharp knife on your cutting board by slicing first and then chopping with your knife.

If you like it, squeeze in the juice of ½ lemon.

Shortening, liquid, and egg are used to bind the ingredients of a dressing together. If you think you would prefer it, you may bind your ingredients together with a little milk, egg, or water— not too much, just enough to dampen and hold the ingredients together.

ROAST LAMB

The leg is the most popular lamb roast, but the shoulder or forequarter is equally tasty. For special events the crown roast or saddle is favored. A crown roast is prepared by the butcher. He takes sections of the loin or rib chops, scrapes the ends of the bones, ties them together into a crown, grinds the trimmings, and fills the center with the ground meat. The saddle is a complete cut across the back of loin cuts. Roast stuffed breast of lamb is another delicious dish.

ROAST LEG, SHOULDER, OR BREAST OF LAMB

COOKING TIME: 30 minutes per pound in a slow oven (300°); by thermometer (leg only), 175°–180°

Wipe the meat and dredge with seasoned flour. If desired, slice an onion, cover the top of the roast with the slices and fasten in place with toothpicks. Place the meat on a rack in an open pan, fat side up. If you like garlic, just before dredging take a clove of garlic and rub over the surface of the meat. Baste occasionally.

CROWN ROAST OR SADDLE OF LAMB

COOKING TIME: 25–30 minutes per pound in a moderate oven (350°)

Wipe the meat, sprinkle with salt and pepper, set on a rack in open roasting pan, and place in the oven. Garlic or onion may be used as in the above recipe. While the crown roast is cooking, it is advisable to place small pieces of salt pork over the ends of the bones to keep them from burning. When the roast is finished, remove the bits of pork and put paper frills (that you buy or make) on each bone.

STUFFED BREAST OF LAMB

PREPARATION TIME: about 45 minutes

COOKING TIME: 30 minutes per pound in slow oven (300°)

For a small family one side of the breast will be adequate. Have the butcher cut a pocket just above the bones. Use any form of dressing you think you would like (p. 100). Grated carrot added to ½ of the basic recipe makes a good stuffing for lamb. Secure the dressing in place, cover with sliced onion, place the meat on a rack in an open roasting pan, and cook.

For a large family or many servings, get a pair of breasts from the butcher. Be sure they are opposites so they will fit together. Put the dressing on the inside or curved part of one breast. Place the other side in place and tie or sew the two breasts together. Cover with onion or rub with garlic, dredge with seasoned flour, place on a rack in a pan, and put in the oven.

ROAST FRESH PORK

PREPARATION TIME: about 10 minutes

COOKING TIME: 30–35 minutes per pound in a moderate oven (375–400°); by thermometer, 185°

The loin is the most popular pork roast. However, leg—whole or half—the shoulder cuts, and pieces known as butts make equally good roasts. As we have repeated, pork must be well cooked.

Wipe the meat and score. Sprinkle well with salt and pepper.

TO SCORE means to cut, with crossed or parallel lines, the surface fat or skin of foods.

Just as some people think lamb or mutton has an odd taste, others think pork has a "pig" taste. An onion or two sliced and pinned to the top of the roast with toothpicks helps to overcome that.

ROAST STUFFED PORK

Have your butcher bone the leg or shoulder. Make your dressing, using the basic recipe for stuffing or dressing (p. 100). A cup of peeled, diced tart apple added to the basic recipe adds zest and flavor. The cooking time and method are the same as for roast pork.

ROAST SPARERIBS

COOKING TIME: 25–30 minutes per pound in a moderate oven (375°)

Have the butcher crack the bones. The ribs may be roasted whole or cut into individual servings before cooking by cutting between the rib bones, leaving about 3 ribs per section. Since there is so much bone, it is well to allow ¾ of a pound per person.

Season the ribs before cooking. Rub some dry mustard on them, sprinkle them with a little powdered sage, salt, and pepper, dust them lightly with flour, and put them in a shallow roasting pan. When they have cooked long enough for the fat to collect in the pan, baste them often to prevent the meat from becoming dry. An onion sliced over the ribs adds flavor.

BARBECUED SPARERIBS

A barbecue sauce poured over the spareribs while cooking and then used for basting gives them an excellent flavor. There are as many barbecue sauces as there are barbecues.

If you have no sauce prepared and want to bring out the flavor of meat, brush it with French dressing seasoned with garlic.

BARBECUE SAUCE

PREPARATION TIME: 15 minutes or longer

This is a basic recipe for barbecue sauce. You may add to or take away according to your personal taste. Whatever you do, you will have a good barbecue sauce.

1 cup salad oil	1 tablespoon salt
1 cup wine or wine vinegar	1 teaspoon black pepper
2 big onions, minced or grated	1 tablespoon smoked hickory
2 cloves garlic, minced	salt

1 teaspoon dry mustard

M E T H O D: Mix the oil and wine or wine vinegar. Beat with a fork until the two are blended. Add the remaining ingredients, mixing well. Store in a jar and allow to stand overnight before using. Stir well before using. Pour onto the meat with a tablespoon and use a spoon for basting, lifting up from the bottom of the pan.

A D D I T I O N S: Any of these may be added to the basic recipe. They are all good. Some people like their sauce hot, some with herbs.

¼ teaspoon Tabasco sauce (for heat)
½ teaspoon chili powder (for heat)
1 tablespoon Worcestershire sauce or A.1
1 teaspoon minced thyme (fresh)
1 teaspoon minced marjoram (fresh)
1 teaspoon minced parsley (fresh)
1 teaspoon minced rosemary (fresh)
1 tablespoon grated fresh horse-radish or 1 teaspoon dry horse-radish

N O T E: If dried herbs are used, use a scant teaspoonful of each.

Any or all of the above may be added to the basic recipe. It will be good, it will be different. Just remember that the 3 essential ingredients for the sauce are oil, wine or wine vinegar (plain vinegar may be used), and salt. From there on follow your own bent.

ROAST SPARERIBS WITH SAUERKRAUT

C O O K I N G   T I M E: 25–30 minutes per pound in a moderate oven (375°)

The preparation of the ribs is the same as for plain roasted.

Put your partially drained sauerkraut in the bottom of the roasting pan. Place the ribs on top of the sauerkraut and bake. Dip the liquid from a corner of the pan and baste several times. If the liquid cooks away in the pan, hot water may be added from time to time. Another good variation is:

ROAST SPARERIBS WITH POTATOES

PREPARATION TIME: about 30 minutes

COOKING TIME: 25–30 minutes per pound in a moderate oven (375°)

Prepare the ribs as for roasting.

Allow 1 medium potato per person and 2 extra. Peel and slice the potatoes. Peel and slice 2 medium onions. Put layers of potato and onion in the bottom of the roasting pan. Sprinkle with salt and a little pepper. Add ½ cup of water. Arrange the ribs on top of the potatoes and roast. Be sure there is enough liquid in the pan for basting purposes.

MUTTON

Any of the mutton cuts may be prepared in the same ways as lamb. Mutton is stronger, having a more pronounced flavor. Rub the roast with a cut clove of garlic. Some people like little slivers of garlic or onion wedged into the meat. Try it if you like the flavor. Follow cooking time given for lamb, but more time will be needed if the mutton is not young.

BRAISED MEAT

Braised meat is first seared or browned in hot fat in a heavy iron frying pan, Dutch oven, or kettle. After browning, it is either simmered in the heavy kettle, covered, on the top of the stove with very little liquid or it is put into the oven and baked covered in a slow to moderate oven (300°–350°) for about 3 hours. Pot roast is the most popular and best known of the braised meats.

It is a waste of good meat to braise anything but the cheaper and tougher cuts. These tougher cuts really have a fine flavor and are delicious when properly prepared. The following cuts are the ones usually braised. The beef cuts are the ones usually used for pot roast. But there is no reason why you should not pot-roast any cut of meat. If you do not have an oven you can do nothing else. The better the cut, the shorter the time it will take for cooking.

Beef	Parts of the shoulder	Veal	Neck
	Chuck		Ribs
	Clod		Shoulder
	Rump		Heart
	Round		
	Short ribs	Lamb	Breast
	Tenderloin tips		Shoulder
	Neck		Shanks
	Brisket or plate		Neck slices
	Thick pieces of shank		Heart
	Ox tails		
	Heart		

M E T H O D: Wipe the meat, dredge with flour, salt, and pepper. For small pieces of meat we have found this method of dredging a great time saver:

Use a 5-pound paper flour bag. Any strong paper bag will do. Put ½ cup of flour, 2 teaspoons of salt, and ¼ teaspoon of pepper into bag. Mix these well in the bag. Then drop the pieces of meat, a few at a time, into the bag and shake well. The meat will be well coated with flour and ready to brown in the hot fat. Use this procedure for short ribs, chunks or cubes of meat, chicken, rabbit, and any other cut that will fit into the bag.

To give a good flavor, mince a clove of garlic and add it to 3 or 4 tablespoons of fat, or use 2 or 3 slices of minced onion if you prefer. Brown the meat on all sides and place it in a casserole or Dutch oven. Rinse the cooking pan with ¼ cup of water and pour it over the meat. Whole or sliced onions should go in at the beginning of the cooking. Other vegetables may be added later as for pot roast. The vegetables may be cubed, diced, chunked, or left whole according to your desires. All you need remember is that braising is really pot-roasting.

GRAVY

PREPARATION TIME: 5–10 minutes

COOKING TIME: 5 minutes after the gravy begins to thicken and bubble

Gravy is made from the juices and drippings of fried, baked, braised, or roasted meats. Meat gravy should be brown; certainly it looks more appetizing than the tattle-tale gray type. There are several ways to be sure of good brown gravy: The flour may be browned in the pan with the drippings, taking care not to burn it, or vegetable coloring can be added. There are many gravy colorings on the market under various trade names. A cup of coffee may be used as part of the liquid to give color.

In some parts of the country gravy is part of the breakfast menu. Breakfast gravy is usually made from the fat of fried meat such as ham, bacon, sausage, or salt pork. When salt pork is used, it is fried or rendered until it is a rich golden brown.

When making gravy, fat or drippings are necessary.

For each tablespoon of fat or drippings, add
1 tablespoon flour
1 cup liquid, water or milk
Seasoning to taste
This makes a thin gravy. If you like a fairly thick gravy, use a heaping tablespoon of flour.

METHOD I: Do not discard the natural juices from the meat which will be in the pan along with the drippings. Since fat rises to the surface above other liquids, you can skim it off.

T O   S K I M means to remove fat, scum, cream, or other matter which rises to the top of a liquid. This is done with a large spoon or, in the case of cream, a regular skimmer.

You may find it a little difficult at first to judge just how much fat you have in your pan. Heaven won't fall if you have a little more or less.

Let us suppose a pint of gravy will be sufficient. Skim off the excess fat, leaving about 2 tablespoonfuls in the pan with the natural juices. Be sure to keep the liquid that is not fat.

Put the fat over a medium heat and add the flour by sprinkling it over the surface of the pan. Use a large fork rather than a spoon for this mixing. Mix the flour into the drippings in the pan and stir constantly while it is mixing and cooking. As the flour cooks, it will brown. Do not allow it to burn. This combination of fat and flour cooked this way is called a *roux*. When the flour is a golden brown, add a little water or stock (part of the 2 cupfuls), mixing rapidly. The gravy will begin to thicken almost immediately. Keep thinning by adding more of the liquid until the roux is all blended with the liquid. You must keep stirring because the flour will begin to cook and thicken in the bottom of the pan unless the gravy is kept agitated. Add seasonings. Cook 5 minutes after the liquid begins to bubble.

M E T H O D   I I: The formula and quantities are the same as for Method I, but it is sometimes necessary to add coloring. Method II seems simpler, quicker, and more satisfactory.

Use the jar method for mixing the flour and liquid.

Put some liquid in the bottom of the jar. Add 1 tablespoon of flour for each cup of liquid, then more liquid. Seal the jar and shake vigorously until the liquid and flour are blended. Add this mixture with the remaining liquid to the drippings in the pan and stir constantly until thick. If it is pale, add a gravy coloring, a little bit at a time, until you have the exact shade you want. Add your seasoning, and the gravy is done.

If your gravy should be lumpy for any reason, do not despair and don't throw it away. Strain it and cast away the lumps.

GRAVY TRICKS: If you are going to have mashed potatoes with your roast, save some of the water in which they were cooked for your gravy liquid. Onion water, carrot water, pea water—in fact, almost any vegetable water—is good in gravy except liquid from the cabbage family and string-bean water.

POT ROAST

PREPARATION TIME: about 30 minutes

COOKING TIME: from 3 to 4 hours, depending on the size and cut of meat, either on top of the stove over a low flame or in a slow oven, covered, at 300° to 350°

Pot roast	1 cup sliced or diced carrots
1 onion, sliced	1 cup diced celery
Salt and pepper	2 small white turnips per person
Flour	1 medium potato per person
Garlic if desired	3 tablespoons cooking fat, preferably
1 cup sliced or diced	bacon drippings
onions	

METHOD: Put the cooking fat in the cooking utensil to heat. If you use salt pork or suet, you will have to try out or render it.

TO DICE means to cut into very small cubes.

TO TRY OUT or RENDER means to cook or fry the fat out of salt pork, bacon, suet, or any other form of uncooked fat. This is done slowly so as not to burn the fat or grease. Some people recommend the top of a double boiler as the safest way to try out.

While the fat is heating, dredge the meat with flour, salt, and pepper.

If you use garlic, take a clove and mince it on your cutting board. Add it to the hot fat. Put the meat in the fat and sear or brown it on all sides. If you are going to continue the cooking in the same pot or pan, add ½ cup of water, a sliced onion, and the seasonings. Try also a crushed bay leaf, a couple of whole cloves, and a few powdered herbs. Remember, not too much. A pinch will give you a suggestion of flavor; more may give you an overdose.

Keep adding small quantities of hot water if necessary.

If you are going to transfer the meat to a casserole, take out the meat, add ½ cup of water to the skillet, and rinse the fat and added water, pouring it over the meat in the casserole. Add the onion and spices, cover, and cook slowly.

About an hour before the meat is to be served, add the vegetables, adding a little more water if necessary.

Cook the potatoes separately.

When the meat and vegetables are done, remove them and make the gravy. You ought to have no less than 2 cups of liquid in the pot. If you do not, add some of the water in which the potatoes have been boiled to make up the required amount, or you may add a small can of mushrooms with their juice.

POT-ROAST GRAVY

For each cup of liquid you will need 1 tablespoon of flour for thickening. Here is a trick for thickening gravies: Put a little cold water in the bottom of a jar which has a tight-fitting lid. Then add the required amount of flour and 1 cup of liquid from pot. Put on the close-fitting lid and shake vigorously. The flour and liquid will be well mixed with no lumps. Add this to the liquid in the pot, stirring constantly so that it thickens evenly. Cook about 5 minutes before serving.

Here is a nice variation for thickening pot roast gravy: Allow 2 gingersnaps per cup of liquid, crush them to powder by rolling with a rolling pin. Stir the powdered snaps into the gravy. This will thicken the gravy, give it an additional rich brown flavor, and surprise you because it is so good.

Another way to thicken pot-roast gravy is to grate a medium-sized potato into the liquid in the pot and cook about 5 minutes.

When ready to serve, pour some of the gravy over the meat and vegetables or serve the gravy separately.

STEWS

There are all types and kinds of stews, and as many opinions as to which particular type or kind is the best. There are brown stews and pale stews. Brown stews are made by searing the meat first in hot fat. Pale stews are made by direct cooking of the meat in water. Both kinds are equally good in flavor, but the brown stew is perhaps the more appetizing in appearance; so the directions given here are for brown stews. But if you are short of time, the meat can be cleaned and put directly into your stewing kettle and nearly covered with boiling water. The searing is actually the only difference between a brown stew and a white one.

If the meat you are to stew is all meat, allow ¼ pound per person. If it is part bone and gristle, allow ½ to ¾ pound per person.

A stew is a complete meal cooked in one pot. Any vegetable that you fancy may be cooked in your stew. It is the combination of flavors which makes the stew such a delightful dish.

PREPARATION TIME: about 30 minutes

COOKING TIME: about 2 hours, or until the meat is tender when tested with a fork

Meat—beef, lamb, mutton, or veal

Fat

1 medium small onion per person

1 medium carrot per person

1 small white turnip per person

1 chunk or piece of yellow turnip per person

1 or more stalks of celery per person, cut in chunks

1 medium-sized potato per person

2 tablespoons chopped parsley

Seasonings—salt, pepper, spices, herbs

METHOD: Dredge the meat in seasoned flour. Melt some cooking fat in a heavy skillet—1 tablespoon of fat is enough for about 2 pounds of meat. Sear quickly on all sides, and when brown transfer to a stewing kettle. Cover the meat with water and simmer over a low flame. The onions, carrots, and turnips may be added when the cooking starts or may be delayed for a half hour. The celery and potatoes should be put in for the last 30–45 minutes of cooking. If you want to add 1 cup of fresh peas and 1 cup of cut string beans, do so. Add anything you fancy to a stew, remembering that you do not want to overcook the tender vegetables, so put them in near the end of the cooking time. This is true of the parsley and thickening, which should be added for the last 5 minutes of cooking.

Most people like their stews thickened, but not too thick. One tablespoon of flour for each 2 cups of liquid will make the juice about half as thick as pot-roast gravy. Use the jar method described under Pot-Roast Gravy (page 111) to mix the flour and liquid. If you are going to have dumplings, do not thicken the liquid until after the dumplings have been cooked.

DUMPLINGS

PREPARATION TIME: about 5 minutes

COOKING TIME: 15 minutes in a closed kettle, in a steaming rack, or on the top of a stew, *never* in liquid

Dumplings are not difficult to make. They need not be tough or soggy. That is up to you. There are two things to remember about dumplings: never let them rest in the liquid; and once they are in the pot and the cover closed, do not look at them to see how they are cooking. They will cook and be good if you leave them alone. A cup of flour makes 4 good-sized dumplings. If you want 8 dumplings, double the quantity. If you will need 12, triple the amounts, and so on.

1 cup flour	1 tablespoon shortening
2 teaspoons baking powder	½ teaspoon salt
½ cup milk, scant	

METHOD: Sift the flour, salt, and baking powder into a bowl. Cut in the shortening.

T O   C U T   I N means to combine fat and flour by using 2 knives and actually cutting the fat into the flour until the fat has been reduced to fine particles. A pastry blender may be used to hasten the work.

After the shortening has been cut in, add the liquid slowly until the dough is wet and sticky but not lumpy or watery.

If the liquid in the kettle comes up over the vegetables, drain some of it off so that the liquid is at least ½ inch below the surface of the meat and vegetables. Drop the dumpling dough by spoonfuls onto the top of the meat and vegetables. Cover the pot tightly and allow to cook for 15 minutes. *Do not remove the lid* until the cooking time is up. Your dumplings will be fluffy and tender, but if you lift the lid for just one peek you're likely to have heavy, soggy dough. Don't be a *pot snooper*. Give your food a chance to be good.

If you have drained off some of the liquid from the pot, make your thickened gravy while the dumplings are cooking. Remove the dumplings from the pot to a warm platter. Add the thickened liquid to the pot, mix, cook a few minutes, and dish up the stew, arranging the meat and vegetables in center of platter, leaving the dumplings at the outer edge. Pour some gravy over the meat and vegetables and serve the balance in a gravy boat.

Mulligan is another name for stew, as is Irish stew. All meat stews are essentially and basically the same and differ only in two ways, whether or not the meat is brown or left *au naturel*. The type, kinds, and amount of vegetables you put into a stew also give it variety.

SWISS STEAK

The most satisfactory cut to buy for Swiss steak is round steak cut from 2 to 2½ inches thick. Other cuts of lean solid meat can be used.

P R E P A R A T I O N   T I M E: about 45 minutes

C O O K I N G   T I M E: about 2 hours

For 6–8 servings you will need:

2 pounds steak   1 medium onion, sliced
½ cup flour   Cooking fat
Salt   2 cups hot water, or 2 cups hot
Pepper   tomato juice

M E T H O D: Mix ½ teaspoon of salt and ⅛ teaspoon of pepper with the flour. (¼ teaspoon of dry mustard may be added). Place the meat on a board and cover with some of the flour. Pound the flour into the meat with a potato masher, the bottom of a cream bottle, or the edge of a heavy saucer. Turn the meat and pound flour into the other side until all the flour has been absorbed by the meat. Heat about 2 tablespoons of fat in a skillet and brown the meat. Add the onion when the meat is browned on both sides. Add the hot water or tomato juice. Cover and cook slowly until tender.

Mashed potatoes, boiled rice, or noodles are good with this dish. Add a green vegetable and you have a savory meal.

GROUND MEAT

The most satisfactory ground meat is top round or sirloin which the butcher will grind for you. The tougher cuts of shoulder are also very good when ground sufficiently. Tough meat should be ground 3 times.

GROUND BEEF OR HAMBURGER STEAK

Individual taste determines how the ground steak should be prepared. Some people like onions and some do not. The entire amount of meat can be molded into one large flat cake to be broiled or pan-broiled, or it can be made into individual cakes and broiled or pan-broiled.

PREPARATION TIME: 15 minutes

COOKING TIME: 8 to 15 minutes

For 3–4 servings you will need:

| 1 pound ground meat | ½ teaspoon salt |
| 1 small minced onion (optional) | ⅛ teaspoon pepper |

1 teaspoon Worcestershire sauce

M E T H O D: Mix the ingredients and mold into 1 large cake or 4 small cakes. If they are to be broiled, make them about ½ inch thick. If they are to be pan-broiled, pat out as thin as possible and cook in a hot skillet, turning often. Cook 8–10 minutes for rare, 12 minutes for medium, and 15 minutes for well done.

If you want thin meat cakes, put a piece of waxed paper on the cutting board and press the meat with the palm of your hand until it is as thin as desired.

Here is a suggestion for cooking ground meat with onions:

For 4 people, separate a pound of seasoned ground meat into 8 equal parts. Make 8 balls and then press them out as thin as possible and still remain cakes. Mince 2 small onions. Take 4 of the thin cakes and divide the minced onion equally, placing it in the center of the 4 thin cakes. Take the remaining 4 cakes and cover the bottom cakes. Press the edges firmly together and pan-broil or broil. The onion is warm and crunchy and gives the dish a delightful flavor.

MEAT LOAF

PREPARATION TIME: about 40 minutes

COOKING TIME: 90 minutes in a 350° oven

A satisfactory meat loaf is one which combines a variety of meats. For 6–8 servings you will need:

1 pound ground beef	2 tablespoons catsup or
½ pound ground veal	chili sauce
½ pound ground lean fresh pork	¼ teaspoon dry mustard
1 minced onion	1 teaspoon salt
1 cup dry bread or cracker crumbs	¼ teaspoon pepper
1 egg, beaten	1 cup milk or tomato juice
1 tablespoon Worcestershire sauce	2 slices bacon

1 cup hot water

Tell your butcher that you would like lean meat for a meat loaf and have him grind the three meats together. Some butchers have the mixture already prepared.

M E T H O D: Put the meat in a large mixing bowl. Add the minced onion and bread crumbs and the dry seasonings. Beat the egg, add the liquids to the egg, and pour over the meat mixture, mixing well. Press the mixture into a loaf pan. Place the strips of bacon over the top, pour hot water over the meat, and bake about 90 minutes.

Some cooks prefer to press the mixture into the loaf pan to form the loaf. They then turn the molded mixture out of the loaf pan onto a roasting pan, cover with bacon, pour the hot water over the meat, and then bake. If this method is used, baste every 15 minutes.

MEAT BALLS

PREPARATION TIME: 30 minutes

COOKING TIME: 30 minutes

For 3–4 servings you will need:

1 pound ground meat	⅛ teaspoon pepper
1 small onion, minced	1 teaspoon salt
1 cup bread crumbs	1 teaspoon Worcestershire sauce
1 egg, beaten	¼ cup milk or tomato juice
2 tablespoons cooking fat	Flour

2 cups hot water

M E T H O D: Mix all ingredients thoroughly except the hot water and form into balls about the size of an egg. Dredge with flour and brown in hot fat. When completely brown, add the 2 cups of hot water and simmer for 30 minutes. Thicken the gravy with 1 tablespoon of flour.

If the meat balls are to be used with spaghetti or macaroni as a sauce, follow the above recipe and in addition add after the meat is browned:

1 cup tomatoes	½ cup minced celery
½ cup minced green pepper	2 cups tomato juice

a pinch of poultry seasoning

Five minutes before serving, thicken the gravy with 3 tablespoons of flour.

BREADED CHOPS, CUTLETS, AND FISH

There are some people who feel that a breaded chop is a waste of good meat. That, of course, is a matter of opinion and taste. Breaded pork chops, breaded veal chops with the kidney included, and breaded pork tenderloin are favorites with many people.

Chops and veal cutlets should be at least ½ inch thick. Pork tenderloins should be split.

T O B R E A D means to cover or coat the food with egg and crumbs prior to frying.

For breading 4 chops, 4 croquettes, or 1 pound of filleted fish, you will need:

1 egg
1 tablespoon milk
1 teaspoon salt
⅛ teaspoon pepper
¼ cup flour
¾ cup bread or cracker crumbs in a deep platter

For fish, corn meal may be substituted for crumbs.

M E T H O D: Add the milk to the egg and beat well until mixed. Mix the seasoning and flour. Dredge the meat with the seasoned flour, then dip it in the egg and then in the crumbs to cover.

If you are going to fry in a skillet, you should have about ⅛ inch of hot fat in the bottom of the pan. Place the breaded pieces in the pan and cook slowly until a rich brown on both sides. Pork and veal should be well cooked. Cover the pan with a lid and cook slowly for about 25 minutes, turning the chops several times. For the last 5 minutes of cooking, remove the lid. This final cooking will dry the breading and make it crisp when served. A gravy made from the cooking fat by adding milk or cream and 1 table-spoon of flour for each cup of liquid is often served over breaded meats. The gravy is particularly good if seasoned with chopped chives or a little onion juice.

ORGAN MEAT

Now we come to the foods that are considered so good for us, that are full of vitamins, flavor and pep. These foods are heartily dis-liked by many people. Your eating habits may already be fixed and if you don't like liver, heart, kidney, sweetbreads, tripe, and brains, you probably never will. Yet many people do like them very much.

LIVER

PREPARATION TIME: 10–15 minutes

COOKING TIME: about 10 minutes for ½-inch slices, longer if the slices are thicker

Liver is fried most of the time, sometimes broiled. Calf's liver is considered the best and is the most expensive to buy. Lamb liver, baby beef liver, and beef liver may be used. Some people prefer pork liver to any of the above. When you buy liver, have your butcher cut the slices about ½ inch thick.

Wash the liver in cold water. Scald pork or lamb liver in boil-ing water for a few minutes; 5 is long enough.

TO SCALD means to pour boiling water over an article or to immerse the article in boiling water, but it does not mean to keep the water at the boiling point for the time specified in the directions for scalding.

After scalding, remove the liver from the hot water and dry with a paper towel or napkin. The liquid may be saved for the gravy. Remove the skin, tendons, and tubes with a sharp knife.

Liver and bacon, like ham and eggs, is a famous combination. If you are going to serve bacon with the liver, you may cook the bacon while the liver is drying. Use the method of cooking bacon that you prefer. Keep the bacon warm.

Use bacon drippings in your skillet, have the bottom well covered. Put the dried slices of liver, dredged in seasoned flour or not as you prefer, in the fat and cook over a slow fire, allowing about 10 minutes for the cooking time. Turn the liver several times. Liver will spatter a great deal when frying. It is well to use a long-handled fork to insure against a fat burn.

A gravy made from the drippings and poured over the liver is relished by many, especially if it is made with milk. It may be served plain, or you may like liver and onions.

FRIED LIVER AND ONIONS

PREPARATION TIME: 15–25 minutes

COOKING TIME: liver 10 minutes or more; onions 20 minutes

Prepare the liver as for Fried Liver.

Serve with onions which have been French fried or have been plain fried in a skillet with a little fat and water. (See Vegetables.)

BROILED LIVER

Brush ½-inch slices of liver with melted butter or oil. Place them on the broiler rack and broil 3 inches from the flame until they just change color—about 3 minutes. Turn and broil the other side.

LIVER LOAF

PREPARATION TIME: about 30 minutes

COOKING TIME: 45–60 minutes in a moderate oven (350°)

If you like liver you will probably enjoy this loaf. It is equally good, hot or cold. It can be used cold as an *hors d'œuvre* or an appetizer by serving thin slices on equally thin pieces of toast.

1 pound liver (beef or pork liver is good)	1 teaspoon Worcestershire sauce
½ pound sausage	1 teaspoon salt
1 cup cracker or bread crumbs, dry	⅛ teaspoon pepper
1 onion	¼ teaspoon dry or English mustard
2 eggs, beaten	1 teaspoon celery salt
Bacon slices to cover loaf	1 teaspoon hickory salt, if you have it
1 tablespoon lemon juice	

½ cup stock from the liver

METHOD: Wash the liver and put it in a stewing pan. Cover it with boiling water and then simmer for about 5 minutes. Remove the liver from the water and save the water for stock. When cool enough to handle, put the pieces of liver and wedges of the onion through a food chopper. Put this in a good-sized mixing bowl. Add the sausage and the crumbs. Beat the 2 eggs lightly and add. Add all the seasonings. Mix thoroughly. You may be one of those people who can do a good mixing job with a spoon, or you may want to wash your hands thoroughly and really get into it. Add the ½ cup of stock gradually so that the mass takes up all the liquid. Shape the mixture and press it into a loaf pan. Cover the top of the loaf with the slices of bacon and put in a moderate oven (350°). Cook at least 45 minutes; a little longer will insure the complete cooking of the sausage. When the loaf is done it will come away from the sides of the pan a little bit. Turn out the loaf onto a platter as soon as baked. For immediate serving, use a hot platter. Let cool before putting in the refrigerator.

There are countless dishes to be made from liver. Now that you have handled it, prepared it, you will be able to face any recipe and know exactly what to do.

ROAST HEART

PREPARATION TIME: 45 minutes

COOKING TIME: 4 or 5 hours in a moderate oven (350°)

1 beef heart	Bacon or salt pork slices
Bread stuffing (p. 100)	Cooking sherry if desired
Seasoning	Herbs and spices if desired

METHOD: Wash the heart thoroughly in cold water. Be sure to remove all clots of blood that may remain. There is a pure food law now which requires the packers to slit the hearts. This slitting simplifies the cleaning but makes the process of stuffing a little more arduous.

After washing, remove fat, sinews, and all the white cartilage from the fleshy part of the heart. If the heart has been slit, sew it together, using a large darning needle and a very light cord.

Prepare the dressing and stuff the cavity. Sew and sprinkle the heart with pepper and salt. Place the heart on a rack in a roasting pan and lard the upper surface with the slices of bacon or salt pork. Baste occasionally. Add herbs to the basting liquid.

One hour before it is done, ½ cup of sherry may be added to the drippings in the pan. Baste more frequently. Make a light gravy from the drippings, adding stock if necessary.

WHOLE HEART, POT-ROASTED

PREPARATION TIME: about 45 minutes

COOKING TIME: 3–5 hours in a heavy kettle over slow heat or in a covered casserole in a moderate oven (350°)

One large beef heart or veal, lamb, or pork hearts may be cooked this way. When buying heart the old rule of ¼ pound of solid meat per person is a good one to follow.

Heart   Bacon or salt pork slices
Bread stuffing   Cooking sherry if desired
Seasoning   Herbs and spices

METHOD : Wash, clean away all blood clots, and remove gristle, fat, and cartilage. Prepare the hearts for the stuffing. If they have been slit, sew up the slits.

Prepare the stuffing and pack the hearts. Tie or sew across the upper cavity to keep the dressing in place.

Use bacon drippings or salt-pork fat in a skillet. When the fat is hot, sear the heart until it is well browned. A clove of garlic minced in the fat doesn't hurt unless you dislike garlic. When the heart is nicely browned, remove to your cooking utensil, either the heavy pot for the top of the stove or the casserole for the oven. Rinse the skillet with a little water and pour the mixture over the heart. Fasten strips of bacon or salt pork in place by using toothpicks or skewers, cover, and cook until done. Add small quantities of water while cooking if necessary. Do not let it stick or burn.

You may add small onions, chunks of carrots, and small white turnips to the pot for the last hour of cooking.

Make a light gravy by adding stock to the drippings. You can also add ¼ cup of cooking sherry to the gravy to give it zest.

BRAISED HEART

PREPARATION TIME: about 45 minutes

COOKING TIME: about 3 hours of simmering

Heart, any type   Fat
Seasoned flour for dredging   Onion
                Seasonings—bay leaf, cloves, garlic

METHOD: Wash and clean the heart, removing all fat, sinews, clots, and gristle. Cut the meat in chunks, dry, and dredge in your paper sack with the seasoned flour. Sear the chunks of meat in the hot fat until nicely browned. Remove the meat to a Dutch oven or casserole. It may be cooked in the oven or on top of the stove.

Rinse the skillet and pour the rinsing water over the meat. Be sure there is about ½ inch of liquid in the bottom of the cooking utensil. Add the bay leaf, 2 or 3 cloves, and a minced clove of garlic. Cover with slices of onions. Simmer covered.

When tender, make a thin gravy from the liquid in the pan. A quarter-teaspoon of dry mustard incorporated in the gravy adds zest without being recognized. Some cooks like to add a tablespoon of Worcestershire sauce. Any seasoning you care to add is fine if you do not add too much. Remember, it is the suggestion of flavor you want, not a full dose of it.

KIDNEYS

Allow ¼ or ⅓ pound per serving. Kidneys need some precooking preparation. Beef, veal and pork kidneys should be washed well, then the fat and tissue removed from the inside of the kidney. This is best done by slitting the kidneys down the middle. A sharp pair of kitchen shears are very helpful in removing the unwanted parts. Rinse the kidneys again, then soak in salted water for about 1 hour. A heaping tablespoon of salt in a bowl of water will be sufficient.

Calf and lamb kidneys should be washed and tissues removed and then soaked for 30 minutes in salted water.

KIDNEY STEW

PREPARATION TIME: about 1 hour

COOKING TIME: about 1 hour of simmering

Beef or veal kidneys, ¼ or ⅓ pound per serving
Seasonings
Onion
½ cup cooking sherry if desired

METHOD: Follow the above instructions for preparing the kidneys for cooking. Wipe the kidneys when taken from salted water. Cut into small pieces and put them into a stew pan. Add 1 or 2 medium onions, sliced. Part of a bay leaf is good if you like the flavor. Add pepper and salt and barely cover the kidneys with cold water. Bring to simmering heat slowly and cook for about 1 hour. If scum forms on the water, skim it off. When the kidneys are tender, thicken the liquid, using 1 level tablespoon of flour per cup of liquid.

Many people like vegetables cooked in the kidney stew. Others prefer them cooked alone. You might add vegetables, following the suggestions for any stew, and see how you like it.

BROILED KIDNEYS

PREPARATION TIME: 60 minutes

COOKING TIME: about 20 minutes

Lamb kidneys—better allow 2
  per person
Cooking fat or oil

Butter
Seasoning
Parsley for garnishing

METHOD: Cut the kidneys in half and remove the tissue and fat. Soak in cold salted water for ½ hour. Drain and dry the kidneys. Coat them lightly with cooking fat or butter—bacon fat is very good. Use your oven broiling pan if you have one. Place the kidneys in the broiling pan or on the broiler and broil slowly in a hot oven (400°) until the kidneys are browned on both sides. Turn them at least once. When they are nicely browned remove the broiler pan from the broiler. Season with pepper and salt and some melted butter. Cover the pan and put them in the oven for about 10 minutes. Serve with parsley as a garnish. If you do not have an oven broiling pan, take the kidneys from the broiler, put in a pan that can be covered, season, add melted butter, cover the pan and place in the oven for about 10 minutes. The fire may be turned out after the broiling is finished. The oven will be hot enough for the 10 minutes the kidneys are to be in the oven.

SAUTÉED KIDNEYS

PREPARATION TIME: 60 minutes

COOKING TIME: 20–30 minutes

Calf or lamb kidneys—¼ or ⅓ pound per serving
Seasoning
  1 tablespoon butter or cooking fat
  2 slices onion, minced
  1 tablespoon flour
¼ cup cooking sherry plus ¼ cup water; or ½ cup stock

METHOD: Wash and clean the kidneys, removing all fat and tissue. Soak in cold salted water for ½ hour. Drain, dry, and cut into small pieces.

Put 1 tablespoon of butter or cooking fat in the skillet to heat.

Mince 2 slices of onion on your board and add to the fat. Season the kidneys with pepper and salt and add to the fat. Cook over low heat. Watch and stir frequently. If the fat cooks away, add more, but do not have the kidneys floating in grease or their own juices. If you have other things to do, cover the pan with a lid but don't forget about them. Be sure to stir them with a fork. When they are tender, sprinkle them with about 1 tablespoon of flour and add the sherry and water or the stock. Cook a few minutes longer.

They may be served plain or on toast.

BEEF AND KIDNEY PIE

PREPARATION TIME: about 1 hour and 30 minutes

COOKING TIME: about 3 hours and 20 minutes

For eight generous servings you will need:

3 pounds stewing beef or a piece cut from the shank
1 beef kidney or 2 veal kidneys
1 pound onions
3 tablespoons flour

1 teaspoon salt
¼ teaspoon pepper
2 cups tomato juice
1 tablespoon Worcestershire sauce

M E T H O D: Wash and soak the kidneys in cold salted water for 30 minutes. While the kidneys are soaking, remove all sinew, excess fat, and gristle from the meat and cut meat into 1- or 2-inch cubes. Arrange the meat in the bottom of a baking dish or casserole that has a tight-fitting cover. Slice the onions, or if they are small they' may be left whole. Mix the flour and seasonings and sprinkle over the meat and onions.

Dry the kidneys. Remove all fat, gristle, and sinews, cut in small pieces, and lay them over the onion. Add the Worcestershire sauce to the tomato juice and pour over the meat. Cover tightly and place in a medium slow oven (250°–300°). You want the meat to be tender but not fall apart. Test it at the end of 2 hours. If it is done, remove from the oven until the crust is ready. The cooking time depends upon the meat. Watch it. It may take the full 3 hours.

The pie must be covered with biscuit dough. Biscuits are very simple really. There is no need for you to worry if you follow the directions under Biscuits. Shape biscuit dough to cover baking dish. Press lightly along the edges. Bake in a preheated oven at 425° for 12–15 minutes.

SWEETBREADS

The chief difficulty which faces any beginner is what to do with the material at hand. A pair of sweetbreads might be a baffling sight. One pair of sweetbreads should serve 2 people. No matter how you serve them finally they must be parboiled first.

First soak them in cold water for about 1 hour. After soaking, they must be parboiled for 20 minutes in acidulated water.

T O P A R B O I L means to cook partially in boiling water for a specified time. Unless boiling water is specified in the directions, start in cold water and cook for the period indicated after the water comes to the boil.

ACIDULATED WATER is ordinary water to which vinegar, lemon juice or some other acid has been added.

To parboil sweetbreads use 4 cups water, 1 tablespoon vinegar, and 1 teaspoon salt.

Drain and plunge the sweetbreads at once into cold water. This will make them firm and easy to handle.

Remove all membrane and stringy tissue. The sweetbreads are now ready for final preparation.

BROILED SWEETBREADS

PREPARATION TIME: 40 minutes

COOKING TIME: about 10 minutes

Cut parboiled sweetbreads in thin slices, season with salt and pepper, brush lightly with butter or cooking oil, and brown in the broiler.

You may gild the lily by pouring over them 2 tablespoons of melted butter to which 1 teaspoon of lemon juice has been added. Sprinkle lightly with chopped parsley before serving.

FRIED SWEETBREADS

PREPARATION TIME: about 45 minutes

COOKING TIME: about 10 minutes

Cut parboiled sweetbreads into slices about ¼ inch thick.

Sweetbreads	Egg
Flour	Seasoning
Milk	Dry bread or cracker crumbs

Cooking fat or oil, to cover the skillet from ⅛ to ¼ inch deep

METHOD: Bread the sweetbreads (p. 6). Place the breaded sweetbreads in hot fat and cook until a rich golden brown on both sides. Do not fry too fast, do not have the fat too hot. If the fat smokes, it is too hot.

When the sweetbreads are cooked pour off all but 2 tablespoons of the fat. Mix 2 tablespoons of flour with a cup of milk and add to the fat to make a gravy or sauce. If the sauce seems too thick, it may be thinned by adding milk until it is the consistency you prefer.

CREAMED SWEETBREADS

Creamed sweetbreads are delicious and may be combined with mushrooms, green peas, or they may be prepared and served as the central filling for a spinach ring, a rice ring, or a noodle ring. They make an excellent luncheon dish and can be served on toast or in pastry shells. In fact, they are a very versatile dish when creamed.

Creamed foods are made by using a white sauce to which the food is added. See page 227 for the method of preparing White Sauce and suggestions for seasoning and uses.

After you have made a medium thick white or cream sauce, add the sweetbreads cut into cubes. A small can of mushrooms may be added to enhance the flavor.

FRIED TRIPE

PREPARATION TIME: 20 minutes

COOKING TIME: about 40 minutes

Allow ¼ pound per person. Honeycomb tripe is best for frying. The preparation is the same for pickled or fresh tripe.

Tripe

1 egg, beaten, for each pound of tripe

Crumbs, dry

Cooking oil or butter to cover bottom of pan

Seasoning

METHOD: Wash and dry the tripe. Beat the egg until well mixed. Cover the tripe with beaten egg and then dip in the crumbs.

Have the butter, cooking oil, or fat hot but not sizzling. Fry the tripe in the hot fat, turning often. After it is browned on both sides, cover the skillet and cook over low heat for another 20 minutes, turning several times to keep the eggs and crumbs from burning. Fried tripe is not particularly tender.

TRIPE AND ONIONS

PREPARATION TIME: about 20 minutes per pound

COOKING TIME: about 1 hour and 40 minutes

Tripe	⅛ teaspoon pepper
3 small onions per pound of tripe	1 tablespoon butter
	1 tablespoon flour
1 teaspoon salt	1 cup milk

METHOD: Wash the tripe and cut it into small pieces about an inch square. Add enough water to cover, add salt and pepper, and simmer for at least 1 hour, longer if possible. Dice the onions.

Add the onions to the tripe and water and simmer for another 30 minutes. Add 1 tablespoon of butter to the tripe. Make a mixture of 1 tablespoon of flour and 1 cup of milk. (See Gravy method for combining flour and liquid.) Add the milk and flour and cook an additional 10 minutes. This is often served with boiled rice.

TRIPE STEW

PREPARATION TIME: about 40 minutes

COOKING TIME: about 90 minutes

Wash the tripe. Cut into small pieces, put in a stewing kettle, cover with water. Add 1 teaspoon salt and ⅛ teaspoon pepper per pound of tripe. Simmer 1 hour.

One pound of tripe will serve 4 people. You may have a number of people in sometime for a Sunday night supper and will want to make a quantity. Use the following amounts of vegetables and milk per pound of tripe:

2 cups diced raw potatoes
2 cups diced onions
2 cups milk

After the tripe has simmered for 1 hour, add the potatoes and onions. Cook for about 20 minutes. Heat the milk in a saucepan or a double boiler. Take some of the liquid from the tripe and allow it to cool. Watch the milk. It must be scalded, but do not let it burn. Make a mixture of the flour and tripe liquid. Add the flour mixture to the tripe. When the entire mixture begins to thicken after the addition of the flour, add the scalded milk. Stir until well blended and serve as a soup or stew. If you like tripe it makes an excellent luncheon or supper dish. Some people even like it for breakfast.

BREADED BRAINS

Brains, like sweetbreads, need preliminary preparation.

First soak them in cold water for at least 30 minutes. After soaking, remove the skin or membrane which covers them, wash off any blood, and cut away stringy tissue. Divide into sections for serving and parboil 15 minutes in salted acidulated water. Drain and drop them in cold water. When cooled, drain until quite dry.

PREPARATION TIME: about 1 hour

COOKING TIME: about 10 minutes

Brains, ¼ to ⅓ pound per serving	Seasoning
Flour	1 egg, beaten, for each pound of brains
Crumbs	Cooking oil or fat

METHOD: Dredge the sections of brains with seasoned flour. Dip in well-beaten egg and then cover with cracker or dry bread crumbs. Cook in a skillet in ⅛ inch of cooking fat or oil until the crumbs are a crisp golden brown on both sides. If you fry in deep fat, use a regular deep-fat frying kettle which comes equipped with a wire basket. Heat the fat to 375°. If you do not have a frying thermometer, drop a piece of white bread into the fat. If it begins to brown after 2 minutes of cooking, the fat is hot enough. Do not have the fat too hot.

Exercise care when doing deep-fat frying. Water will make the fat sputter and jump. It is safest to put the articles to be cooked in the basket and then immerse the basket in the hot fat. Cook the brains in deep fat for about 8 minutes or until nicely browned and crisp.

If you fry in deep fat, the fat should be saved for future use. Keep a can for your deep-frying fat. Line a sieve with a cloth. Strain the fat into the can or peel a potato, cut in chunks, and drop into gently cooking fat and cook until particles adhere. Remove potato. Cool and store in the refrigerator.

A nicely seasoned sauce should be served with the brains. (See White Sauces for suggestions.)

CHAPTER VIII

FISH AND SEA FOOD

T H E term "sea food" should cover all varieties of fish, but it is often used to mean only shellfish.

Fish should be fresh. The flesh of slices and fillets should be thick and firm. The scales of whole fish should be bright and stiff, the eyes full and prominent.

Fish may be fried, broiled, boiled, or baked. Cooked fish makes good salads and is excellent creamed.

When buying fish with large bones, allow ½ pound per person per serving. For fish steaks, fillets, or small fish, ⅓ pound per person per serving is usually adequate. When buying lobster in the shell for salads, etc., allow ½ pound per serving. For hard clams and oysters in the shell, allow 6–8 per serving. Increase the allowance for steamed clams. Six or 8 clams or oysters, shelled, in juice make an adequate serving.

When you buy fish at the market, it is usually ready for cooking. Wipe it with a clean cloth to be sure.

Do you know what to do with a nice fresh fish just out of the water, one you may have caught yourself, or the gift of a generous friend? Now is the time to learn how to scale and clean a fish.

HOW TO CLEAN A FISH

Most fish have a lingering and persistent odor. The first step in the preparation of a fish is plenty of newspaper spread over the sink or table where the operation is to take place. If you can do the cleaning out of doors or under running water, do so.

Wet the fish and place it on the paper. Take a good strong sharp knife and start to scale the fish. Begin at the tail and work toward the head with a scraping motion of the knife. This will loosen the scales and separate them from the body skin. As the scales are likely to stick to the edge of the knife, wipe the blade on a piece of paper. Always scale toward the head. Scale both sides.

Unless the fish is to be baked, the head can be cut off as soon as the scaling is finished. If it is a large fish and is to be baked, cut through the loose flesh under the mouth. Insert a sharp knife and cut toward the tail through the soft belly flesh to the end of the cavity. The entrails can be easily removed. For small fish, cut off the head. Remove the tail and all the fins. A sharp pair of kitchen scissors will help in removing the fin bones along the backbone or spine.

If the fish is fair-sized, perhaps you would like to fillet it. Use a sharp knife. Lay the fish flat and cut along the fin bones on the back. Keep cutting close to the bone, lifting the flesh as you cut into the fish. Cut away the meat from the spinal bone from the head to the tail. This is not difficult and needs but little practice. When one side has been filleted, turn the fish and repeat the operation on the other side. When the meat is cut away you will have nothing left but the skeleton of the fish, which your cat will enjoy, if you have one.

Wash the cleaned or filleted fish well. Roll up all papers and burn them if possible.

Dry the washed fish on paper toweling, rub with salt, and put in the refrigerator until needed for cooking.

When preparing fish be sure that it has been well scaled and is absolutely clean. Be particularly careful with small fish: smelts, butterfish, herring, and trout. If you have caught and cleaned your own fish, you know they are clean. If you buy them at the market, check to be sure.

COOKING FISH

Fish should be well seasoned.
Fish fry better if dredged.

Many people prefer to dredge their fish for frying by using corn meal instead of flour.

FRIED FISH

Fish may be fried in a skillet with about ⅛ inch of cooking fat in the bottom of the pan, or it may be fried in deep fat. If fried in deep fat, bread the fish first by dipping in egg and then in corn meal. Breaded or batter fish may be fried in deep fat. (For batter recipe, see page 143.) For deep-fat frying, the heat should range from about 375°–390°. The cooking time in deep fat ranges from 2 to 6 minutes, depending upon the size and thickness of the fish. Fish such as cod, halibut, and thick fillets take the maximum time. Smelts should cook in 2 minutes; butterfish, herring, and small trout in 3 minutes.

For pan-fried fish the time, of course, is longer. Small fish should be done in 10 minutes; larger and thicker pieces of fish take 15 to 20 minutes.

BROILED FISH

PREPARATION TIME: 5–10 minutes

COOKING TIME: 5–20 minutes, depending on size and thickness of the fish

Fillets, cod, halibut, swordfish, or salmon steaks, split shad, mackerel, blue fish, or flounders are delicious broiled. Besides the fish you will need:

Lemon	Salt and pepper
Fat	Slices of salt pork or bacon
1 tablespoon chopped parsley per pound of fish	1 tablespoon melted butter per pound of fish

METHOD: Be sure the fish is clean and dry. Sprinkle with salt and pepper and squeeze lemon juice over it. Cover it with the slices of salt pork or bacon and place on a well-greased shallow pan, skin side down, and broil. With mackerel, salmon, or shad you need not use the pork or bacon as the fish is oily enough.

Remove from the broiler to a hot platter, cover with melted butter, and sprinkle with chopped parsley. Quarters of lemon may be served with the fish.

If you are broiling with a wire rack over coals or embers, have the rack well greased. Cook with the white or fleshy side toward the coals until done. Turn the rack after the flesh is cooked and heat until the skin crisps, then serve. If you are broiling fish steaks, broil on both sides.

If you have never cooked fish, you will realize before you have finished that it is a smelly job. Pans in which fish are cooked seem to retain the odor. If you are going to do a great deal of fish cookery, it is wise to have separate utensils for the fish.

If you use your regular equipment you can get rid of the fish odor by first removing all the grease with a paper towel. Then rinse well with hot water and wash with rich soapsuds. After that has been done, fill the skillet or pan with water and add 2 tablespoons of washing soda and bring to a boil. Wash again with soap and water and allow to air.

BAKED FISH

COOKING TIME: about 20 minutes per pound

The larger fish such as bass, bluefish, cod, mackerel, salmon, shad, trout, and weakfish are delicious when baked. The job is most successfully done if the head is left on the fish. Clean the fish thoroughly and scale it. Stuff with a well-seasoned bread stuffing. Besides the fish, you will need:

Seasoning	Stuffing
1 onion, sliced thin	1 lemon
1 cup hot water	Slices of salt pork or bacon

Sew up the cavity and place the fish in a well-greased baking pan. Sprinkle with salt and pepper and squeeze lemon juice over it. Cover or lard with slices of pork or bacon and then cover the larding with thin slices of onion. Salmon, mackerel, shad, and naturally fat fish do not need to be larded. Pour a cup of hot water in the bottom of the pan and bake in a moderate oven (375°).

BOILED FISH

PREPARATION TIME: 15–20 minutes, depending on the size of the fish

COOKING TIME: 5–10 minutes per pound for small pieces; 10–15 minutes per pound for large pieces

If you like fish, you will want boiled fish occasionally. A fish kettle is a good investment and should be used for nothing but fish. A plate to hold the fish and a piece of cheesecloth should be kept for boiling fish. If you keep them all in the fish kettle, you will have all your material in one place when wanted.

Wash and prepare the fish. Sprinkle with salt, place on a plate that will fit in your kettle, and tie the plate and fish in a piece of cheesecloth. Put 2 quarts of water in the kettle for a 2-4-pound fish. Have the water very hot but not boiling. Add 1 tablespoon of either lemon juice or vinegar and 1 teaspoon of salt. Put in the fish and bring to a boil. Then reduce the heat so the fish simmers but does not boil.

If you have discovered that you are partial to herbs, try boiling a fish in a courtbouillon instead of plain acidulated water. Bring your 2 quarts of water to a boil and throw into it the following:

1 carrot, diced	6 whole cloves
1 onion, minced	6 peppercorns
1 green pepper, diced	6 whole allspice
1 sprig parsley, diced	1 clove garlic, minced
1 small bay leaf	Pinch of thyme

½ cup diced celery or a handful of celery tops

Simmer the seasonings and herbs in the water for 20 minutes, then put in the lemon juice or vinegar. Lower the fish into the water and cook as directed above.

This list of seasonings is only a starter. You will want to change it to suit your taste—more garlic, sage instead of thyme, more spices or fewer, and so forth.

Boiled fish is particularly good when served with an appropriate sauce. Any of the following is good:

Butter sauce	Hollandaise sauce
Parsley butter	Tartar sauce
Fitzsauce	Horseradish sauce
Egg sauce	Mustard sauce

The recipes will be found in Chapter XI.

PREPARED FISH

Smoked, canned, salted, and dried fish are delicious when properly prepared. All dried and salted fish need freshening. Follow the freshening directions which come with the package of dried or salted fish. But if you buy dried or salted fish without directions on the package, use the following directions for freshening: Soak in lukewarm water according to Method I or Method II below:

METHOD I: Soak the fish overnight. Wash and rinse in the morning and soak in fresh water until wanted for use.

METHOD II: Leave the fish under the spigot with a light stream of water running into the bowl. This method will take less time.

Smoked fish can generally be freshened by soaking in cold water for about an hour. Remove the fish from the cold water and put in boiling water for 5 minutes. Remove the fish and dry.

CREAMED FISH

A delicious luncheon or supper dish may be made from boiled fish, canned salmon or tuna, salted or dried fish. You will need for each cup of flaked fish:

1 cup milk	2 tablespoons butter
2 tablespoons flour	Salt and pepper

METHOD: Put ¼ cup of milk in the jar which you use for mixing flour and liquid, add the flour, cover, and shake until the flour is blended with the milk. Turn the flour and milk mixture into a pan, add butter and the remaining milk and a little pepper. Cook, stirring constantly, until the mixture thickens and comes to a boil. Add the fish, stir well, and place in the top of a double boiler over hot water until wanted for use; or place the pan in hot water.

A beaten egg per cup of fish may be added. If you use egg, beat and stir in just before serving. If you cook the mixture with the egg in it, it may curdle.

FISH CAKES OR FISH BALLS

PREPARATION TIME: about 1 hour

COOKING TIME: 2–5 minutes

You will need for each cup of flaked fish:

4 cups well-beaten mashed potatoes	1 egg
3 tablespoons milk or cream	Pepper and salt
3 tablespoons butter or other fat	Flour

METHOD: Mix the fish and the mashed potatoes; add the well-beaten egg and butter and pepper. Mix. Add a little milk or cream gradually until the mixture is moist but not runny. Do not add all the milk or cream unless needed—it may make the mixture too wet. You want to be able to shape and pat the mixture into cakes.

FISH CAKES: Flour your hands, take a good heaping table-spoon of the mixture, shape into a flat cake, and fry in a little fat in the skillet. Cook gently until browned, then turn and brown on the other side. This will make from 8–10 cakes.

FISH BALLS: Shape the mixture into balls instead of cakes and cook in deep fat for 2–5 minutes.

SALMON PATTIES

These are quickly prepared and are delicious.

1 6–8-oz. can salmon	Bread or cracker crumbs
1 egg	Salt and pepper

METHOD: Remove the skin and bones from the salmon. Flake into a bowl and add a little of the oil in which the fish was packed. Add the egg and mix thoroughly. Add the crumbs a little at a time until the mixture becomes stiff and thick enough to shape into patties. Flour your hands and pat a tablespoon of the mixture until it is a flat cake. Fry in hot fat until crisp and brown. Turn and brown the other side. This makes 4 patties.

Any flaked fish may be made into patties.

FISH ROE AND MILT

The roe of a fish is really a mass of eggs in a sack. The milt is the part of the male fish that takes the place of the roe.

To prepare roe and milt, parboil them first in salted acidulated water (1 dessertspoon of salt and 1 tablespoon of vinegar or lemon juice to each quart of water). Simmer the roe or milt for 10 minutes. Drain, cool, and pick out the pieces of membrane. They are then ready for any recipe.

They may be fried, broiled, or mixed with scrambled eggs.

FRIED ROE: Cook about 10 minutes, 5 on each side, in butter or bacon fat or other cooking fat.

BROILED ROE: Place on a greased broiler, brush with butter or suitable fat, and broil for 5 minutes on each side.

ROE WITH SCRAMBLED EGGS: Use 1 heaping table-spoon of roe to each beaten egg. Proceed as for scrambled eggs.

OMELET WITH ROE: A fried roe rolled in a plain omelet is a neat trick and surprisingly good.

OYSTERS

To be good, oysters must be fresh. Buy them from a reputable market and buy them in the shells. They taste better. If you are forced to buy them opened, be sure the liquid is clear. Don't trifle with any sea food unless you are sure it is absolutely fresh.

Don't be appalled by the casing of an oyster. It is not nearly as formidable as it looks. Wash the shells thoroughly, otherwise the liquid from the oyster when opened will be dirty.

Take the oyster and hold the thick part of the shell in the palm of one hand. Take a good strong knife and whack the thin edge of the oyster with the back of the knife. The shell is quite brittle and a piece will break off. Insert a strong thin knife in the open-ing and work it toward the edge of the shell. Move the knife up until it severs the muscle which holds the shell together. Run the knife up along the inside top shell until you have cut the muscle. The top shell will then open or come off. Cut the muscle from the bottom shell and drop the oyster in a bowl which you have had ready to catch the liquor which runs from the shell.

The oysters are now ready for use. If you are to fry them, put them in a strainer. If they are to be creamed or put in stews, soups, or chowders they can be lightly drained.

OYSTERS ON THE HALF SHELL

After the oyster is opened and freed from the bottom shell, place the bottom shell with the oyster coyly nestling in its natural abode on a plate of crushed ice. Allow 6–8 oysters per person. Serve with cocktail sauce, a wedge of lemon, and a little Tabasco, which should be optional with your guests; or some people prefer horse-radish.

OYSTER STEW

PREPARATION TIME: about 10 minutes

COOKING TIME: about 15–20 minutes

For 4 servings you will need:

2 cups oysters and juice   1 teaspoon Worcestershire sauce
4 tablespoons butter   Pepper and salt
4 cups rich milk or cream   Paprika
                     Nutmeg or mace

METHOD: You will need 2 saucepans, one for the oysters and one for the milk or cream. Use the large pan for the oysters because you will add the milk to that pan later.

Measure your milk or cream into one pan and scald it, being careful not to scorch it.

TO SCALD MILK means to heat it *slowly* until small beads or bubbles appear around the edge of the pan. It may be done over a low flame, but is safest in a double boiler.

While the milk is being scalded, put the oysters, butter, a dash of salt (more can be added later if needed), a little pepper, and the Worcestershire sauce in the other pan. Simmer gently until the oysters begin to curl at the edges. Do not overcook oysters; it makes them tough. When the edges begin to curl, add the scalded milk or cream and serve at once, sprinkling each portion with a little paprika and a little mace or nutmeg. Pilot or soda crackers should be served with all fish stews and chowders.

This makes a delicious clear stew. If you like your stew slightly thickened, you may add 2 tablespoons of flour, mixing it with cold milk before scalding.

CREAMED OYSTERS

For creamed oysters, add 8 tablespoons of flour to the recipe for Oyster Stew.

Follow the directions for Oyster Stew with this exception: Mix the milk and flour by adding the flour to some milk in a jar. Cover the jar tightly and shake well until the flour is dissolved. Add the milk and flour mixture to the remaining milk and scald, stirring constantly as the milk scalds to prevent lumps. Combine the hot thickened milk or cream with the oysters, mix, and serve at once.

FRIED OYSTERS

PREPARATION TIME: about 20 minutes

COOKING TIME: 2–4 minutes per oyster

Allow 3 or 4 large oysters per serving. Drain the oysters.

METHOD: Dip the oysters in the dry flour and shake off the excess flour. Dip them in batter, allow the batter to run off, dip in flour again, and then in the batter. Drain slightly and drop into hot deep fat (375°–390°) and cook from 2–4 minutes. Or fry gently in ⅛ inch of butter or suitable cooking fat in a skillet.

BATTER

½ cup flour	1 teaspoon salt
¾ cup milk	1 egg, beaten
Extra flour or crumbs	

METHOD: Put the flour in a bowl. Make a well or hole in the center of the flour and stir in the milk gradually until the flour is absorbed and the mixture smooth. Add the salt and beaten egg and mix well. The batter should be a thick liquid about the consistency of thick gravy. A little more milk or flour may be used to get the proper consistency.

CLAMS

To a New Englander, and particularly a Cape Codder, a clam is that mollusk which has a soft shell and a long neck and is dug from its dark and dismal lair about a foot deep in sand.

The hard-shelled fruit of the sea is commonly called a Quahog.

It is, however, a clam. It is the hard-shelled clam which is eaten raw when small and is called Cherrystone and Little Neck.

The recipes in this section mean clams, whichever are available. The soft-shelled variety make the best steamed and fried clams. They are equally good in cooking but need more care and attention because they are likely to be filled with sand unless carefully washed. The soft-shelled clam also has the long tough neck which can be used in chowders, fritters, pies, scalloped dishes, etc., if it is put through the food chopper.

Don't trust a clam any more than you would an oyster. They can be dangerous if dead. Buy them in the shells. The Quahog or hard clam is more difficult to open than the oyster, but it is not a difficult task if you go about it properly. The process of opening clams and oysters is also called "shelling" or "shucking."

HARD CLAMS, OR QUAHOGS

Wash well and place them in a basket or bucket and do not disturb for an hour. Whether they go to sleep under this treatment or simply relax, they are definitely off guard. Have a strong sharp knife available. Lift the unsuspecting clam gently, and before it can become aware of your nefarious intent, slip the knife gently but firmly between the front lips and cut the hard muscle. If you are clumsy and knock the clam, it will shut up tightly and you won't be strong enough to pry the shell open with a knife. Trying to crack the edge of a clam shell is a messy job. The shell breaks and you find yourself rather involved. A live clam closes its shell tightly. If you come across a flabby and unresisting one, discard it.

If this live method seems too much for you, put your washed clams in a kettle with 2 cups of water, or enough to cover the bottom of the kettle, and steam them until they open. Take them from the shells. Save the clam broth or liquor in the steaming kettle. This method is the simplest, but it robs the clam of some of its flavor.

SOFT CLAMS

These are no problem to open. Use a firm sharp knife and insert the blade along the edge of the upper shell and cut the shell away. Make a cut in the neck or siphon, cut the clam away from the bottom shell, and pull the skin from the neck. Some people throw the necks away, but they can be chopped or ground for use in pies, chowders, and scalloped dishes.

STEAMED CLAMS

Wash soft-shelled clams in many waters. Allow at least a quart of clams, 15–20 per person. Place the well-washed clams in a kettle, being careful not to break the shells. Add 1 to 2 cups of water. If you like onion as a flavoring, slice one onion and place it over the top of the clams. Cover the kettle and cook for about 10 minutes after the water boils. The small amount of water does not cover all the clams. The steam generated cooks the clams not in the water.

Serve with individual dishes of melted butter and a wedge of lemon for those who like it. Provide plates for the empty shells and many paper napkins; there is nothing dainty about steamed clams. One must get into them with one's fingers really to enjoy them. Save the broth in the pot and serve hot in cups with a dab of butter or use later for a bisque.

FRIED CLAMS

Allow 6 to 8 soft clams per serving. Wash well to be sure they are free of sand and grit. Open and dry on a soft cloth.

The clams may be dipped in batter, or in egg and cracker or bread crumbs, and fried. For dipping in batter, see Fried Oysters. For dipping in egg and crumbs: Beat 2 eggs well. Put your crumbs on a separate plate. Dip the clams in the egg, drain a moment, and roll them in the crumbs. If you like plenty of covering, dip them in the egg a second time and then in the crumbs again.

Have a skillet ready with about ¾ of an inch of hot fat over the bottom.

Put the clams in the hot fat one at a time until the bottom of skillet is covered and cook them until brown. The fat should be hot enough to brown them within three minutes. Remove from the fat and serve at once.

CLAM CAKES

PREPARATION TIME: 20 minutes if the clams are shelled

COOKING TIME: 20 minutes

2 cups flour	1 cup milk, about
2 teaspoons baking powder	2 cups chopped clams
¼ teaspoon salt	Salt and pepper
2 eggs, lightly beaten	Cooking fat

METHOD: Sift the flour and baking powder with ¼ teaspoon of salt. Start your batter by mixing the eggs into the flour mixture. Add a little milk at a time, not too much because you want a batter halfway between wet dough and a heavy liquid. Add the clams and then more milk until the mixture will drop from a spoon but is not runny—the consistency of griddle cake mixture is ideal. Have a skillet or griddle hot and grease it well with fat or bacon drippings. Drop the mixture by spoonfuls, 2 tablespoons per cake. Fry brown on both sides and serve at once.

CLAM PIE

PREPARATION TIME: about 45 minutes

COOKING TIME: 60 to 70 minutes

This is a dish to dream about if you are fond of clams. It really is a pie, crust and all; but it is a meat course and not a dessert. So make the rich crust first. When baking pies, preheat your oven to the desired temperature, usually very hot (450°) for the first 10 minutes to set the pastry.

For 4–6 servings, you will need:

1 recipe Rich Pie Crust	1 medium onion, minced, if de-
2 cups chopped clams, drained	sired
¼ cup clam liquor	1 egg, well beaten
½ cup cracker crumbs	1 cup milk
1 tablespoon butter, melted	1 teaspoon poultry seasoning
⅛ teaspoon pepper	

M E T H O D: Prepare a pie shell as described under Rich Pie Crust below. Mix all the ingredients together and pour into the shell. Cover with the upper crust and bake in a very hot oven (450°) for 10 minutes. Reduce the heat to medium (315°–350°) and bake for 50–60 minutes.

RICH PIE CRUST

P R E P A R A T I O N T I M E: about 30 minutes for blending and rolling. Chill at least 15 minutes if possible

C O O K I N G T I M E: 10 minutes in a very hot oven (450°), then at reduced heat. Follow individual recipes for exact time

Rich crust contains more shortening than the regular recipe.

1½ cups flour	¼ cup ice water (be sure it is
½ cup shortening (lard is	very cold)
good)	1 teaspoon salt
1 teaspoon baking powder	

There are a few simple rules for making good pie crust. They are not tricks, they are common sense. The first rule is to have everything you use as cold as possible. Leave your shortening in the refrigerator until you are ready to use it.

M E T H O D: Sift the flour, salt, and baking powder into a bowl. Take half of the shortening and cut it into the flour mixture with 2 knives or a pastry blender until it resembles coarsely ground corn meal. Add the balance of the shortening and cut in until the pieces are about the size of a dried pea.

Add the water, a tablespoon at a time, and mix or blend it in lightly. *Always* work pie crust lightly. As soon as the dough can be lifted in a ball, stop adding the water. The less moisture you have, the better the crust will be. The dough must, however, hold together.

If you have time, make your crust and put it in the refrigerator to chill before rolling. It can be made the day before or made in the morning and used at night. Some cooks keep prepared pastry dough in their refrigerators at all times to take care of an emergency. It is smart to chill all dough for at least 15 minutes after mixing. It will roll better.

To roll pastry you will need a board and a rolling pin. The canvas cloth and stockinette cover for the rolling pin make rolling easier. A board must be lightly floured. Flour must be rubbed into the canvas if you use it. The rolling pin must be lightly floured or flour rubbed into the covering for the pin.

If you are going to make a 2-crust pie, divide the dough into 2 parts. The portion for the bottom crust should be slightly larger than the one for the upper crust. The crust when rolled should be larger than the surface to be covered—in this case a 9-inch pie plate—to allow for shrinkage.

Flour the board and rolling pin or canvas and covering. The flour prevents the pastry from sticking.

Roll the dough. Do not pound or press. A light touch, remember. Roll the dough away from the center of the wad, not back and forth. Do not try to stretch the dough, or it may run to peaks. It will probably do all sorts of contrary things.

Your first pie will not be easy, but don't be discouraged. Just remember, you are the boss. If the dough runs to points, cut off the long point and use the piece to fill in the gaps near the center of the pastry. You want a piece large enough to cover the bottom of the pan.

Once the dough is rolled, you may wonder how you are going to get it into the pan. The dough may have stuck to the board. Take a spatula and work it under the pastry to loosen it from the board. Fold the dough over lightly, lift to the pan, and turn back the folds, or you may roll the dough around the pin, lift the pin with the dough rolled about it to the pan, and unroll across the pan. Either method takes some practice.

Once the dough is in the pan, fit it into place. Allow a good overlap on the edges. When the filling (on Cape Cod it is sometimes called "pie timber") to be baked is moist, brush the inside of the bottom crust with white of egg or melted butter to prevent a soggy crust.

When the bottom crust is in the pan and prepared, add the filling.

Roll out the top crust, following the directions for rolling dough. Cover the top of the pie. The edge of the bottom crust may be moistened with water and the top crust pressed into it, or the bottom edge may be folded over the top to seal the edge. Make a few small gashes in the top crust with a sharp knife to allow the steam to escape.

There are gadgets on the market to put in pies to keep the juices from running out. A homemade trick is to insert a couple of pieces of macaroni about 3 inches long inside the gashes. Put a cookie sheet on the bottom of the oven to catch any juices which may happen to boil over.

CHOWDERS

Now we come to a controversial dish, clam chowder. A New England clam chowder is made with milk. Manhattan clam chowder and Rhode Island clam chowder are something else again. They all have their advocates, so all 3 kinds are given here.

CLAM CHOWDER

PREPARATION TIME: about 60 minutes

COOKING TIME: about 35 minutes

For 8 servings you will need:

4 slices salt pork or bacon, diced	2 cups chopped clams
4 cups clam juice and water	4 cups milk
4 cups diced raw potatoes	4 tablespoons flour
1 large onion, diced	1 teaspoon salt
	⅛ teaspoon pepper

M E T H O D : Put the diced pork or bacon in a kettle and fry it gently until the fat is rendered. Do not cook the bacon or pork too much; it should not be brown. Add the diced onion to the fat and fry the onion in the fat for a few minutes. Add the combined clam liquor and water and the potatoes. Cook until the potatoes are done but not soft. While the potatoes are cooking, mix the milk and flour together by the jar method—a little milk in a jar, then the flour, some more milk, cover tightly and shake well until mixed. Scald the milk and flour, stirring to prevent lumps. When the potatoes are done, add the chopped clams, allow the mixture to come to a boil, and turn off the heat. Now add the hot milk and flour liquid to the clams and potatoes. Mix well and serve at once.

Serve hard biscuits or pilot crackers with chowder. Some people like their chowder thickened with crumbled pilot crackers. Others serve them on the side and let those who will crumble them into the chowder themselves.

RHODE ISLAND CLAM CHOWDER

Follow the recipe for New England Clam Chowder, but add 1 cup of tomatoes, either canned or fresh, to 3 cups of clam juice and water.

MANHATTAN CLAM CHOWDER

Follow the recipe for New England Clam Chowder, but omit the milk and flour and add 1 cup of tomatoes, 1 cup of corn, ½ teaspoon of thyme, 1 cup of diced carrots, and 1 cup of diced celery. With the extra vegetables it will be necessary to add more water, which will take the place of the milk. About 4 cups of additional water will suffice. Remember to add the clams last in all chowders or they will be tough.

FISH CHOWDER

PREPARATION TIME: about 60 minutes

COOKING TIME: about 45 minutes

4 slices salt pork or bacon, diced	3 medium onions, diced
	4 cups milk
4 cups water	4 tablespoons flour
2 cups diced raw fish	1 teaspoon salt
4 cups diced raw potatoes	Pepper
Paprika	

METHOD: Fry the pork in a deep kettle but do not brown. Add the onion and sauté for a few minutes, then add the water, salt, fish, and potatoes. Cook until the potatoes are done but not soft. While the fish and potatoes are cooking, mix the flour and milk by the jar method and scald the milk mixture. When the fish and potatoes are done, add the thickened scalded milk, mix, and serve at once with pilot crackers.

NOTE: Add 1 cup of diced carrots and 1 cup of diced celery to the above recipe if you like a variety of vegetables in your fish chowder.

OTHER CHOWDERS

To make any other chowder, use the basic recipe for all chowders, which is:

4 slices salt pork or bacon, diced	4 cups water
	4 cups diced raw potatoes
1 cup onion, diced	4 tablespoons flour

Fry the pork or bacon but do not brown. Add the onions, cook for a few minutes in the fat, add the water and potatoes, and cook until the potatoes are done but not soft.

While that is cooking you can prepare corn or other vegetables and lobster, crab, or shrimp, either fresh or canned.

Scald 4 cups of milk thickened with the flour. Add 2 cups of corn, lobster, shrimp, or crab. Canned products do not need to be cooked but may be added in the last few minutes just before the thickened milk is combined with the basic liquid.

LOBSTER

A good live lobster has a mottled dark green shell. Don't buy a dead green lobster; be sure it is alive.

If you buy a boiled lobster it will be a bright red. You will want to be sure that it was cooked alive. Take the lobster in your hands and straighten out the tail. If it springs back into its curved position, it was alive when boiled. Don't trifle with shellfish unless you feel sure they are fresh, or were when cooked.

BOILED LOBSTER

Have a kettle of boiling water seasoned with 1 tablespoon of salt. Lobsters bought at the market have their claws pegged to prevent them from nipping unwary fingers. If you are lucky enough to get them fresh from the sea, beware of their claws. They are powerful, and once they clamp shut they are likely to stay shut. If a lobster has not been pegged, do not approach it from the front. Lobsters are surprisingly quick with their nippers. It is always wise and sensible to have a pair of tongs. If you do not own tongs, lay a wooden spoon or a stick over the claws and then lift the lobster from the back, putting your hand down on the body part close to the tail joint.

Plunge the lobster head-down into the boiling water, cover the kettle, and keep the water boiling. A medium-sized lobster will cook in about 20 minutes. A very large lobster will take half an hour. If the lobster is not to be served hot in the shell, lift it from the kettle and plunge it into cold water. Let it stay until cool enough to handle.

Then break off or chop off the claws near the body. Turn the lobster on its back and split the front down the middle, using a heavy knife. You may have to tap the back of the knife with a hammer.

TO CLEAN LOBSTER: Remove the stomach, which you will recognize, also the sac just in back of the head. Remove the black intestinal canal. This is a threadlike membrane which runs from the stomach down to the end of the tail. Take out all of the intestine, even if you have to do it bit by bit. If you are going to serve the lobster in the shell, you need take out nothing more. There is a spongy substance, the lungs, between the body frame and shell which you do not eat. The creamy green substance is the liver. The pink coral is the spawn in female lobsters. The coral may be removed and added to mayonnaise, butter, or cream sauce. It is really delicious.

Crack the claws with a hammer or a heavy nutcracker.

Serve boiled lobster cold with mayonnaise or, after it has been opened and cleaned, brush it with butter and put it under the broiler for a few minutes and serve with melted butter. For each serving allow half of a large lobster or a whole small one.

The meat may be taken from the tail, body, and claws and used in stews, chowders, patties, creamed, or in salad.

BROILED LIVE LOBSTER

Kill the lobster quickly by inserting a sharp knife between the end of the body casing and the first of the tail sections. Split the lobster lengthwise and take out the stomach and intestinal canal. Crack the claws and lay the two halves on a broiler, shell side down. Brush the meat with butter and season with pepper and salt. Broil for about 20 minutes, or until the flesh is a delicate brown. Then, to finish cooking without losing the juice, set the broiler in the oven, reduced to 350°, for another 10 or 15 minutes. Extra butter may be added when the lobster is placed in the oven.

CREAMED LOBSTER

PREPARATION TIME: 5–10 minutes

COOKING TIME: 20–30 minutes

For 4 servings you will need:

2 cups freshly boiled or 2 8-oz. cans canned lobster
2 tablespoons butter
8 tablespoons flour
4 cups milk
1 teaspoon salt

¼ teaspoon pepper
½ teaspoon Worcestershire sauce
2 tablespoons cooking sherry if desired

METHOD: Put some of the milk into a jar and add the flour and more milk. Cover. Shake until the flour is blended. Turn the milk and flour into the top of a double boiler and cook over direct heat. Add the butter and seasoning and keep stirring the mixture until it begins to bubble. Stay with it, stir it, watch it if you don't want lumps. After the milk bubbles, add the lobster and put the top of the double boiler over hot water until served.

NOTE: Oysters, clams, crab, salmon and tuna may be creamed this way by substituting any of them for the lobster.

CRABS

The Atlantic and Gulf crab is commonly known as a "blue claw." These crabs vary in size, but they average from 3 to 5 inches in body length. The frontal approach to a crab is risky because they, like the lobster, have dangerous claws. If you catch them yourself or get them from a fisherman, you will find them both lively and dangerous. There is one safe way to pick up a crab: catch it at the back close to the shell, behind its smallest leg. The claws cannot reach you there. Do not pick up or hold the crab in any other position, or you will find that the crab has taken hold of you.

The Pacific Coast crab is a much larger species. It has a thicker and meatier body, and its claws are smaller and less dangerous.

Crabs shed their shells in the spring and summer. When the time is right, they emerge from their old shell and for a few days are soft-shell crabs.

If you can get soft-shell crabs, you will find them delicious. Be sure they are alive. Hard or soft, dead crabs are not good.

BOILED CRABS

Allow 2–3 Eastern crabs per person; 10–12 crabs will yield 2 cups of meat.

Allow ½–1 Western crab per person; 2–3 crabs will yield 2 cups of meat.

COOKING TIME: about 30 minutes

Plunge the hard-shell crabs into a kettle of boiling water with 1 tablespoon of salt. It is advisable to use tongs for crabs. Cook for a half hour. Drain and cover with cold water.

TO CLEAN BOILED CRABS: Remove the apron on the underside. This apron is long and pointed on the male and rounded on the female. When the apron is broken off, insert the thumb in the opening at the back and separate the upper and lower shells. Discard the spongy material which covers the body. Break the crab in half, discarding the material in the middle section. The meat is in the body casing. Pull off the legs and discard. Crack the claws and take out the meat.

The crab is now ready for use in salad, or any dish you may fancy, such as Creamed Crab.

CREAMED CRAB

Follow recipe for Creamed Lobster (p. 154), substituting crab flakes for lobster meat.

SOFT-SHELL CRABS

To prepare soft-shell crabs for cooking, take the points at each end of the body and pull back about halfway. Remove the spongy substance which covers the body on both sides. Cut out the eyes and mouth section with a sharp knife. Remove the apron on the underside. Wash the crabs and drain.

FRIED SOFT-SHELL CRABS

Allow 2 small or 1 large crab per serving.

Crabs may be dipped in flour or corn meal and fried in butter or suitable cooking fat for about 10 minutes, turning often to keep them from burning.

Crabs may be dipped in beaten egg and then dredged in crumbs and fried in deep fat 3–5 minutes.

Or they may be dipped in batter (page 143) before frying in deep fat.

Serve with melted butter, lemon juice and chopped parsley, or a tartar sauce.

SHRIMP, PRAWNS, AND CRAWFISH

Fresh or uncooked shrimp are sometimes called "green shrimp." Prawns are much larger than the shrimp, usually 5 or 6 inches long. The crawfish comes from fresh water and resembles a lobster but is much smaller.

The shells of these fish turn a pinkish red when cooked. They should be washed and cooked in boiling salted water for about 15 minutes.

The crawfish must be cleaned. See directions for cleaning lobster.

Shrimps and prawns must be shelled and the intestinal thread, a black line that runs the length of the body, removed.

N O T E : When you cream them or make stews or any other liquid dish, save 2 cups of the liquid in which they have been cooked. It gives added flavor.

The meat of these fish may be substituted for crab or lobster in many dishes. They are delicious in salads too.

FRIED SHRIMP

Use fresh, or green, shrimp. A pound will serve 4 people generously.

You will need hot fat, either deep fat or about an inch of fat in your skillet. Do not boil the shrimp; but shell and remove the intestinal thread. Cut them in half and flatten them out after washing. Dry well and dust with flour.

Make a batter using:

2 tablespoons flour	¼ teaspoon baking powder
½ cup milk	½ teaspoon salt

1 egg, well beaten

Make a paste by adding a little milk to the flour and baking powder and blend well. Add the balance of the milk, the seasoning, and the beaten egg. Mix well.

Dip the floured shrimp into the batter. Dust with flour and dip in the batter again. Drain slightly, then drop into the hot deep fat (375°). Cook until a rich golden brown. It takes 3–5 minutes. Drain on absorbent paper in the oven and serve with catsup to which is added about ½ teaspoon of English mustard. Mix powdered English mustard with a little water to make a paste before adding to the catsup.

CANNED SHRIMP

Canned shrimp may be used in any recipe calling for cooked shrimp. Just be sure that you buy a good brand; and if the little black thread has not been removed, take it out.

CHAPTER IX

POULTRY AND GAME

THE term "poultry" includes all the domesticated birds that find their way to our dinner tables. The most popular is chicken—known as roasters, fryers, broilers, fowl, and capons. Turkey is justly famous. We all know it as a roast bird. Young turkeys, broiled or fried, are delicious. Ducks or ducklings, squabs, pigeons, and geese complete the list of commonly used birds. Guinea hens or guinea fowl should be better known.

WHAT TO DO WITH A LIVE BIRD

It is just possible that some day you may have to kill a bird. You may win, be presented with, or otherwise acquire a bird that will have to be dealt with. The simplest and easiest way to approach the task is to assure yourself that the bird is food. Once your mental attitude is adjusted, the rest will be relatively easy. A block of wood, an ax, a hatchet, a cleaver, or a heavy kitchen knife will do the trick if you are properly determined.

Tie the bird's legs together and hold it by the legs near the feet. Put the head on the block of wood and cut. If you are going to do it, aim straight and look where you aim. Don't be like the man who couldn't, or didn't, look at what he was doing and finally had to call his wife to finish the job.

Most people prefer to prepare home-butchered fowl at least 24 hours before it is to be used. After fowl is prepared, refrigerate for several hours at least.

Once the head is removed, hang the bird by the feet for 10–15 minutes to permit proper bleeding.

The feathers are the next thing to worry about. A bird may be dry-picked, which takes a long time and the feathers are hard to control. Scalding the bird makes plucking easier.

To scald a bird you will need a bucket of boiling water. After the water has boiled, add 2 cups of cold water. Hold the bird by the legs and immerse in the hot water for about 2 minutes, covering all the feathers. Drain for a moment and start to pick the feathers. They will come off easily. Tail and wing feathers will have to be pulled individually. Pick the bird clean.

The next step is to singe off the hairs from the carcass. To do this, hold the bird over an open flame until the hairs have been burned off. If the bird is too heavy to handle conveniently, leave the singeing until after it has been drawn.

TO PLUCK POULTRY means to pull off the feathers.

TO DRAW POULTRY means to cut open and remove the entrails.

At this point the bird is described as "dressed," which means that it has been plucked but not drawn. When you buy poultry at the market, you buy it by "dressed weight." After the butcher weighs it he draws it.

WHAT TO BUY

What kind of chicken to buy depends upon how you intend to cook it. Broiling, frying, and roasting demand young birds; fricassee and stew are better made with older birds, called fowl.

Broiling chickens are 2–3 months old and weigh from a pound up to 2½ pounds. Fryers are 3½ to 5 months old and weigh 2½ to 3½ pounds. Roasting chickens, including capons, run from 5 to 10 months old and from 3½ to 6 pounds in weight. Anything older than that is a fowl. All these weights are dressed weights —that is, when the bird is plucked but not drawn.

When you are choosing full-grown poultry, look for a soft, smooth skin without blemishes, short legs, plump breast, and back and thighs well covered with fat.

PREPARING WHOLE BIRDS FOR COOKING

POULTRY BOUGHT AT THE MARKET: If you buy your poultry, preparation for cooking begins with singeing. The butcher will have removed the entrails and tucked the giblets— liver, heart, and gizzard—back into the body. Take them out and put aside.

After singeing, pluck out the pinfeathers still left on the bird. Wash the carcass thoroughly, inside and out. Let water run through the body cavity of a whole bird. Also, thrust your hand into the cavity and feel along the backbone for the lungs and kidneys and pull them out. The butcher always misses them when he draws a bird. Discard them. Wash off the giblets. Squeeze the heart as you wash to force out any blood clots. There may be some pieces of the tough inner sac still clinging to the gizzard. Peel them off and discard them. Wipe the skin dry, and you are ready to stuff for roasting, dredge for frying, or whatever you plan to do with your bird.

POULTRY NOT YET DRAWN: After singeing, pluck out the pinfeathers still left on the bird. Wash off the skin and then cut off the head and feet. To remove the feet, make a cut just below the drumstick, but do not cut the tendons. Then place the cut over the edge of a table and bend downward to break the bone. Pull the feet, and the tendons should come off with the feet.

The next step is drawing the bird. Lay the bird on its back. Make an incision at the lower end of the breastbone and cut through the soft skin toward the tail. Insert your hand in the opening and carefully loosen the entrails from the back and sides and pull them toward you through the opening. With a little skill you will be able to bring out the whole mass with one motion. Make sure the lungs and kidneys, which lie close along the backbone, have been removed. With a sharp knife cut out the oil sac, which is found on the upper surface of the tail, under the little white knob.

Separate the heart, liver, and gizzard from the entrails and throw out the rest. Attached to the liver you will find the gall-bladder, a small greenish sac. Cut it away carefully without breaking it because the gall is very bitter and will spoil the taste of the meat if it breaks. Cut through the thick outer part of the gizzard down to the inner skin, but do not cut through that. Pry the thick flesh apart and it will peel away from the inner sac, which you then discard.

Save the soft layers of rich yellow fat which cling to the side skin of the bird.

Roll back the loose neck skin and slit it down the back. Cut the neck off short where it joins the body and set it aside with the giblets. Reach down into the body and pull out the windpipe and crop.

Wash the bird thoroughly in running water, inside and out. Drain and wipe with a clean soft cloth. The bird is now ready for stuffing.

PREPARING BIRDS FOR OTHER METHODS OF COOKING

FOR BROILING: Singe the bird and cut off its head and feet as described above. Make an incision at the back of the neck and cut along the backbone the entire length of the bird. Open it up and remove the contents. Save the giblets and clean as instructed above.

Wash thoroughly, drain, and dry with a cloth.

FOR FRYING, STEWING, or FRICASSEE: Singe. Remove head and feet and oil sac as described.

Hold the legs away from the body and cut the skin with a sharp knife. Press the legs toward the back and cut at the body joint. In large birds, divide the leg into 2 sections by cutting at the knee joint. Remove the wings from the body by cutting at the body joint.

Cut the skin at the tip end of the breastbone. Cut down each side to the back, being careful not to puncture the intestines. Bend the tail back toward the neck and cut where it breaks. The intestines will come out easily now. Remove and clean the giblets. Cut through the ribs toward the neck. Bend the breast and neck apart and separate. Cut the breast in half. Wash thoroughly, drain, and dry. Be sure to remove all lung and kidney tissue. Save the layers of fat.

CHICKEN

ROAST CHICKEN OR ROAST CAPON

PREPARATION TIME: 30 minutes or longer, depending on size of bird

COOKING TIME: in a moderate oven (350°)
Small birds 30 minutes per pound
Large birds 25 minutes per pound

Allow ⅓–½ pound per serving.

Rub the bird inside and out with half a lemon. Put a light sprinkling of powdered ginger inside and then sprinkle salt and pepper over the ginger. Prepare stuffing (p. 100).

Put some of the stuffing in the chest cavity over the breast and the remaining stuffing inside the lower cavity. Do not overstuff; the dressing needs room for expansion. Sew up the opening with a large darning needle and light cord, or use skewers.

The bird is now ready for trussing. Bend the wings back so that the tips rest on the back of the bird. Tie a piece of string around the neck, leaving 2 long ends to the string. Pull the neck over the back of the bird. Press the thighs close to the body. Pass a piece of the twine attached to the neck over each thigh. Cross the string over the body, bring it back, and tie it under the tail.

If it is a lean bird, coat it with melted fat or bacon drippings, or lay strips of bacon or salt pork over the back.

Roast on a rack, breast side down, for the entire cooking period.

When cooking birds this way, it is not necessary to baste. The juices stay in the bird and keep the flesh moist. If the bird seems to be browning too rapidly, place wet parchment paper over it to retard the browning. Or you may soak cheesecloth in bacon drippings and cover the bird with it. At the end of the cooking time and before removing bird from the pan, puncture the skin in several places to allow the juices to run into the pan. Use the juices for the gravy.

To make the gravy, follow the recipe for Turkey Gravy (page 170).

POULTRY GIBLETS

Some people like the giblets chopped up and added to the gravy. Others still prefer the old-fashioned way of serving them whole. In either case, the gizzard needs long, slow cooking. Simmer it for 45 minutes in some seasoned water, along with the neck and wing tips. The heart can be simmered with the gizzard, nearly if not quite as long; but the liver should be added only for the last 10 minutes.

If you are serving roast chicken with whole giblets, simmer the gizzard and heart as directed, then put them in the oven for 10 minutes to dry a little. In this case don't simmer the liver at all, but put it in the oven with the heart and gizzard.

For fried chicken, simmer the heart and gizzard as directed, then remove and coat with seasoned flour. Fry 10 minutes or until golden brown. The liver needs only to be coated and fried—no simmering.

For broiled chicken, simmer the gizzard and heart as directed, then place on the broiler rack, along with the liver, for the last 10 minutes of cooking.

BROILED CHICKEN

PREPARATION TIME: 20 minutes

COOKING TIME: 30–45 minutes

First be sure the chicken is young. Broilers are best when halved or quartered. Wash, clean, and dry. Sprinkle with salt and pepper. Put them in the broiler with the inside to the fire. Brush lightly with butter or bacon drippings and cook with oven at about 400°. Turn the chickens frequently, brushing lightly with the fat at each turning.

PAN-FRIED CHICKEN

PREPARATION TIME: 30 minutes

COOKING TIME: 30–45 minutes

Use only young, tender, disjointed chicken. Wash, drain, and dry. Clean the giblets and simmer in 2 cups of seasoned water.

Put ½ cup of flour, 1 teaspoon of salt, and a dash of pepper in a paper bag. Dredge the chicken pieces in this mixture by dropping them in the bag and shaking until they are well coated.

Melt ¼ cup of cooking fat in a skillet. Put the chicken in the fat and fry until brown and tender. When the flesh admits the tines of a fork without pressure, the chicken is done. Keep the chicken warm until it is all cooked. Serve with

CHICKEN CREAM GRAVY

1 cup milk	Salt
1 cup giblet stock	Pepper
2 tablespoons flour	2 tablespoons fat

METHOD: Remove all chicken from the skillet. Save 2 tablespoons of the cooking fat. Put ½ cup of milk in a jar, add 2 tablespoons of flour, seasonings, and add another ½ cup of milk. Shake until the milk and flour are well blended. Add the milk and flour mixture to the grease in the skillet and keep stirring to prevent lumps. Add 1 cup of the giblet water and cook until the gravy thickens. Serve the gravy separately.

FRIED CHICKEN

PREPARATION TIME: 30 minutes

COOKING TIME: about 60 minutes

Follow the recipe for pan-fried chicken, browning all pieces. After the pieces of chicken have been browned in fat, place the chicken in a casserole or baking dish and bake, covered, in a moderate oven (300°–350°) for about an hour, or until the flesh admits the tine of a fork without pressure. Serve with Chicken Gravy.

Hot biscuits and honey are a traditional accompaniment.

SMOTHERED CHICKEN

PREPARATION TIME: 45 minutes

COOKING TIME: about 75 minutes

Follow directions for Fried Chicken. Stew the giblets in 2 cups hot water until tender. Season with pepper and salt. A small onion may be added for flavor.

Make Chicken Gravy. Then place the browned chicken in a casserole, pour the chicken gravy over it, sprinkle the gravy with 2 tablespoons of minced onion and 1 tablespoon of minced parsley. Cover and bake in a moderate oven (300°–350°) for 1 hour and 15 minutes, or until the chicken is done by the fork test.

FRICASSEED CHICKEN

PREPARATION TIME: about 30 minutes

COOKING TIME: 1–4 hours

Fricasseed chicken is cooked in liquid. Some people make their fricassee without browning the chicken in fat; others think it is sacrilege not to brown it. If you want it browned, dredge the chicken in seasoned flour and brown in hot fat.

Cover the chicken with water, just enough to cover. Add 1 teaspoon of salt and a dash of pepper. If desired, add 3 tablespoons of minced onion, 1 tablespoon of chopped parsley, and 3 tablespoons of chopped celery or 1 teaspoon celery salt. Cover and simmer until done by the fork test. A young chicken will cook in about 1 hour. An old bird or a fowl will take 2–4 hours.

A 3-pound bird will serve 4 to 6; a 4-pound bird will serve 6 to 8.

Serve with dumplings (p. 113) or boiled rice.

When the chicken is tender, remove from pot and keep warm. Thicken the stock or liquid with 2 tablespoons of flour. Mix the flour and liquid by the jar method or mix the flour with water until it is a smooth liquid paste and add to the liquor in the pot.

Place chicken and dumplings on a platter and serve with the thickened gravy.

CHICKEN STEW

PREPARATION TIME: about 45 minutes

COOKING TIME: 2–3 hours, longer if the bird is old

A fowl is good for this dish. It will take 2–3 hours for the chicken to cook. A 2-pound bird will serve 4; a 3-pound bird 4–6.

1 chicken, cut up	1 teaspoon salt
4 medium potatoes, sliced	Dash of pepper
1 clove garlic, minced, if desired	3 small onions, sliced
	1 cup diced celery
½ teaspoon poultry seasoning	

METHOD: Wash and drain the chicken. Put the pieces in a pot with the salt, pepper, poultry seasoning, and onion. Cover with water, bring to a boil slowly, and simmer 2–3 hours. About 30 minutes before the dish is done, add the potatoes and celery. If you are going to serve dumplings, cook the potatoes for 15 minutes, then drain off and save all but about 2 cups of liquid. Prepare the dumpling (p. 113), drop onto the chicken and vegetables, cover, and cook for 15 minutes without lifting the lid. In case you have forgotten, there is no finesse to one peek at a dumpling. You will spoil them if you remove the lid before the full cooking time has expired.

CHICKEN PIE

PREPARATION TIME: about 60 minutes

COOKING TIME: 2–3 hours

You will need a 3-pound bird for 4–6 servings.

Chicken	1 medium onion, sliced
1 teaspoon salt	Piece celery or 1 teaspoon cel-
Pepper	ery salt
Flour for thickening	Sprig parsley
	Rich pie crust

METHOD: Put the chicken, seasoning, onion, celery, and parsley in a kettle. Cover with water and simmer until the chicken is tender. While the chicken is cooking, prepare a rich pie crust, using twice the quantities given in the recipe on page 299. You will need more crust because you are going to use a deep baking dish, one 9 or 10 inches in diameter and 3 inches deep. And you will want the top crust to be thicker than for ordinary pie. Put prepared dough in the refrigerator to chill.

When the chicken is done, remove from the kettle and make a thick gravy by adding 2 tablespoons of flour for each cup of liquid.

Remove chicken from the bones. Roll out the crust and line the bottom and sides of the baking dish. Place an inverted cup in the bottom of the dish, lay pieces of chicken around the cup, and sprinkle with salt and pepper. Add the chicken in layers until it is all in. Fill up the dish with the gravy and put on the top crust. Bake in a hot oven until the crust is done, 30–45 minutes in a hot oven (450°). If you have extra gravy after filling the pie dish, serve it with the pie.

NOTE: A pinch of saffron may be added to the gravy to give it a rich golden color.

Cooked small onions, diced carrots, and cooked peas may be added to the pie when the chicken is put in. Some people feel cheated if there is anything in chicken pie other than chicken and gravy. If there is plenty of chicken, the few vegetables do not hurt and make it a one-dish meal.

CHICKEN SOUP.—See p. 246

CREAMED CHICKEN

PREPARATION TIME: about 20 minutes

COOKING TIME: about 30 minutes

To serve 4, you will need:

2 cups cooked chicken	1 teaspoon salt
2 tablespoons flour	⅛ teaspoon pepper
1 cup milk or cream	1 teaspoon chopped chives or
2 tablespoons butter	½ teaspoon onion juice

1 tablespoon chopped parsley

METHOD: Put some of the milk into a jar and add the flour and more milk. Cover and shake until the flour is blended. Turn the milk and flour into a pan with the butter and seasoning added. Keep stirring until the mixture thickens and begins to bubble. You are really making a white sauce, and you must keep stirring every minute until it has thickened and is bubbling. If you don't, it will lump. When the sauce is thick, add the chicken, chives, and parsley. Put the pan in a pan of hot water to keep warm until ready to use, or use the double boiler. Serve on toast or in ramekins.

CHICKEN SALAD

PREPARATION TIME: 30–45 minutes

To serve 4, you will need:

2 cups cooked chicken	Crisp lettuce
1 cup diced celery	Mayonnaise
Pepper and salt	1 tablespoon minced onion

M E T H O D : Cut the chicken into small pieces and mix with the diced celery. Add enough mayonnaise to make a binding paste for the chicken and celery. Season with pepper and salt. Make a bed of lettuce leaves, mound the chicken and celery mixture on the lettuce, and garnish with wedges of cooked eggs, tomatoes, asparagus tips, slices of avocado, thin strips of cooked beets, chopped parsley, and chopped chives. All or any of the garnishes may be used or the salad may be served plain. Some people like a wedge of fresh lemon with their salad.

TURKEY

ROAST TURKEY

Stuff and truss the turkey as described under Roast Chicken.

Roast on a rack in a slow oven (300°), breast down for the entire cooking period.

C O O K I N G   T I M E : about 15 minutes per pound for large birds from 20 to 25 pounds; 20 minutes per pound for birds from 15–18 pounds; and 25 to 30 minutes per pound for smaller birds

One nice thing about cooking breast down on a rack at low temperature—basting is not necessary, and it is almost impossible to overcook the bird. If you are careful when preparing the bird and do not break the skin, all the juices stay inside the bird, making the meat deliciously moist.

If the back seems to be browning too rapidly, soak a clean cloth in bacon drippings or vegetable oil and cover the back for the last few hours of cooking. Remember that it takes many hours to cook a turkey.

Simmer the giblets as directed under Poultry Giblets. Chop and add to the gravy.

When the turkey is cooked, puncture the skin in several places to allow the juices to run into the pan, remove to a platter and garnish with sprigs of parsley, orange halves, and a few ripe cranberries.

TURKEY GRAVY

It's nice to have a lot of turkey gravy. If there is any left over, it goes into the turkey-bone soup later. *Warning:* Keep gravies and soups in the refrigerator at all times. Put them in the refrigerator as soon as they are cool and keep them there.

Cut the cooked giblets in small pieces. Leave about 6 tablespoons of the turkey drippings in the roasting pan and all the natural juices from the bird. Use 1 tablespoon of flour and 1 cup of liquid for each tablespoon of fat. Use a jar with a tight-fitting lid. Put some of the giblet water in the jar and add the flour. Add more giblet water and shake well until the flour is blended with the liquid. To make your gravy different, save ½ cup of morning coffee to add to it; and use some of the water in which the potatoes have been boiled and some of the water from the onions as well as the giblet water.

Put the roasting pan over a burner, add the liquid and the flour mixture, and salt and pepper to taste. Keep stirring, blending the liquid with the fat and juices in the pan. Stir until the gravy thickens and bubbles. Add the cut-up giblets and cook 3 minutes longer.

WHAT TO DO WITH THE BONES

Never discard the bones of roast turkey or chicken. Make Turkey-Bone Soup or Chicken-Bone Soup out of it, as described in Chapter XII.

GOOSE

ROAST GOOSE

COOKING TIME: 30 minutes in a hot oven (450°), then 20 minutes per pound in a moderate oven (350°)

Trust your butcher to get you a young goose. The best geese do not weigh much over 8 pounds.

Prepare the goose as for Roast Chicken.

Geese are quite fat, so it is wise, if you stuff them, to use a bread stuffing (p. 100) as a base and then add a cup of diced apples. Some cooks add a cup of diced prunes as well as the apples. Bread, celery, apple, onion of course, and the spices make a good combination.

A goose need not be stuffed at all.

If you roast it without stuffing, rub the inner cavity with a cut onion. It will do no harm to leave the onion in the carcass. A piece or two of coarse celery may be left inside too.

Salt and pepper the dressed and trussed goose, sprinkle it with flour, and put it in a very hot oven (450°) for 30 minutes. At the end of 30 minutes drain the fat from the pan. Return the goose to the oven and cook in a moderate oven (350°), allowing 20 minutes per pound.

Prick the skin with a fork every 20 minutes to let the fat escape. Baste and sprinkle again with flour. Do this throughout the cooking time. A cup of hot water may be added to the pan after the first half hour to aid in the basting.

While the goose is roasting, simmer the giblets, and when tender cut them up in small pieces for the gravy.

When the goose is done, remove from the roasting pan. Remove about half the fat in the pan, then add 2 cups of hot water and thicken if necessary. The flour used during the roasting usually makes the gravy thick enough. Add the giblets and serve.

Baked apples or applesauce should be served with roast goose.

DUCK

ROAST DUCK

Follow the directions for Roast Chicken.

Ducks, like geese, are rich in fat and need not be stuffed. In that case rub the interior with a cut onion and put in the body cavity a quartered onion and some quartered tart apples or pieces of celery.

However, they are excellent stuffed with dry bread crumbs, diced apple, minced onion, a little sage, and a little thyme (see p. 100). Try grating the rind of an orange into your duck stuffing.

When the duck is stuffed, place it in a moderate oven (350°) and allow 25 minutes per pound for roasting time. Prick the skin with the tines of a fork every 20 minutes to allow the fat to escape. After the first 45 minutes, drain off most of the fat and add 1 cup of orange juice to the remaining fat and baste the duck. Baste every 20 minutes with the orange juice, adding more if necessary, until the duck is done.

Cook the giblets and add to the gravy. Make the gravy as directed for Turkey Gravy (p. 170).

Applesauce, currant jelly, and green peas are usually served with roast duck.

Now, if you are an epicure, you will prefer your duckling rare and without stuffing. Prepare your duck for roasting, omit stuffing, sprinkle it inside and out with salt, pepper, and flour. Place the duck in a 500° oven which has been preheated to that temperature and cook from 20 minutes to a half hour. The time depends on the type of epicure you are. Remember this method is used for young birds only, and usually Canvasback.

SQUAB

Squabs are best when broiled, although they may be stuffed and roasted.

BROILED SQUAB

Split the squab down the back. Clean and wipe with a damp cloth. Brush lightly with melted butter, season with pepper and salt, and put in the broiler. Keep brushing them with the melted butter until they are nicely browned. Turn them often. They should be done in 15–20 minutes, depending on the heat of your broiler.

Serve the broiled squab on toast, covering with melted butter.

ROAST SQUAB

Prepare as for Roast Chicken. Stuff the birds, cover the breasts with salt pork or bacon, and roast in a moderate oven (350°) 30–45 minutes. Baste frequently.

PIGEONS

Pigeons are usually tough and need long cooking. They are best when pot-roasted, stewed, or made into pies. They take 2–3 hours of slow cooking to become tender.

PIGEON STEW

Cut up the pigeons, put in a stewing kettle, and barely cover with water. Add salt and pepper, 1 small onion, minced, and simmer until tender. Mushrooms may be added when the liquid is thickened. To thicken the liquid, use 1 tablespoon of flour for each cup of liquid. The addition of a tablespoon of butter usually adds to the flavor of the dish.

PIGEON POT ROAST

Clean the birds, stuff, and brown lightly in fat. When lightly browned, cover with water and simmer tightly covered for 2–3 hours. Thicken the gravy and serve on toast.

RABBIT

In certain sections of the United States, particularly in California, millions of pounds of rabbit are eaten yearly. It is a light, delicious meat, rich in food value and preferred by many to chicken.

Rabbits are generally purchased at the market. If, however, you are presented with a wild rabbit or hare, there is the problem of cleaning and preparing it.

The first thing to do is to cut off the front feet at the first joint.

Cut out the tail. With the point of a sharp knife, cut the skin from the tail opening to the first joint on the hind legs. With the fingers separate the skin from the leg meat. Tie the hind legs together and hang the rabbit by the tied legs to a nail. Pull the loosened leg skin down over the body until the neck is reached, then pull the skin over the front legs. Cut off the head and you are free of the skin.

With the point of a sharp knife inserted at the edge of the breastbone, cut the stomach skin upward toward the rectum. Remove the intestines, reserving the heart, liver, and kidneys. Take out and discard the lungs.

It is advisable to wash fresh rabbit in water to which 1 tablespoon of soda has been added. Drain the rabbit and put in the refrigerator until ready for use.

If the rabbit is to be roasted, leave whole. If it is to be fried or cooked in a casserole, cut it up. The hind legs are the largest. Make a triangular cut to the back joint at either side, bend the hind leg back, and remove. This leaves a good portion of meat on the back. Remove the front legs. Cut the back into 3 sections across the spine. Cut the breast open and cut down the spine, making 2 sections.

A 2-pound rabbit will serve 4 people, but not too generously. A 3-pound rabbit will more than generously serve 4 people.

RABBIT CASSEROLE

PREPARATION TIME: about 20 minutes

COOKING TIME: about 90 minutes

Rabbit	4 tablespoons fat
4 tablespoons flour	2 cups hot water
1 teaspoon salt	1 clove garlic if desired,
⅛ teaspoon pepper	minced
¼ cup cooking sherry	

METHOD: Wipe the disjointed rabbit. Dredge in a paper bag

into which ½ cup of flour, 1 teaspoon of salt, and ⅛ teaspoon of pepper have been put. Shake the pieces of rabbit in the bag until they are well coated. Melt the fat in a skillet and brown the rabbit on all sides. Transfer to a casserole. Mince the clove of garlic, or if you want just a touch of flavor you may rub the skillet with the garlic clove before melting the fat. If you use the garlic itself, add the minced garlic to the fat after the rabbit has been browned. Add the flour and mix the fat and flour together with a fork. Add the salt and pepper and the hot water and cook until the gravy thickens. Pour the gravy over the rabbit in the casserole, cover, and bake in a moderate oven (350°) for at least 1 hour and 15 minutes, or until the rabbit meat is tender. A few minutes before serving add the sherry to the gravy. Serve hot.

FRIED RABBIT

PREPARATION TIME: about 20 minutes

COOKING TIME: about 75 minutes

Rabbit	Seasoned flour for dredging
1 teaspoon salt	4 tablespoons fat
⅛ teaspoon pepper	Clove of garlic or 1 small onion

Dredge the disjointed rabbit in seasoned flour (see Rabbit Casserole for quantities). Rub a skillet with a clove of garlic or mince the garlic or onion and add to the fat. Brown the rabbit in the hot fat, then transfer to a baking pan. When all the rabbit is fried, pour ¼ cup of hot water into the skillet, rinse well, and pour the water and fat over the rabbit in the baking pan. Place the baking pan in a moderate oven (350°) and bake uncovered for at least 1 hour, or until the rabbit is tender.

FRICASSEED RABBIT

Follow the directions for Fricasseed Chicken, substituting rabbit for chicken.

COLD RABBIT

Cold cooked rabbit may be used in any recipe calling for chicken. It is delicious creamed, is good in a salad, and makes very palatable sandwiches.

VENISON

Venison is prepared and cooked much like beef, and the amounts per serving are the same as those for beef.

Venison is considered to be at its best when rare. If you do not like rare meat, cook it longer.

BROILED VENISON STEAK

PREPARATION TIME: about 10 minutes for a medium steak

COOKING TIME: rare 12–15 minutes; medium 15–20 minutes; well-done 20–25 minutes

Venison steak
1 cut clove garlic
1 tablespoon butter or cooking oil
Seasoning

METHOD: Wipe the steak with a damp cloth. Rub with the cut clove of garlic, then rub in the butter or cooking oil. Season and broil. The steaks should be cooked quickly until they are crisp and brown on the outside. Serve with a tart jelly.

ROAST VENISON

The saddle or leg are the favorite roasts.

PREPARATION TIME: 20–30 minutes

COOKING TIME: in a moderate oven (325°)

Rare   18–20 minutes per pound
Medium   20–25 minutes per pound
Well done 27–30 minutes per pound

5–7-pound roast

1 clove garlic

2–3 tablespoons butter or cooking oil

¼ pound salt pork or bacon

2 teaspoons salt

¼ teaspoon pepper

¼ cup port wine or claret

Grated rind of 1 lemon

METHOD: Wipe the roast with a damp cloth. Rub with the cut clove of garlic and then with the butter or cooking oil. Sprinkle with salt and pepper. Lard the roast by covering it with salt pork or bacon. Bake in an uncovered pan. When the roast is done, make gravy (p. 108). Add to the gravy the ¼ cup wine and the grated lemon rind.

VENISON POT ROAST OR STEW

Follow the recipes for beef Pot Roast or Beef Stew. Or first marinate the venison from 12 hours to several days in the following mixture:

1 cup wine—claret or port

1 cup water

2 teaspoons salt

8–10 peppercorns

1 bay leaf, broken

8–10 whole cloves

1 medium onion, sliced

½ clove garlic, minced

Keep the venison covered with the liquid. For a larger amount of meat, double the above quantities. Turn the meat several times.

Save the liquid after you remove the meat. Drain the meat and dry. Dredge in seasoned flour and then follow the pot-roast or stew recipe, using the liquid left after marinating instead of water. Save any remaining liquid to be used in the gravy. A little more wine and the juice of a lemon may be added to the gravy.

Wild rice goes well with venison, and a tart jelly is always advisable.

CHAPTER X

VEGETABLES

VEGETABLES should be fresh and firm to the touch. Never buy withered, wilted, old, or moldy vegetables.

All vegetables, particularly the head and leaf variety, should be well washed to remove "spray poisons" which might be present.

The colored vegetables should show their true colors. Cauliflower should be white and solid with no marks. If a cauliflower is yellowed, it has passed its prime. Carrots should be a bright orange color. Beets should be firm, their tops freshly green and their roots a dark dusky red. String beans and peas should be bright green and the pods brittle. Onions should be firm and dry. A wet soggy onion is no good. A bud of garlic should be firm and dry. Parsley and other fresh herbs should be freshly crisp and of bright color. Green celery should be a rich dark green; blanched celery should be white and crisp to the touch. Asparagus should be firm at the tip with no indication of going to seed. Lettuce, cabbage, and other head vegetables should be firm and solid with no waste leaves. Summer squash should be tender. If the skin can be easily punctured with the thumbnail, the squash may be cooked with the skin on. Otherwise it is best to peel.

All root vegetables, turnips, rutabagas, kohlrabi, and potatoes, should be firm and suggest crispness. Broccoli should be bright green and the heads compact and tight. Globe or French artichokes should be solid. If the leaves are tightly placed one over the other, they are best. If the leaves have begun to separate, the bud was getting ready to blossom before it was picked.

HOW MUCH TO BUY

When buying fresh vegetables it is often a problem to know how much to buy per person. The list on pages 182 and 183 will be very helpful. When buying bulky vegetables or vegetables in pods, allow from ⅓ to ½ pound per person per serving.

COOKING TIME FOR VEGETABLES

It is impossible to give accurate times for boiling vegetables because the time varies with the age and quality of the vegetables and with the tastes of the people who eat them. Modern cookery stresses more and more that vegetables should be cooked as short a time as possible and remain crisp and crunchy. Many people, however, still prefer the old-fashioned "until tender" method. In the recipes in this chapter two sets of time ranges are given. The first one is the time range for cooking the vegetable until done but still crisp. The second range, in parentheses, is the time required to cook the vegetable thoroughly, until tender.

FROZEN VEGETABLES

The average 10- to 12-ounce package will net about 4 servings because the vegetables are ready for cooking and there is no waste. Frozen vegetables are a boon to the busy housewife or the woman who works but enjoys cooking her own food.

ARTICHOKES

The French or globe artichoke should be a solid head. If the upper leaves at the tip have begun to separate, the artichoke was preparing to blossom before it was picked.

BOILED FRENCH ARTICHOKES

Allow 1 artichoke per person; or if they are very large, ½ artichoke.

PREPARATION TIME: about 20 minutes for 4
COOKING TIME: 25–30 (45–60) minutes

Soak the artichokes in cold salted water for 15 minutes. This will crisp and freshen the bud, and also drive out any small insects which may have been looking for a safe place to hide. Cut off the sharp points of the leaves with a pair of shears or a sharp knife.

Have enough boiling water ready to float the artichokes. Add 1 tablespoon of salt and 1 tablespoon of vinegar or lemon juice. For definite flavor, 1 tablespoon of olive oil, 3–4 whole cloves, and a clove of garlic may be added. Boil 45–60 minutes, or until the base of the bud can be pierced with a sharp fork.

Drain the artichokes and cut off the stem close to the base of the bud so that it will stand on a plate. Serve hot with melted butter or Hollandaise sauce, or cold with mayonnaise.

At the table, when all the outer leaves have been pulled off and the soft ends consumed, the fuzzy hair, or choke, must be removed before the heart can be eaten. The choke scrapes off easily with a knife or fork.

If you enjoy a mingling of rare flavors, try this: Take a bite of artichoke (no sauce), then a sip of tea without sugar or cream. It's a delicious combination.

JERUSALEM ARTICHOKES

The Jerusalem artichoke is a tuber, or root vegetable. It rather resembles a small potato with severe cramps.

One pound serves 3 or 4.

BOILED JERUSALEM ARTICHOKES

PREPARATION TIME: about 20 minutes per pound

COOKING TIME: 15–25 (30–45) minutes

These artichokes should be washed and scraped.

TO SCRAPE VEGETABLES means to remove the outer skin by scraping the surface with a sharp knife.

Put them in a kettle and cover with cold water. Add 1 teaspoon of salt, cover the pot, and allow the water to come to a boil over a medium flame. They are done when they can be pierced with the tines of a sharp fork. Serve with melted butter and a sprinkling of parsley.

Cold cooked Jerusalem artichokes may be creamed or added to salads.

ASPARAGUS

Asparagus should be fresh and crisp. If it is old and withered it will be tough and tasteless. It is generally green at the tips, fading to a purple-white at the stem or cut end. The green portion only is edible. There is, however, the Oyster Bay asparagus which is creamy white with a purple tip. Some 4 to 5 inches of the tip end of asparagus is edible.

BOILED ASPARAGUS

PREPARATION TIME: about 15 minutes per pound

COOKING TIME: 15–20 (30) minutes

Have boiling water ready. Wash the asparagus and cut off the tough ends, leaving 4–5 inches. Scrape or cut off the scales and wash again. Tie in bunches which are easy to handle.

Set the asparagus bunches upright in a tall, narrow kettle, stem ends down. Add 1 teaspoon of salt per pound of vegetable. Pour in boiling water, allowing 1 inch of the tips to remain uncovered. Cover the kettle and cook for 15 minutes. After 15 minutes, remove the lid and continue cooking until the stem ends are done by the fork test. Lift out the bunches, drain, untie, and arrange on a hot plate. Serve with butter or Hollandaise sauce. Save the water for soup.

Cold asparagus may be creamed or used in salads.

Vegetable	Servings Per Pound	Preparation Time, Minutes Per Pound	Cooking Method
Artichoke, globe	2–3	20	boil
Artichoke, Jerusalem	3–4	20	boil
Asparagus	2–3	15	boil
Beans, dried	4–6	Soak overnight	simmer
			bake
Beans, lima	2	15	boil
Beans, string	3–4	10	boil
Beets	2–3	5	boil
Beet greens	2–3	15	boil
Broccoli	3	30	boil
Brussels sprouts	3–4	45	boil
Cabbage	3	20–30	boil
Carrots	3–4	15	boil
Cauliflower	2–3	35	boil
Celery	3–4	15	boil
Celeriac or celery root	3–4	20	boil
Chard	2–4	20–30	boil
Corn, 1 or 2 ears per person		2–3 per ear	boil
Eggplant	2–3	20	oven-fry
			fry
			boil
Kale	3–4	20	boil
Kohlrabi	3–4	15	boil
Leeks	2–3	6–10	boil
Mushrooms	3–4	20	
Okra	4	15	boil
Onions	4–6	20	boil
			French fry
			fry
Parsnips	3–4	20	boil
Peas	2	10–15	boil
Potatoes, White	2–3	10–15	boil
			bake
			raw fry
Potatoes, Sweet	2–3	5	boil
			bake
Salsify or Oyster plant	3–4	20	boil
Spinach	3	20–30	boil
Squash, Summer	3–4	10	boil
			bake
Squash, Winter	3	10	steam
			bake
Tomatoes	3	about 3 per tomato	bake
			stew
			broil
			fry
Rutabaga	3–4	15	boil
Turnips, White	3–4	15	boil
Turnip greens	3	30	boil

CHART

183

| Cooking Time in Minutes | | No. of Cups, Cooked, in 1 Pound | No. of Cups, Raw, in 1 Pound |
Tender	Crisp		
45–60	25–30		
30–45	15–25	2	
15–30	15–20	1½	
120			
6–8 hours			
15–30	15–30		1, shelled
20–30	20–30	3½	
60	20–60	2, sliced	
20–30	10–20	2	
20–30	15–25		
15–30	10–20	3	
7–30	5–15	3	5, shredded
30–45	10–25	3, diced	3¼, diced
10–30	10–20	2, broken	
15–30	10–20	3, sliced	3, diced
30–45	10–20	2½, sliced or diced	
20–30	10–15	2	
3–10	3–10		
30–45	25		
15	5–10		
30–45	10	1¾	
50–60	10–25		
15–25	15–25	2	
20	15–20		
5 up	5 up		
15–40	15–25	3	
30–45	20–40	2½	3, diced
3–5	3–5		
20	10–15		
45	30–40	2½	
10–20	10–20		1
30–50	20–40	2	
45–60	45		
30–45	25		
30–45	20–30	1½, mashed	
45–60	30–40		
30	20–40	2, sliced	
10–20	5–10	2, chopped	3, tightly packed
20–30	10–15	2½, sliced	
45–60	45		
30	30	1, mashed	
120	45		
30	30		
15–30	5–15		
20	3–5		
10–15			
45–60	30–45	3, mashed	
30–45	15–30	2, diced	
20–30	10–20		

BEANS, DRIED

Dried beans, any variety, are often used as a winter vegetable. Soak them overnight after washing them, then cook them in the water in which they have been soaked.

BOILED DRIED BEANS

PREPARATION TIME: beans must be washed and soaked overnight

COOKING TIME: about 2 hours

2 cups dried beans	⅛ teaspoon pepper
¼ pound salt pork or bacon	1 teaspoon salt
1 minced onion	Water to cover

In the morning pick over soaked beans, discarding any imperfect ones. Put the beans in a kettle with the pork or bacon, onion and seasoning. Cover with water in which they were soaked. Add more water if necessary to cover. Bring to the boil and simmer for about 2 hours. Serve the beans in their own juice.

PURÉED DRIED BEANS

Purée hot boiled dried beans, using 1 cup of the liquid to wash the purée through the sieve.

TO PURÉE means to press through a coarse sieve or a food mill.

The puréed beans may be put in a greased baking dish covered with slices of the pork with which they were cooked and baked in a moderate oven (350°) for 45 minutes.

DRIED BEAN SOUP

Use all the liquid when puréeing the beans. Add 1 cup of milk for each 2 cups of pulp and juice, 1 tablespoon of minced parsley, 1 tablespoon of butter, and extra seasoning if needed. Return to the stove and cook until the flavors are blended.

MOCK BAKED BEANS

Prepare Boiled Dried Beans. Drain off the water into another dish and save it. Turn the beans into a greased baking dish or casserole, and add:

½ teaspoon dry mustard 2 tablespoons molasses
Slices of the pork with which they were cooked

Pour the water you have saved over the beans, enough to cover. Bake in a slow oven (300°) for at least 1 hour.

CASSEROLE OF DRIED BEANS

Prepare Boiled Dried Beans. Drain off the water into another dish and save it. Turn the beans into a greased casserole and add:

1 green pepper, minced 2 tablespoons brown sugar
2 medium tomatoes, peeled 1 tablespoon Worcestershire
   and cubed   sauce
1 cup diced celery ½ teaspoon dry mustard
1 teaspoon salt 1 cup diced carrots
⅛ teaspoon pepper

Pour the water you have saved over the beans, enough to cover. Cover the casserole and bake in a slow oven (300°) for 2 hours. Dried lima beans are particularly good prepared this way.

BOSTON BAKED BEANS

PREPARATION TIME: the beans must soak overnight
COOKING TIME: 6–8 hours

There is no quick method for real Boston Baked Beans. It is a dish that takes time in the preparation, but the results more than repay the patient cook. Since considerable time is consumed in preparation, why not cook a good quantity? They keep well, are good reheated. When mashed and mixed with chili sauce, they make delicious sandwiches and are good in a cooked vegetable salad.

4 cups dried small beans (2 pounds)
1 medium onion, minced
½ pound salt pork streaked with lean
1 teaspoon salt
2 teaspoons dry mustard
4 tablespoons molasses
1 tablespoon Worcestershire sauce if desired

M E T H O D: In the evening of the day before the beans are to be served, wash the beans, removing any imperfect or broken beans. Imperfect beans become mushy when cooked. These beans should be firm. Put the beans in a large bowl and cover well with water, allowing room for them to expand. Let them soak overnight.

In the morning drain the beans (save the water) and place them in the bean pot. Add the salt, dry mustard, minced onion, molasses, and the Worcestershire sauce if you use it. Now add the water the beans were soaked in, pouring slowly until the beans are just covered. Mix well with a spoon and bury the chunk of salt pork deep in the beans. If the water does not cover the beans because of the addition of the pork, add just a little more to cover. Put the lid on the bean pot and put the pot in a slow oven (300°). Let them cook all day until the evening meal is to be served—at least 6–8 hours.

Every hour or two take the lid from the pot and stir the beans carefully so as not to break them. Be sure they are just covered with water.

About 2 hours before the beans are to be served, lift the pork to the surface of the beans so it will brown.

Boston Baked Beans are a traditional Saturday night supper in New England when served with boiled ham and brown bread.

QUICK BAKED BEANS

PREPARATION TIME: about 10 minutes

COOKING TIME: 1 hour or more

Take 1 large can of baked beans. Be fussy about the brand.

Pick a good brand, one that is *oven-baked* or *bean-hole baked*. (Do not buy beans baked with tomato sauce for this recipe.) Put the canned baked beans in your bean pot. Add 1 small onion, minced, stirring carefully. Sprinkle 2 or 3 tablespoons of water over the top of beans. Put the lid on the pot and cook in a slow oven (300°) for at least 1 hour; better 2 hours. Remove the lid of the bean pot during the last 15 minutes so the beans will brown.

BEANS, FRESH

BOILED LIMA BEANS

PREPARATION TIME: about 15 minutes per pound

COOKING TIME: 20–30 minutes (if freshly picked, 10–15 minutes)

When buying fresh lima beans, see that the pods are freshly green, free from small holes, and well rounded over the bean itself. Allow ½ pound of beans in the pod per serving.

Cover the beans with boiling water and boil until tender. Just before the beans finish cooking, add ¼ teaspoon of salt per cup of beans and a little pepper. Add a lump of butter and drain for a dry vegetable, or serve them in the liquid in which they were cooked.

If you drain the beans, save the liquid. It will be excellent and nutritious in soup.

BOILED STRING BEANS

Both the long green and the yellow wax bean can be boiled as described here.

The beans should be fresh and crisp; they should snap when bent between the fingers. They are known as "snap" beans in some parts of the country. Allow ⅓ to ¼ pound per person for a generous serving.

PREPARATION TIME: about 10 minutes per pound, longer if cut into thin slivers. The beans may be cut in 1-inch pieces, cooked whole, or cut into long slivers, sometimes called French beans. If you want to sliver or shred the beans, there is a very practical gadget on the market for the purpose.

COOKING TIME: 20–30 minutes

Cover the prepared beans with boiling water and boil rapidly until tender. Add ½ teaspoon of salt, a little pepper, and 1 table-spoon of butter just before the beans finish cooking. Drain and serve. Two tablespoons of bacon drippings may be added to the beans before cooking starts, in which case omit adding butter at end. Or the beans may be cooked with a piece of bacon or salt pork, about ¼ pound per pound of beans. If cooked with pork they should boil gently for about an hour.

BEETS

The roots should be round and firm, the tops green and fresh. Beets may be boiled or steamed. Allow 2 medium beets per serving.

BOILED BEETS

PREPARATION TIME: about 5 minutes per pound

COOKING TIME: 20–60 minutes. Beets should be tender to the tines of a fork.

Wash the beets and remove the tops and long stem end. Place in a pot and add 1 teaspoon of salt for each 6 beets. Cover generously with cold water and cover the pot. Bring to a boil and boil until tender.

When the beets are done, turn into cold water and slip off the outer skin with the fingers. Keep the beets warm. Serve with butter and pepper and salt, with or without vinegar.

PICKLED BEETS

Slice cold beets into a jar with slices of onion, add vinegar to cover, and serve as a pickle.

BEET TOPS OR GREENS

PREPARATION TIME: 30 minutes for about 2 pounds

COOKING TIME: 10–20 (20–30) minutes

The young beet plant, leaves, and small root ends are used. The leaves should be fresh and crisp. All greens reduce in bulk when cooked, so allow ½ pound of uncooked greens per serving.

Soak the greens for a few minutes in salted water and wash carefully. Remove all grit and any old leaves.

Put the greens in a kettle with 1 teaspoon of salt and I cup of boiling water. Cover and cook until the greens are wilted and just tender. Drain and chop. Add butter, pepper, and more salt if necessary. Some people like vinegar with their greens, so have a cruet ready for those who do.

BROCCOLI

The head or flower of broccoli should be tight buds, and the whole plant should be a fresh bright green. This is one of the vegetables which gives off an unpleasant odor while cooking. A crust of bread in the kettle, on top of vegetable, helps to keep down the unpleasant smell. An open window is essential.

BOILED BROCCOLI

PREPARATION TIME: about 30 minutes per pound

Soak the broccoli in plenty of salted water to which 1 tablespoon of vinegar has been added. This will bring out any small worms or insects that might be hiding in the heads. Soak for about 20 minutes, then trim off the large and old leaves and the thick tough end.

COOKING TIME: 15–25 (20–30) minutes, uncovered

Broccoli, like asparagus, should be cooked stem end down in salted water. Divide large stalks and flowers or split the ends of the stems. Place the broccoli in a kettle of boiling water. Do not submerge the heads. Boil rapidly uncovered, until the stems are tender to the tines of a fork. When done, lift the broccoli and drain off excess moisture. Serve with butter or Hollandaise sauce.

Save the water, purée any cold broccoli remaining, and use for cream soup.

BRUSSELS SPROUTS

Sprouts should be green and crisp-looking. They, too, have a cooking odor. A crust of bread should be in the kettle on top of vegetable during the cooking time. Allow ¼ pound per serving.

BOILED BRUSSELS SPROUTS

PREPARATION TIME: about 45 minutes per pound

COOKING TIME: 10–20 (15–30) minutes

Soak the sprouts in salted acidulated water for 30 minutes. After soaking, cut off the stem and remove any dead or yellow leaves.

Cover the sprouts with boiling water, add 1 teaspoon of salt, and boil until tender. When done, drain. Serve with butter or a cream sauce.

CABBAGE

Cabbage should be crisp and the heads solid to the touch. A pound serves 3.

BOILED CABBAGE

PREPARATION TIME: about 30 minutes for a small head

COOKING TIME: young cabbage, 5–10 minutes of boiling is the way some like it; others prefer 15 minutes; older cabbage, 20–30 minutes

Cut the cabbage into 6 or 8 sections and remove the hard core from each section. Soak 20 minutes in salted water.

Drop the chunks of cabbage into boiling salted water and cook uncovered with a slice of bread on top the cabbage. The cabbage should be crisp and crunchy when done. (There was a time when cabbage was cooked for hours, but now we know that overcooking toughens the fibers.) Serve with melted butter and pepper and salt, or creamed.

CARROTS

Carrots should be bright orange, crisp and plump, with fresh leaves. Young carrots are sweeter than the large winter carrots.

BOILED CARROTS

PREPARATION TIME: about 15 minutes per pound

COOKING TIME: 10–25 (30–45) minutes, depending upon their age and how they are cut up

Cut off the tops and the roots. Scrub with a brush and scrape if desired. Winter carrots may have to be peeled. Very young carrots may be cooked with their skins on.

Slice the carrots, cut them in long thin strips, or in chunks. Very young carrots can be cooked whole.

Put the carrots into a kettle which can be tightly covered. Pour 1 cup of water over them and add ½ teaspoon of salt. Cover and bring the water quickly to a boil. Reduce the heat and cook until the carrots are tender when pierced with a fork.

If preferred, carrots can be cooked in an uncovered kettle in a large amount of salted water. For variety, add to the water 1 small onion, minced, 1 tablespoon of chopped parsley, or other herbs to taste.

Drain, saving the water for soup, and add butter, pepper, and salt.

MASHED CARROTS

Mash boiled carrots before adding butter and seasoning.

CREAMED CARROTS

Serve boiled carrots with a cream sauce (p. 232), either alone or mixed with peas.

BAKED CARROTS

Prepare whole baby carrots as for Boiled Carrots. Put them in a greased shallow covered casserole with generous dottings of butter and salt and pepper. Cover tightly and bake in a moderate oven (350°–375°) 30–45 minutes, or until tender. Sliced carrots or carrot chunks may be baked the same way.

If you are having roast lamb, peel whole carrots and put in the roasting pan about 45 minutes before the lamb is done.

CARROT SANDWICHES

Cold mashed carrots mixed with grated cheese make surprisingly good sandwiches.

CAULIFLOWER

Cauliflower should be white, tightly formed, and spotless.

BOILED CAULIFLOWER

PREPARATION TIME: about 35 minutes

COOKING TIME: 10–20 (30) minutes uncovered

Remove excess leaves and the thick woody stem. Retain fresh green leaves and ribs. Soak in a deep bowl or pan of salted water, head down, for about 30 minutes.

Cook the washed cauliflower in boiling salted water until tender. A bread crust in the water helps to kill the odor while it cooks. Very young, fresh, home-grown plants will cook in from 8–10 minutes. The heads bought at the market usually take a little longer. When done, drain. Serve with melted butter and a sprinkling of paprika, or with cheese sauce or cream sauce.

CELERY

Celery should be crisp and the tops fresh. Blanched celery is white. Green celery is delicious too.

BOILED CELERY

PREPARATION TIME: about 15 minutes for a medium-sized head

COOKING TIME: 10–20 (15–30) minutes

Peel off the outer stalks and save the small heart to be eaten raw. Save some of the top leaves; they make excellent flavoring for stews, stuffings, and casseroles. Wash the stalks and cut away any dark or brown spots. Wash thoroughly because celery is sometimes sprayed with arsenic. Cut the stalks into 1-inch pieces. Place in a stew pan and cover with boiling water. Add ½ teaspoon of salt and boil until tender. Serve with butter, pepper, and salt.

CREAMED CELERY

Prepare Boiled Celery and make a cream sauce as follows:

½ cup of water in which celery was boiled
½ cup milk or cream
2 tablespoons flour
2 tablespoons butter or fat

Use the jar method for thickening (see Method II, p. 229). Or combine the fat and flour in a saucepan, mixing until blended. Add the celery water and milk, stirring constantly until smooth and thick. Add the drained celery, season, and serve.

CELERY ROOT OR CELERIAC

Celeriac is a knobby root vegetable whose leaves look and smell like celery leaves. The roots should be firm.

BOILED CELERIAC

PREPARATION TIME: about 20 minutes per pound
COOKING TIME: 10–20 (30–45) minutes

Cut off the tops and scrub the root well to remove all earth. Pare off excess root fibers. Cover with cold water to which 1 teaspoon of salt has been added. Boil covered until tender. Serve with butter, a dash of paprika, salt and pepper. Cold boiled celeriac, sliced or diced, is delicious in salads with French dressing.

CREAMED CELERIAC

Boil celeriac and make a cream sauce as for Creamed Celery.

CHARD OR SWISS CHARD

Chard is a large leafy vegetable. It is plain green with a white rib, or the rhubarb or beet chard is dark red. The leaves should be crisp and the midrib fairly brittle. It is easy to clean. The midribs may be taken out and cooked separately, or may be cut into small pieces and cooked with the leafy part. For a time this vegetable was known as Swiss Chard, but now the "Swiss" seems to have been dropped.

Like all greens, chard loses a great deal of its bulk when cooked. Allow at least ¼ pound of fresh chard per serving.

BOILED CHARD

PREPARATION TIME: 20–30 minutes per pound
COOKING TIME: 10–15 (20–30) minutes

Soak the chard in cold water for a few minutes. Rinse the leaves well and cut or break them into fairly small pieces. Take out the midrib and boil separately or cut it up and add to the leafy section. Chard needs very little water for cooking, but since it scorches easily, add ½ cup of boiling water when you put it over the fire. When tender, drain and chop, season with salt and pepper, and serve.

VARIATIONS: Some people like olive oil and vinegar with chard; others prefer it dotted with butter. A little basil, marjoram, savory, or tarragon may be added to the greens while cooking. Remember, a little of the herbs. You want a suggestion of a flavor while retaining the original goodness of the chard.

Two tablespoons of bacon fat may be added to the chard before cooking if you like the flavor.

The midribs may be boiled separately and served as a separate vegetable, or they may be marinated after cooking and served as a salad.

TO MARINATE means to soak in oil and acid. The simplest and easiest way is to soak in a good French dressing, either your own or a prepared dressing bought at the market.

CORN ON THE COB

The husks covering the ears should be fresh and green. When a little of the husk is pulled back, the kernels should be tender to the touch, soft and milky if you pierce a kernel with your thumbnail. Leave the husks on the corn until just before the corn is to be cooked.

PREPARATION TIME: 2–3 minutes per ear

COOKING TIME: 2–3 minutes for really young, fresh corn; 6–10 for older ears

Remove the husks and all the silk. Drop the ears into rapidly boiling salted water to cover. When done, place a napkin on a platter. Put the hot corn on napkin, cover with the ends of the napkin, and serve at once.

EGGPLANT

A good eggplant should be surprisingly light for its size. Don't try to buy a heavy one. It should be a rich dark purple, the skin smooth and glossy.

OVEN-FRIED EGGPLANT

PREPARATION TIME: about 20 minutes for a medium eggplant

COOKING TIME: 25 (30–45) minutes in a hot oven (400°)

Cut the eggplant in slices ½ inch thick. Peel and sprinkle lightly with salt. Beat 1 egg for each medium-sized eggplant. Dip the slices into the egg and then in cracker or bread crumbs. Place the covered slices on a greased cookie sheet and bake for at least 30 minutes. A dab of butter added to the top of each slice just before going into the oven helps the flavor.

SAUTÉED EGGPLANT

Prepare the eggplant as directed for Oven-Fried Eggplant and fry in a small amount of fat in a heavy skillet. Drain on absorbent paper before serving.

FRENCH-FRIED EGGPLANT

Prepare as for Oven-Fried Eggplant. Fry in hot deep fat (375°–385°) until browned. Drain on absorbent paper before serving.

KALE

Kale is a green vegetable of the cabbage family. It should be green and sturdy, crisp and curly.

PREPARATION TIME: about 30 minutes for 1½ pounds

COOKING TIME: 25–50 minutes

Wash the kale thoroughly. Cut away the tough midrib of the leaves.

1½ pounds kale   Salt and pepper
    ⅛ pound salt pork or 3 tablespoons bacon fat

METHOD: Place the kale and pork or fat in kettle. Cover with boiling water and boil for 25–50 minutes. Add salt and pepper.

Drain, chop, and serve at once, adding a little of the juice from the pan if you like a moist green.

KOHLRABI

Kohlrabi is a knobby vegetable. It looks something like a misplaced root, since the knob grows above the ground. The leaves grow out of the surface of the knob. The leaves should be pale green, fresh and crisp. The knobs should be about the size of a medium-sized onion. Allow about 1½ per serving.

BOILED KOHLRABI

PREPARATION TIME: about 15 minutes for 6 knobs

COOKING TIME: 15–25 minutes

Cut off the leaf stems close to the knob, then peel. Be sure to remove the woody fibers in the outer surface and at the root juncture. Cube the kohlrabi and cover it with boiling salted water. Boil until tender and drain. Serve with butter, pepper, and salt.

CREAMED KOHLRABI

Boil the kohlrabi as directed above. Make a cream sauce and add to it ½ cup of grated cheese.

LEEKS

A leek looks like an overgrown scallion. It is a compact sheaf of white leaves and should be at least an inch thick. The white bottom or stem end should blend into the bright green of the leaves. It should be firm to the touch, and the green of the leaves bright and brittle.

The leek has a delicate flavor all its own. It is delicious as a vegetable. One leek per person is a generous serving.

BOILED LEEKS

PREPARATION TIME: about 2 minutes per leek

COOKING TIME: 15–20 minutes

Cut off the whiskers or roots at the base. Use all of the green leafy part which is neither browned nor wilted. Cut into chunks 1 inch long or cook whole.

Drop the leeks into boiling salted water and boil uncovered for 15–20 minutes. When done, drain (save the liquor), arrange on a platter, bathe with melted butter, sprinkle with pepper, and serve hot.

LEEKS AU GRATIN

Prepare boiled leeks and place them in a buttered shallow baking dish. Cover with ½ cup grated cheese, dust with salt and pepper, and put under the broiler long enough for the cheese to melt and turn slightly golden.

AU GRATIN literally means "with bread crumbs." But it has come to be associated with cheese dishes so that now it usually refers to a baked casserole dish in which the food, usually moistened with a cream sauce, is covered with grated cheese or buttered crumbs, or both, and baked or broiled until the top is brown.

MUSHROOMS

Unless you know what you are doing, do not pick mushrooms in the fields. Be safe and buy them at your market unless you want to strum a harp or stoke a fire, because some varieties are deadly poison.

Mushrooms should be fresh. The tops should be creamy white. Dark or spotted tops usually indicate age.

Allow about 6 fair-sized mushrooms per serving.

TO PREPARE MUSHROOMS

PREPARATION TIME: about 20 minutes per pound

Break off the stalk or stem. Pare the caps of large mushrooms by peeling toward the center from the edge. Young tender mushrooms may be brushed and not peeled. When prepared, drop the mushrooms into acidulated water, using either 1 tablespoon of lemon juice or vinegar. This will keep them from darkening. If the stems are tender, they may be served with the caps. Tough stems and the peelings may be cooked in a small amount of water and used for stock and flavoring for sauces.

SAUTÉED MUSHROOMS

COOKING TIME: 5–10 minutes

6 mushrooms per serving	Pepper
Butter	1 slice toast per serving

METHOD: Prepare the mushrooms as directed above. Have your toast ready and keep it warm. Heat a skillet that can be tightly covered. Brush the skillet with butter. Place the mushrooms in the skillet, topside down. Into the hollow of the mushroom place a small piece of butter and sprinkle with salt and pepper. Cover the pan and cook over a medium flame from 5–10 minutes. Each cap will be filled with its own juice, mingled with the melted butter. Lift carefully from skillet to the toast and serve at once.

CREAMED FRESH MUSHROOMS

COOKING TIME: about 15 minutes

To serve 4 you will need:

2 cups fresh mushrooms	½ cup cream
2 tablespoons butter or fat	⅛ teaspoon pepper
1 tablespoon flour	1 teaspoon salt
½ cup boiling water	

Prepare the mushrooms as directed above. Make a sauce of the fat, flour, cream, and seasoning by blending the flour and fat in the bottom of a saucepan or double boiler. Add the cream, stirring constantly. Add the seasoning. Pour the ½ cup of boiling water over the mushrooms in a saucepan and boil gently until tender, 6–8 minutes. When the mushrooms are done, pour them with their liquid into the cream sauce. Mix, reheat, and serve on toast.

CREAMED CANNED MUSHROOMS

COOKING TIME: about 5 minutes

2 cups canned mushrooms	1 cup milk
1 tablespoon fat	⅛ teaspoon pepper
2 tablespoons flour	1 teaspoon salt

METHOD: Make a cream sauce of the fat, flour, milk, and seasonings. Add the cooked mushrooms to the sauce and cook gently about 5 minutes or until very hot. Serve on toast.

OKRA

Okra has a tradition behind it. It is associated with fine Southern cookery, but many people object to it because of its sliminess. It is rarely served alone, but is good with contrasting vegetables, particularly the tomato.

Okra should be fresh and young. It is a fuzzy vegetable, a pod about 3 inches long. It is 5-sided, has a broad top and a pointed tip. The pods should be crisp to the touch and break easily. Do not buy soft or withered okra. Okra is sold by the quart or the pound. Allow 1 pound for 4 servings.

BOILED OKRA

PREPARATION TIME: about 15 minutes per pound

COOKING TIME: 15–25 (40) minutes

Wash and clean the okra, being careful not to injure the pods as they become quite sticky. Cut off the stem and the tip. Slice the okra about ½ inch thick, using a sharp knife. Cover the slices with boiling water and cook gently until tender. Drain, place in a hot serving dish, and cover with 6 tablespoons of melted butter. Sprinkle with salt and pepper, 2 tablespoons of lemon juice. Serve hot.

GUMBO

2 cups sliced okra	4 tablespoons bacon fat
4 ripe tomatoes or 2 cups thick tomato paste	1 green pepper, minced
	1½ teaspoons salt
1 onion, minced	⅛ teaspoon pepper
1 tablespoon chopped parsley	6 cups boiling water

METHOD: Cook the onion and pepper in the fat for a few minutes. Add the okra and tomato, stirring constantly, and cook a few minutes. Add the seasoning and the boiling water and simmer for about 2 hours. Serve on boiled rice or add 1–2 cups of boiled rice the last few minutes.

VARIATIONS: In the last 5 minutes add 2 cups of cooked crab, shrimp, or chicken; or a combination of crab, shrimp, and fresh oysters is delicious. Serve on hot boiled rice.

ONIONS

"If you have tears, prepare to shed them now."

All onions, regardless of color, should be firm to the touch. The small white varieties are best for boiling. The large Italian Red and the Bermuda are perfect for sandwiches or raw sliced onions. Medium-sized onions are best for French-frying. Any onion is good just plain fried.

Each cook has her own ideas about how to prevent tears when peeling and preparing onions. Some suggest putting a crust of bread in the mouth. Others say peel them under water. If you can do it successfully, try to breathe through your mouth while preparing onions, and you will reduce the tears to a minimum. Keep your hands away from your face if possible, but it is more than likely that while peeling onions a fly will try to settle on your forehead, or the tip of your nose will itch. We have had interested friends stand watching us prepare onions. It has been a touching scene because they had the tears streaming down their faces while we did the work.

BOILED ONIONS

Allow 3 or 4 small onions per serving.

PREPARATION TIME: about 20 minutes per pound

COOKING TIME: 20–40 (30–45) minutes

Peel the onions. Cut off the fibrous root end and any remnants of the leaves. Wash in cold water. If it is not possible to get small onions, larger onions, quartered, will do.

Cover the peeled onions, bring to a boil, and simmer gently for 20–40 minutes. There is no point in cooking an onion until it is mush. Drain when tender and save the water for soups. Place the onions in a hot dish, cover with 2 tablespoons of melted butter, sprinkle with salt and pepper, and serve hot.

VARIATION: Boiled onions to which a tablespoon of sage has been added after draining is a delicious accompaniment to Roast Pork.

CREAMED ONIONS

Boil the onions as directed above. After draining, pour over them 1 cup of medium cream sauce for each pound of onions.

FRENCH-FRIED ONIONS

COOKING TIME: 3–5 minutes

Peel medium-sized onions and cut into slices ⅜ inch thick. Separate the rings. Have at least 1 inch of hot fat (360°–375°) in a deep skillet or kettle. Drop in the onion rings and cook until light brown (3–5 minutes). Lift out, drain on paper, sprinkle with salt and pepper, keep hot in the oven and serve hot.

VARIATIONS: Some people like to drop the onion rings in a bowl of milk for a few minutes and then fry. It makes the grease spatter more. Others dip them in seasoned flour or egg and crumbs before frying.

PLAIN FRIED ONIONS

COOKING TIME: 20 minutes

Allow 2 medium-sized onions per serving.

Peel and slice the onions into a skillet into which you have melted 4 tablespoons of bacon fat. Sprinkle the onions with salt and pepper, add ¼ cup of water, cover the skillet, and allow the onions to simmer for 10 minutes. Remove the lid and cook for 10 minutes longer, stirring the onions to keep them from burning.

Onions fried this way are often served with liver or with broiled steak.

PARSNIPS

Parsnips are best after the first frost. They are a white carrot-shaped root vegetable. They may be served boiled, creamed, fried, or roasted in a pan in which lamb is being cooked. They are good in soups.

Parsnips should be creamy white and firm. If a parsnip is too large, it is probably old and will have a woody center. They come in assorted sizes. A pound will serve 3 to 4 people.

BOILED PARSNIPS

PREPARATION TIME: about 20 minutes per pound

COOKING TIME: 30–40 (45) minutes

Wash and scrape the parsnips. Cover with cold water and cook in a covered kettle until tender. An older parsnip may take an hour's cooking. Drain, cut into small pieces, cover with melted butter, salt, and pepper, and serve hot. If the center core is woody or fibrous, always remove it.

MASHED PARSNIPS

Prepare Boiled Parsnips. Mash the parsnips, dot with butter, and sprinkle with salt and pepper and a little minced parsley. Serve hot.

FRIED PARSNIPS

METHOD I: Prepare Boiled Parsnips. Slice in long thin strips, season with salt and pepper, dust with flour, and fry in fat until a golden brown.

METHOD II: Prepare Boiled Parsnips and mash them. Put 2 cups of parsnip pulp in a bowl. Add 1 well-beaten egg, 1 tablespoon of flour, 1 teaspoon of salt, 1 teaspoon of sugar, and mix well. Cover your fingers with flour and shape each tablespoon of the mixture into a flat cake, cover lightly with flour, and fry in fat until brown.

CREAMED PARSNIPS

Slice boiled parsnips. To each 2 cups of parsnips add 1 cup of medium white sauce to which 1 tablespoon of chopped chives and 1 tablespoon of chopped parsley have been added.

BAKED PARSNIPS

Cut boiled parsnips in halves, bathe them in the grease in the pan in which a lamb roast is cooking, and brown for the last half hour of roasting.

PEAS

Pea pods should be a fresh, clear green, the pods well rounded and full. Allow ½ pound of peas in the pod per person. Peas should not be shelled too long before cooking.

BOILED PEAS

PREPARATION TIME: 10–15 minutes per pound

COOKING TIME: 10–20 minutes

Wash the freshly shelled peas and put them in a saucepan. Add as little boiling water as possible (¼–½ cup) and a few of the freshest and greenest of the pods. *Please do not* sprinkle them with sugar. Boil gently. Test them at the end of 10 minutes. When tender, add salt, ½ teaspoon per pound, a little pepper, and a generous lump of butter. Serve hot. If you drain them, save the water in which they were cooked. It is far too good to throw away and can be used in soup or a cream sauce.

Frozen peas are delicious when cooked according to the instructions on the package.

PEPPERS

Sweet peppers can be either red or green. When fresh the skin should be firm, shiny, and have no wrinkles. Don't buy peppers willy-nilly. Ask the market man for sweet peppers. A hot pepper can be most awfully hot, and the tiny reddish-brown chili peppers are extremely hot.

Peppers are rarely cooked and served alone. They are generally served in combinations with other vegetables or in sauces. Stuffed Peppers, however, are a popular dish.

STUFFED PEPPERS

Peppers can be stuffed with almost any mixture that you care to make. Boiled rice, chopped meat, onion and tomato, is a popular combination. In a pinch, if you want to have a quickly prepared dish, you could open a can of corned beef, loosen it, stuff the peppers, cook and serve them with a tomato sauce or just plain. Large peppers are best for stuffing.

To prepare peppers for stuffing, cut across the pepper about ½ inch below the stem, saving it for a cap. Remove the seeds and the white pith from the inside of the pepper. Fill the peppers with any prepared mixture and place them in a saucepan. Put about ¼ inch of hot water in the bottom of the pan, cover, and simmer until the peppers are tender. If you have difficulty keeping the cap on, you may tie the pepper with fine kitchen cord. Do not overcook the peppers. About 15 minutes should make them tender and heat the filling. Sprinkle them with fresh minced dill.

POTATOES

A book could be written about the potato and the many ways to prepare it for the table. It is the vegetable we meet most often in the course of a lifetime. The potato has been in bad grace with the thousands of girls and women who have been dieting, but nevertheless it is still, and justly so, the mainstay of the dining table. There are few foods which can vie with a good boiled potato, bathed in butter, sprinkled with parsley, and properly seasoned.

Potatoes should be firm to the touch. New potatoes have a red or a cream transparent skin. As the potato ages, its skin darkens and becomes thicker. At the end of winter potatoes often begin to grow short green sprouts. These sprouts do not spoil the potato unless they are allowed to grow too long. Break them off before using the potato.

BOILED POTATOES

PREPARATION TIME: 2–3 minutes to peel 1 potato

COOKING TIME: 20–40 (30–50) minutes, depending on age and size of potato. New potatoes take longer than old ones.

Potatoes may be peeled and boiled or boiled in their skins or jackets. Peel potatoes as lightly as possible, removing all spots and eyes in the surface. Potatoes to be boiled in their jackets should be well washed, scrubbed, and rinsed.

Cut large potatoes in half; boil small ones whole. Put the potatoes in a saucepan and cover with water. Add 1 teaspoon of salt for 4–6 potatoes. Cover and bring to a boil. Boil gently until they are soft to the fork test. Drain off the water and shake the pan over the heat to dry the potatoes. If boiled with their skins on, they can be peeled quickly or served in their jackets, as preferred.

Serve peeled potatoes plain or coat them with butter and sprinkle with parsley.

MASHED POTATOES

PREPARATION TIME: about 15 minutes

For 4 servings you will need:

6 medium potatoes	3 tablespoons butter
½ cup or more hot milk or cream	½ teaspoon salt Dash white pepper

METHOD: Boil the potatoes and drain. Dry by holding the pot over the flame for a moment. Mash the potatoes thoroughly, add the hot milk or cream, beat, add the butter and salt and dash of white pepper, then beat some more. The mixture should be beaten or whipped until light and fluffy. An electric mixer may be used. Serve in a hot serving dish.

TO MASH POTATOES means to break them down to a mushy consistency by using a round wooden potato masher, a wire one, or if you are without either, a clean warmed milk bottle will do the trick.

RICED POTATOES

TO RICE POTATOES means to put hot boiled potatoes through a ricer.

To serve 4, boil 6 medium-sized potatoes. Dry by shaking the pot over the flame. Run the potatoes through a ricer, put them in a hot dish, dot with 3 tablespoons of butter, sprinkle with salt and a dash of white pepper, and serve hot.

POTATO SOUFFLÉ

PREPARATION TIME: 15–20 minutes

COOKING TIME: about 90 minutes

For 4 servings you will need:

2 cups hot mashed potatoes	2 tablespoons butter or fat
2 eggs, separated	½ teaspoon salt
1 cup hot milk	Dash white pepper

METHOD: To the 2 cups of mashed potatoes, add the fat, the egg yolks, well beaten, and the hot milk. Stir until well blended and add the seasoning. Beat the egg whites until very stiff. Fold the stiff egg whites into the potato mixture until blended. Carefully transfer the mass to a greased baking dish. Place the baking dish in a pan of hot water and put in a moderate oven (375°) for 30 minutes. Serve at once. All soufflés have a tendency to fall as soon as they are taken away from the heat.

POTATO CAKES

PREPARATION TIME: 20 minutes

COOKING TIME: about 10 minutes

For 4 servings you will need:

2 cups cold mashed potatoes	Flour
1 egg, beaten	Cooking fat
Salt and pepper	

Moisten the mashed potatoes with 1 beaten egg. Mix well. Shape the potato and egg mixture into small cakes. Dust in flour and fry in a greased skillet until crusty brown on both sides.

POTATOES AU GRATIN

PREPARATION TIME: about 20 minutes

COOKING TIME: 45–60 minutes

For 4–6 servings you will need:

6 medium-sized potatoes	½ teaspoon paprika
3 tablespoons butter	Dash white pepper
½ cup or more of hot milk	½ cup grated cheese
½ teaspoon salt	½ cup buttered crumbs

Peel and boil the potatoes. Drain and dry them by holding the pot over the fire for a moment. Mash or rice them.

Add the butter and the hot milk. Whip until smooth and fluffy, using more milk if necessary. Add the seasoning. Turn the fluffy potato mixture into a greased baking dish. Sprinkle the top with the grated cheese, then cover the cheese with the buttered crumbs. Put in a hot oven (450°) and bake 10–15 minutes. The cheese should melt and the buttered crumbs should be brown.

TO BUTTER CRUMBS means to mix crumbs and butter or fat together. This is done by melting fat in a skillet, then putting crumbs in the hot fat and mixing thoroughly. Butter is the best fat, but bacon fat does very well for some dishes. The ratio is 4 to 1. If your recipe calls for ½ cup buttered crumbs, use 2 tablespoons of fat. In other words, use 4 times as much crumbs as fat.

CREAMED POTATOES

PREPARATION TIME: about 15 minutes

COOKING TIME: about 20 minutes

For 4 servings you will need:

2½ cups cold boiled potatoes, diced
1½ cups medium white sauce
Seasoning

METHOD: For creamed potatoes, if you have at least 1 baked leftover, use it to add flavor. Make your cream sauce (p. 228). A little chopped parsley and chives or a tablespoon of minced onion takes the curse off the plain cream sauce. If you do not have the herbs, you may use 1 teaspoon of celery salt and 1 teaspoon of onion salt as seasoning.

Add the diced potatoes to the sauce and cook gently until the potatoes are hot.

DELMONICO POTATOES

PREPARATION TIME: about 20 minutes

COOKING TIME, INCLUSIVE: about 30 minutes

Prepare Creamed Potatoes as directed above. Pour the creamed potatoes into a buttered baking dish, cover with ½ cup of buttered crumbs, and bake in a hot oven (400°) about 10 minutes, or until the crumbs are nicely browned.

HASHED BROWN POTATOES

PREPARATION TIME: 15 minutes

COOKING TIME: about 20 minutes

For 4 servings you will need:

2 cups finely diced or chopped cold potatoes	5 tablespoons fat
	1 teaspoon salt
⅛ teaspoon pepper	

METHOD: Melt the fat in a frying pan, add the seasoned potatoes, stir and fry for a few minutes until the fat has mixed with the potatoes. Press the potatoes gently to the bottom of the pan. Continue frying until the potatoes are browned on the bottom. Take a broad spatula or pancake turner and fold one half of the potatoes over the other half. Slide from the pan to a hot plate and serve at once.

LYONNAISE POTATOES

PREPARATION TIME: about 15 minutes

COOKING TIME: about 15 minutes

For 4 servings you will need:

2 cups cold boiled potatoes, diced	1 tablespoon minced onion
	2 tablespoons butter or fat
1 tablespoon chopped parsley	

METHOD: Melt the fat and sauté the onion in it until golden brown. Add the potatoes and stir until the potatoes absorb the fat and are browned on all sides. Add more fat if necessary as they cook. Be careful not to break the potatoes; you do not want fried mush. When done, serve on a hot dish. Sprinkle the parsley over the top.

BAKED POTATOES

PREPARATION TIME: 5 minutes per pound

COOKING TIME: 45 (60) minutes

For individual servings, select smooth-skinned, medium-sized potatoes. If large Idahoes are used, they may be split in half after baking to make 2 portions.

Wash the potatoes well, remove any blemishes. Rub the skin with grease, if you like. It is recommended for soft-skinned potatoes. Prick the skin several times with the tines of a fork. They sometimes explode in the oven if you forget to do this. Bake in a hot oven (450°) for 45 (60) minutes.

Do not test baking potatoes with a fork. Test them with your fingers, but be sure to have something over your fingers. Use a soft pot holder or a folded towel. Press the sides of the potato. If the potato yields to the pressure of your fingers, it is done. To prevent baked potatoes from becoming soggy, crack the skin or slit them with a knife. Keep hot and serve with butter.

PEELED BAKED POTATOES

PREPARATION TIME: 4–5 minutes per potato

COOKING TIME: 45 (60) minutes

Peel baking potatoes and remove any blemishes. Rub the entire potato with bacon fat, then roll it in flour, dusting completely. Place in a shallow pan and bake in a hot oven (450°) until done.

BAKED POTATOES FRANCONIA

PREPARATION TIME: 4–5 minutes per potato

COOKING TIME: 90 minutes or more

Peel medium-sized potatoes. Be sure they are dry. Place them in a baking pan with a roast which is cooking. Baste them with fat from the bottom of the pan.

Their cooking time will depend upon the temperature you use for your roast. At 350° (moderate) it will take at least 90 minutes for them to bake.

In order to be sure that your Franconia potatoes are ready when the roast is done, parboil them for 15 minutes before adding them to the roasting pan. They are sure to cook in an hour if parboiled first. If you want them to be crisp and a delicious brown, baste them often with the fat from the bottom of the pan.

BAKED POTATOES ON THE HALF-SHELL

PREPARATION TIME: about 15 minutes

COOKING TIME: 1 hour at 400°

Bake medium-large or large potatoes, allowing 1 potato for 2 servings. When the potatoes are baked, cut them in half and scoop out the potato, being careful not to break the shells. Mash the pulp and mix with hot milk and butter until fluffy. Season with salt and pepper. Return to the shell, piling in the mashed potato lightly. Place the shells in a shallow pan and return to the hot oven (400°) for 10–15 minutes, or until browned on top.

A tablespoon of chopped chives and some parsley added to the potatoes when mashed and creamed makes them really delightful.

OVEN-FRIED POTATOES

PREPARATION TIME: about 20 minutes for 4 medium-sized potatoes

COOKING TIME: 20–30 minutes in a hot oven (450°)

Cut raw peeled potatoes into long thin strips. Dip the strips of potatoes in melted fat and lay them in a shallow pan or on a cookie sheet. Do not let the pieces overlap. Bake in a hot oven (450°) until they are browned on top. Turn carefully and bake until they are browned on all sides and resemble French-fried potatoes. When done, sprinkle with salt and pepper and serve piping hot.

BAKED POTATO AND SAUSAGE

Allow 1 medium-sized potato, 1 link sausage, and 1 slice of bacon for each serving.

PREPARATION TIME: about 30 minutes for 6 potatoes.

COOKING TIME: 60 minutes or longer

Peel the potatoes. With an apple corer make a hole through the center of each potato and insert a sausage in each hole. Put the prepared potatoes in a baking pan or a casserole. Cover each potato with a slice of bacon, sprinkle lightly with pepper, and bake in a hot oven (450°–500°) until the potatoes are tender. Baste them while cooking with the drippings from the bacon and sausage. If the drippings are scant, add a very little hot water to the bottom of the baking dish.

RAW-FRIED POTATOES

Allow 1½ potatoes per serving. They shrink some and are so good that they disappear rapidly.

PREPARATION TIME: 5 minutes per potato

COOKING TIME: 25 (30–45) minutes

Peel the potatoes. Cut into 3 sections lengthwise of the potato. Slice the potato sections crosswise, about ⅛ of an inch thick, into a skillet in which 3 tablespoons of bacon drippings or fat have been melted. When the potatoes are all in, allow to fry gently. Sprinkle with salt and pepper before turning them over. When they begin to brown, lift up with a pancake turner by sections and turn them over. Several turnings will be necessary. Fry them until most of the thin slices are crisp. Add more fat if necessary to keep them from burning.

Thin slices of 1 onion may be added for flavor and variation.

POTATO PANCAKES

PREPARATION TIME: about 40 minutes

C O O K I N G   T I M E: about 30 minutes

For 6–8 servings you will need:

3 cups grated raw potatoes
2 eggs, beaten
1 onion, grated

1 teaspoon salt
Pepper
Cooking fat

M E T H O D: Peel and grate raw potatoes and drain off the excess potato water. Put the well-drained grated potato into a bowl. Add the grated onion, the 2 beaten eggs, and the seasoning. Mix well.

Heat a generous amount of cooking fat in a skillet. Drop the potato mixture into the fat a tablespoon at a time. Spread the mixture thin to make large cakes. Fry until a golden brown. Turn and fry on the other side.

Serve with applesauce or with sour cream. With a strip or two of bacon, some applesauce, and a salad, good potato pancakes make a meal.

SCALLOPED POTATOES

P R E P A R A T I O N   T I M E: 30 minutes

C O O K I N G   T I M E: 60 (90) minutes

For 4 servings you will need:

4 medium-sized potatoes
2 tablespoons flour

3 tablespoons butter
Salt and pepper

Milk

M E T H O D: Peel raw potatoes. Cut them into thin slices across the potato. Put a ½-inch layer of sliced potatoes in the bottom of a lightly greased baking dish or pan. Sprinkle with some of the flour, a little of the butter, pepper, and salt. Keep making layers until the potatoes are used up. Add the remaining flour and butter to the top layer. Now add milk until the potatoes are almost but not quite covered. Cover the dish and place in a hot oven (400°) and cook for at least 90 minutes. The potatoes must admit the tines of a fork for them to be done. Take the cover off for the last 20 minutes to let the top brown. If they do not brown and are done, run them under the broiler for a couple of minutes, but watch or they will blacken. You want them a golden brown.

SWEET POTATOES

Sweet potatoes and yams should be firm to the touch. Do not buy soft or leathery sweet potatoes or yams. Get fairly well rounded tubers if possible.

BAKED SWEET POTATOES

Follow the recipe for Baked Potatoes. Bake 30–40 minutes.

BOILED SWEET POTATOES

Follow the instructions for Boiled Potatoes. Boil 20–30 minutes.

CANDIED OR GLAZED SWEET POTATOES

PREPARATION TIME: 5–10 minutes

COOKING TIME: 20–30 minutes

Use either freshly boiled, cold cooked, or canned sweet potatoes. If freshly boiled, peel and cut into thick slices. If cold or canned, cut into slices.

For 6 servings you will need:

6 sweet potatoes	2 tablespoons sherry if desired
1 cup brown sugar	Butter
¼ cup of water	Pepper and salt

METHOD: The simplest and most satisfactory way to candy sweet potatoes is to mix the sugar and water and boil for a few minutes. Dip the slices into the syrup and lay them in a greased baking dish. Dot the potato slices with butter, season with pepper and salt, and pour over them any syrup remaining after the dipping. Bake in a hot oven (450°) until they are browned. Watch them, for they will brown quickly and the sugar may burn if left in the oven too long. If you use sherry, add it to the syrup.

FRIED SWEET POTATOES

Slice cold boiled sweet potatoes, dip the slices in seasoned flour, and fry in hot fat until brown.

SALSIFY OR OYSTER PLANT

This vegetable looks like a thin parsnip. It is usually sold by the bunch. The roots are cream colored or light chocolate. They should be firm.

CREAMED SALSIFY

PREPARATION TIME: 20 minutes per pound

COOKING TIME: about 20–40 minutes

Scrape the salsify roots. They discolor quickly, so it is wise to have a bowl of water to which 1 tablespoon of vinegar has been added. Wash the roots and scrape and drop into the acidulated water at once. Cut them into slices and cook in boiling salted water until tender—about 30 minutes. When cooked, combine with medium white sauce to which some chopped chives and 1 tablespoon of minced parsley have been added. Use 1–1½ cups of salsify to 1 cup of medium white sauce for 4 servings.

FRIED SALSIFY

Boil the salsify whole in boiling salted water. Fry as directed for Fried Parsnips.

SQUASH

Squash are generally divided into summer and winter squash. The summer squash are the button or patty-pan squash, yellow crook necks, and Zucchini or Italian squash. Varieties of winter squash are: Banana, Table Queen or Des Moines, sometimes called Acorn, and the Hubbard, either green or orange-skinned. All squash should be fresh and firm. The younger they are, the better.

Young tender summer squash may be cooked without peeling or removing the seeds. But if there is any doubt about the age of summer squash, peel and remove the seeds.

All summer squash may be steamed, boiled, baked, or French-fried. But since squash is such a watery vegetable, steaming or baking is the most satisfactory method. A pound of squash serves 3–4.

BOILED SQUASH

PREPARATION TIME: about 10 minutes

COOKING TIME: 10–15 (20–30) minutes

Wash, peel, and seed any but very young squash. Cover with boiling salted water and boil until tender. Drain thoroughly. Young squash may be served whole with a dressing of melted butter and pepper.

STEAMED SQUASH

PREPARATION TIME: about 10 minutes

COOKING TIME: about 30 minutes

Wash and seed all but very young squash. The winter varieties are good when steamed and save considerable cooking time.

If you are using winter squash, it is wise to buy a section from the market. A large squash is much too much for a small family. Buy a 2- or 3-pound piece. Cut into serving pieces.

Place the squash in the steaming basket or compartment. Do not allow the water to touch the squash. Cover tightly and steam until tender.

Butter the pieces of cooked squash, season, sprinkle with brown sugar and a little cinnamon, and bake in a moderate oven (350°) for about 20 minutes.

Or scrape the steamed squash from the shell, mash, pile into a baking dish, dot with butter, sprinkle with seasoning, and bake in a moderate oven for half an hour, stirring a few times to blend the butter and seasoning through the squash. A well-beaten egg mixed with the squash makes it fluffy.

FRIED SUMMER SQUASH

PREPARATION TIME: 10 minutes per pound

COOKING TIME: 4 to 5 minutes

Peel the squash, seed, and cut in ½-inch slices. Salt lightly, dip in fine bread crumbs, and shake. Dip in beaten egg and then in the crumbs again. Fry in deep hot fat for 4–5 minutes. The fat should be 390°. If you have no thermometer, test with a 1-inch cube of white bread. The bread should brown in 40–60 seconds. Fry a golden brown, drain on absorbent paper, and keep warm in the oven until ready to serve.

BAKED WINTER SQUASH

Wash winter squash and cut into sections. Remove the seeds and pulp, sprinkle lightly with salt, and bake until tender, 45 minutes (2 hours) in a moderate oven (350°).

Scrape the squash from the shell, mix with butter and seasoning, and return to the shell. Reheat for a few minutes in a hot oven (450°).

Or coat the baked squash with brown sugar and butter, season with pepper and salt, and bake until the butter and sugar glaze the surface. A sprinkling of cinnamon is good, or some nutmeg.

Summer squash may also be baked. It takes much less time than the winter varieties.

SPINACH

Spinach is spinach. You like it or you don't, and that's that. The fact that it is rich in iron and is good for you has nothing to do with the case.

When buying, be sure to get crisp green leaves free from worm-holes and brown edges. New Zealand spinach, available in summer, is good. It has a flavor all its own and is easier to clean than ordinary spinach. Note to gardeners: New Zealand spinach is easy to grow.

The regular spinach is likely to be full of sand and grit. It should be soaked in several changes of water. If the leaves float, so much the better.

Because spinach, like other greens, loses so much in bulk when cooked, allow about ⅓ to ½ pound of uncooked spinach per serving.

Wash and pick over spinach leaves. If you buy New Zealand spinach, discard the stems, using nothing but the leaves.

BOILED SPINACH

PREPARATION TIME: about 20 minutes per pound

COOKING TIME: 5–10 minutes

Put the washed spinach in a covered kettle. Enough water clings to the leaves to prevent burning. Place the kettle over a medium flame and cook covered 5–10 minutes, or until tender. Drain the spinach. Chop, turn into a bowl, dot with butter, sprinkle with pepper and salt, and serve with lemon juice or vinegar on the side.

CREAMED SPINACH

PREPARATION TIME: 20–30 minutes

COOKING TIME: 5–10 (10–20) minutes

For 4–6 servings you will need:

2 pounds spinach	4 tablespoons thick cream or
4 tablespoons butter	¼ cup thin white sauce
Pepper and salt	

METHOD: Drop the washed spinach into a kettle of boiling water. Cook 5 minutes and drain. Chop the spinach in a chopping bowl or put it through the coarse blade of a food chopper. Melt the butter and add the cream or white sauce and seasoning. Heat and add chopped spinach, stir while cooking for 5–7 minutes. Serve hot.

SUCCOTASH

Succotash can be made from fresh or dried beans and corn.

SUCCOTASH I

PREPARATION TIME: soak overnight

COOKING TIME: about 2 hours

For 4–6 servings you will need:

1 cup dried or parched corn	Salt and pepper
1 cup dried beans	½ cup milk
2 tablespoons butter or fat	

METHOD: Soak the beans and corn separately overnight. Next day simmer the beans in the same water in which they were soaked. Simmer 1 hour and 15 minutes, then add the corn and the water in which it soaked. Simmer another 45 minutes, add the milk, and heat well. Stir in the butter and seasoning and serve.

SUCCOTASH II

PREPARATION TIME: about 30 minutes

COOKING TIME: 30–45 minutes

For 4–6 servings you will need:

2 cups string beans	Salt and pepper
2 cups corn cut from cob	1 cup milk
4 tablespoons butter or fat	

METHOD: String the beans and cut them into small pieces. Cut fresh corn from the cob with a sharp knife and gently scrape the cob to get all the natural juice.

Put the beans in a pan with ½ teaspoon salt and 1 cup boiling water. Boil 20–30 minutes, until tender. Watch them and add more hot water if the beans show any tendency to boil dry. When the beans are done, scald the milk and add to the beans and their liquid. Add the corn. When the combined mixture starts to boil, add the butter or fat and boil for 3–5 minutes. Add pepper and serve in the liquid.

LIMA-BEAN SUCCOTASH

PREPARATION TIME: about 30 minutes

COOKING TIME: 30 minutes

For 4–6 servings you will need:

2 cups fresh lima beans	½ teaspoon salt
2 cups fresh corn cut from cob	Pepper
4 tablespoons butter or margarine	

METHOD: Shell and wash the lima beans. Cut the fresh corn from the cob with a sharp knife and gently scrape the cob to get all the natural juice. Cook the limas in 2 cups of boiling water until tender. Add the salt, the corn, and the butter or margarine. Bring the mixture to a boil and cook for from 3 to 5 minutes. Some cooks like to add 1 cup warm milk. Add a sprinkling of pepper and serve in the liquid.

SHELL-BEAN SUCCOTASH

PREPARATION TIME: about 30 minutes

COOKING TIME: about 90 minutes

For 4–6 servings you will need:

½ pound bacon or	2 cups fresh corn cut from cob
¼ pound lean salt pork	¼ teaspoon salt
2 cups fresh shell beans	Pepper

METHOD: Put the bacon or pork in 4 cups of boiling water, add the shell beans, and simmer gently for at least 1 hour. More hot water may be added if necessary. The liquid will begin to turn coffee-colored as the beans cook. Fifteen minutes before the dish is to be served, add the corn and simmer gently until done.

Small new potatoes are in the market when shell beans are available. A dozen or more small new potatoes, scraped, washed, and cooked in the succotash for about 40 minutes will make a 1-dish meal out of the succotash. Serve it in a soup plate, have a green salad and some fruit, and feel that you have dined well.

TOMATOES

Tomatoes should be red and firm when bought at the market. Do not take tomatoes that are soft, bruised, or have black dots on their skins. When buying for several days, select some that are half ripe. They will ripen at home.

Canned tomatoes may be substituted for fresh in nearly all recipes except where it is obvious that fresh tomatoes must be used.

HOW TO SKIN TOMATOES

When fresh tomatoes are used, they are usually skinned. An easy way to skin them is to cover them with boiling water for a minute, then plunge them into cold. The thin skin will peel off easily. Cut away the stem end and any green spots. Or hold them on a long-tined fork over a hot flame for a few seconds. The skin will blister and peel off easily.

When tomatoes are to be served raw, and you do not want to have the pulp softened by heat, hold the blade of a paring knife perpendicular to the skin and rub the whole surface of the tomato, much as though you were scraping a carrot, only taking care not to break the skin. This will loosen the skin which can then be stripped away.

BAKED TOMATOES

Allow 1 medium-sized tomato per serving.

PREPARATION TIME: about 20 minutes for 6 tomatoes

COOKING TIME: about 30 minutes

You will need:

Tomatoes	½ cup bread crumbs
Butter	Salt and pepper

METHOD: Select firm tomatoes. Peel or leave skins on according to your preference. Cut out the stem end, making a fairly deep hole. If you don't know what to do with the extra piece, eat it as you work. Fill the hole made by the deep cut with bread crumbs, top the crumbs with a piece of butter, and sprinkle with pepper and salt. Place in a greased baking dish. Repeat this process with each tomato. If any crumbs are left, sprinkle them in the dish to take up the juices which will escape from the tomatoes. Bake for at least 30 minutes in a slow oven (300°). Remove carefully with a spatula or pancake turner when ready to serve.

BAKED TOMATOES IN CASSEROLE

PREPARATION TIME: 20 minutes

COOKING TIME: 30 minutes

For 4–6 servings you will need:

6 medium tomatoes or 2 cups canned tomatoes	1 cup bread crumbs
4 tablespoons butter or other fat	1 tablespoon sugar
1 sliced onion (optional, but good)	Pepper and salt

Skin and slice the fresh tomatoes. Butter the crumbs by warming them in a skillet with the fat. Put a layer of tomatoes in the bottom of a greased casserole, sprinkle with salt and pepper, and add a layer of buttered crumbs. If the onion is used, put the slices in the middle layers. Add another layer of tomatoes and more crumbs. Use all the crumbs, adding some dry crumbs if necessary. Dot the top with flecks of butter and bake in a hot oven (400°) about 30 minutes.

BROILED TOMATOES

COOKING TIME: 6–10 minutes

Select firm tomatoes. Cut them in half, sprinkle with salt and pepper, and place on a greased broiler. Broil about 3–5 minutes. Turn the halves carefully and broil on the other side for another 3–5 minutes. Cover with melted butter when serving.

FRIED TOMATOES

COOKING TIME: 10 (15) minutes

Select firm ripe tomatoes. Wash and cut them in ½-inch slices. Dip the cut slices in flour or fine crumbs and fry in hot fat about 5 minutes on each side. Serve hot, sprinkled with salt and pepper.

Green tomatoes also may be fried in this manner. They should be cooked 7–8 minutes on each side.

STEWED TOMATOES

PREPARATION TIME: about 15 minutes

COOKING TIME: 5–15 (15–20) minutes

For 4 servings you will need:

6 medium tomatoes or 2 cups canned tomatoes	1 teaspoon salt
4 tablespoons butter	Dash pepper
	½ cup bread or cracker crumbs
½ minced onion if desired	

Skin and cut up fresh tomatoes. Add no more than ¼ cup of water. They may be stewed in their own juice without any water. Simmer for 15–20 minutes, until soft. Add the butter, 1 teaspoon salt, a dash of pepper, and the crumbs to thicken juice. Serve hot.

TURNIPS

There are two varieties of turnips: the white turnip and the yellow turnip, or rutabaga. The white turnip is an early summer vegetable. The yellow turnips are definitely winter vegetables. They keep well long into the winter.

All turnips should be firm when bought. Dry or withered turnips will be tough. Yellow turnips are likely to be pithy.

CREAMED TURNIPS

PREPARATION TIME: about 15 minutes

COOKING TIME: 15–30 (30–45) minutes for white turnips; 30–45 (45–60) minutes for yellow turnips

For 3–4 servings you will need:

1 pound turnips
2 cups medium cream sauce
Salt and pepper

METHOD: Peel and slice or dice the turnips. Start them in cold water with 1 teaspoon of salt. Cover and cook until tender. When tender, drain, add to the cream sauce, and serve hot. One tablespoon of chopped parsley may be added to the cream sauce.

MASHED TURNIPS

PREPARATION TIME: about 15 minutes

COOKING TIME: 30–45 minutes

Boil 1 pound of turnips as directed above. Drain, dry over the flame a moment, and mash. Add 4 tablespoons of butter, season with salt and pepper, and serve hot.

RUTMUS

It is an old custom in some parts of the country to combine mashed potatoes and yellow turnips for holiday dinners. The combination is almost always served with fresh roast pork. Boil the turnips and potatoes separately, drain, mix, mash, add a good lump of butter, season, and serve well blended. The potatoes and turnips may be cooked in the same pot if the turnips are started first.

Mashed turnips and mashed winter squash may be mixed and served together.

TURNIP GREENS

PREPARATION TIME: 10–20 (20–30) minutes per pound

COOKING TIME: 30 minutes

Turnips are sometimes grown for the greens alone. The fresh green tops of young white turnips may be used as a green. Turnip greens may be combined with spinach, chard, or other greens; or they may be cooked and served alone. When served as a special dish, they are generally cooked uncovered in boiling salted water, with a piece of salt pork or bacon, for half an hour.

The advocates of turnip greens like some of the pot liquor served with them. They also like a hot sauce.

CHAPTER XI

SAUCES

A M A N is known by the company he keeps. And good cooks become famous for the sauces they serve.

You have all heard the story of the French chef who labored for an hour making a special sauce for the dish he was serving to an American tourist. He had put all his art and a little of his soul into the preparation of the sauce. He knew it was exactly right, served it with a flourish, and waited for just one word of delighted appreciation. The tourist tasted the concoction, looked up and said, "Pass me the catsup."

Catsup is fine. So are chili sauce and all the prepared meat sauces available on the market. They have their place in cooking, are particularly good with certain foods. But there are other sauces.

There is nothing less palatable than an improperly made pale white sauce. Too often it is not cooked long enough. There is no excuse for the uncooked, starchy taste of practically raw flour. There is nothing inviting about a white sauce in which little lumps of tough dough offend the palate. But if the proper materials are used, if directions are carefully followed, even a plain white sauce should be appetizing in spite of its pallor. There are ways to give it a creamy tinge. A drop or two of kitchen bouquet will soften the white, or the butter may be browned a little in the pan —browned, not burned. Or a little paprika may be added to give color.

WHITE SAUCE

A good white sauce must be well cooked. Its flavor improves if it is made ahead of time and kept warm in a double boiler because the ingredients have a chance to blend.

White sauces need not be made with milk or cream alone. Stock can be used or vegetable water. For example: If you are going to cream celery, don't throw down the drain the water in which the celery has been cooked. Save it. You want your dish to have a celery flavor. What better way to be sure of it than to use at least half celery water for the liquid required for the white sauce?

If you plan to serve creamed chicken, the chicken had to be cooked. If you are using the remains of a roasted chicken you must have at least a half cup of chicken gravy to use for your sauce. If the chicken was boiled, surely there is some of the broth left. If not, why don't you open a can of chicken soup and use it for the liquid? You want your creamed dish to taste like chicken.

If you boil green shrimps for later creaming, save some of the liquid for the white sauce.

The habit of saving broths and liquids is a good one to follow.

Why not, if you are going to cream onions, save some of the onion water to add to the sauce? Too much flavor goes down the drainpipe because we fail to stop and think.

Remember this about making white sauce: *You must stay with it every minute until it is done.*

White sauce is made of butter, flour, and milk, with seasoning added. It can be made over direct heat or in a double boiler. Until you are an experienced cook, you had better use the double boiler because the direct heat demands speed and efficiency on your part.

METHOD I: White sauce may be made by blending the fat, flour, and seasonings together in the bottom of the saucepan and then adding the milk or liquid a little at a time, mixing well, stirring constantly so that you have a smooth paste at first and then a smooth, balanced liquid which you continue to cook and stir until it begins to thicken. The white sauce should not only thicken, it should be cooked and stirred at least 10 minutes after thickening in a double boiler and for 5 minutes at the slow bubbling stage over direct heat.

When using vegetables for flavoring sauces, if you want a sharp flavor, sauté the vegetables for a few minutes in the fat before adding the flour and liquid. If you want mild flavor, add the vegetables when the sauce has finished cooking.

M E T H O D II (JAR METHOD): This method can be used over direct heat or with a double boiler. Over direct heat saves time, and there is very little chance of lumping if you stay with it and keep stirring.

First, melt the fat over a low flame or in the double boiler. Sauté vegetables in the fat if you want a sharp flavor.

Second, add the seasonings.

Third, take a jar with a tight-fitting lid. Put ½ cup of the liquid in the jar, add the flour, add ½ cup of remaining liquid. Shake well until the flour and liquid are well mixed with no lumps. Pour this liquid and flour mixture into the pan with the melted fat and begin to stir and keep stirring, particularly if you are cooking over direct flame. Do not answer the telephone or the door until you remove the sauce from the source of heat. Keep stirring the sauce every second while it is in contact with heat. When it thickens, continue the cooking for 5 minutes over direct heat, or for 10 minutes in a double boiler. If you use the direct-heat method, cook in the top of the double boiler until the sauce is done, then put the top back on the double boiler over hot water to keep the sauce warm and blend the flavors.

The chart on page 230 gives the ingredients for 1 cup of white sauce, thin, medium, thick, and very thick, with the uses for each kind. If you need 2 cups, double all quantities except salt. If you want 3 cups, treble all quantities except salt. In any cooking at all, if you increase the quantities of ingredients, salt sparingly. It is easy to put in too much salt.

It is up to you to make a good white sauce. You can do it. Remember all the herbs, condiments, and food liquors at your disposal. Use them! For example, 1 or 2 tablespoons of cooking sherry will give added zest to cream sauce used with sea food.

White sauces are thicker when cold than when hot. Do not thin a cold sauce before it has been thoroughly reheated.

Some white sauces call for stock. Use any of the following when stock is called for:

STOCK FOR SAUCES AND SOUP RECIPES

Canned consommé

Canned bouillon

The liquor from cooked vegetables which we hope you have stored in your refrigerator

SUBSTITUTE FOR STOCK: Use chicken, beef, or vegetable bouillon cubes, 1 or 2 cubes for each cup of boiling water.

If a recipe calls for a light stock, use consommé, chicken, or vegetable cubes, pea or carrot water. Never use any dark liquids.

TYPES OF WHITE SAUCE

	Thin	Medium	Thick	Very thick
INGREDIENTS				
Butter or fat	1 tablespoon	1 tablespoon	1 tablespoon	2 tablespoons
Flour	1 tablespoon	2 tablespoons	3 tablespoons	4 tablespoons
Salt	¾ teaspoon	¾ teaspoon	¾ teaspoon	¾ teaspoon
Pepper	Dash	Dash	Dash	Dash
Milk, liquid, or cream	1 cup	1 cup	1 cup	1 cup
USES	To cream starchy vegetables To make cream soups	To cream non-starchy vegetables, fish, eggs, chicken, etc. To make cream soups	For scalloped dishes	For croquettes and soufflés

When in doubt about quantities, use the chart. You can now make a good white sauce. Taste it. If it is a little flat, if you think it needs pepping up or feel that it lacks that provocative something which the sauces served in good restaurants always have, do something about it. Seasonings to be used in sauces and gravies are given in the list on page 232. Use them sparingly, rather a pinch at first than too much. Taste and add seasoning a little at a time until it is just right. Too little is as bad as too much. Have your guests say, "I don't know what they do to their food, but it always tastes so good," rather than, "They use too much thyme," or "Everything tastes of chili powder." For your own enjoyment, develop variety. This list does not attempt to give you all the seasonings nor all their uses. You will undoubtedly develop some preferences yourself.

SAUCE RECIPES

ANCHOVY BUTTER

¼ cup butter	4 drops onion juice
1 teaspoon anchovy paste	¼ teaspoon lemon juice
Few grains cayenne pepper	

T O C R E A M butter or fat means to work, or press it with a spoon or flat knife until it is soft and creamy.

M E T H O D: Cream the butter. Mix in the anchovy paste, onion, and lemon juice and beat. When completely blended, add the cayenne.

This butter is served with broiled or fried fish. Some people like it on broiled steak. It makes a delicious canapé.

ANCHOVY SAUCE

1 cup medium white sauce	1 teaspoon anchovy paste
Few grains cayenne pepper	

M E T H O D: Use a saucepan or a double boiler. Blend the paste well with the sauce, add the cayenne, and serve with fish.

SEASONINGS, HERBS, AND CONDIMENTS

Seasoning	Amount to Add to 1 Cup of Sauce or Gravy	Combines Well with:
Anchovy paste	1 teaspoon in white sauce	Fish
Capers, chopped	1½ tablespoons	Fish, boiled meats
Catsup	1 tablespoon	Beans, fish
Cayenne pepper	Few grains	Meat, fish, cheese, bland vegetables
Celery salt	1 teaspoon	
Chili powder	Pinch or two	Fish, vegetables, meats
Garlic salt	1 teaspoon	Meat, fish
Herbs:		
Basil	¼ teaspoon fresh or powder	Meats, cheese
Chervil	1 teaspoon fresh	Eggs, cheese, meats
Chervil	½ teaspoon powder	Eggs, cheese, meats
Chives	1 tablespoon fresh	Eggs, vegetables, fish
Garlic, chopped	⅛ teaspoon	Meat, fish
Onion, chopped	1 teaspoon	Eggs, fish, meat, vegetables
Parsley, fresh	1 tablespoon	Potatoes, vegetables, meat, fish
Sage, fresh	Pinch	Meat, fish
Savory, fresh	¼ teaspoon	Meat, vegetables
Tarragon	Pinch or two	Fish, meat
Thyme, powdered	Pinch	Meat, poultry, fish
Cummin seed, powdered	Pinch	Meat, beans, greens
Curry powder	1 teaspoon	Fish, eggs, meat
Dill, fresh	1 teaspoon	Vegetables, meat, fish
Dill, seed	½ teaspoon	Vegetables, meat, fish
Horse-radish, prepared	1 teaspoon	Meat, fish
Leeks, chopped	1 tablespoon	Potatoes, meat, fish
Lemon juice	1 teaspoon	Fish
Lemon rind, grated	½ teaspoon	Fish
Mustard, dry	½ teaspoon	Fish, meat, cheese, eggs
Mustard, prepared	1 teaspoon	Fish, meat, cheese, eggs
Onion juice	1 teaspoon	Fish, meat
Onion salt	1 teaspoon	Fish, meat
Paprika	Dash	Fish, meat, eggs, cheese
Pepper sauce	3 drops	Fish, meat, eggs, greens
Pickles, chopped	1 tablespoon	Makes a mock caper sauce for fish and meat
Poultry seasoning	⅛ teaspoon	Fish, meat, poultry
Sherry	2 tablespoons	Fish, cheese, poultry, eggs
Tabasco sauce	3 drops	Fish, cheese, poultry, eggs
Worcestershire sauce	1 teaspoon	Fish, meat, poultry

Remember, a pinch is a few grains, a dash of liquid is a few drops, a dash of powder is a light sprinkling.

BUTTER SAUCE OR PARSLEY BUTTER

¼ cup butter   1 tablespoon chopped parsley
½ tablespoon lemon juice   ½ teaspoon salt
                    ¼ teaspoon pepper

M E T H O D: Cream the butter. Add the lemon juice and seasoning and mix well. Spread this over boiled potatoes.

If you want to use butter sauce on fish, add:
½ tablespoon lemon juice   1 teaspoon Worcestershire sauce

BREAD SAUCE

1 cup soft white bread crumbs   ½ teaspoon salt
2 cups milk   ⅛ teaspoon pepper
1 medium onion, grated   3 tablespoons butter
              1 tablespoon chopped parsley

M E T H O D: Take ¾ cup of the bread crumbs, add the milk, seasoning, and onion. Cook over direct heat for 15 minutes, watching to prevent scorching, or cook for 30 minutes in a double boiler. When done, add 1 tablespoon of the butter and the parsley.

Take the remaining ¼ cup of crumbs and the remaining 2 tablespoons of butter and sauté the crumbs in the butter until a light brown. Put the browned crumbs over the sauce and serve. Bread sauce is a must for game. It is equally good with poultry.

CAPER SAUCE

1 cup medium white sauce   3 tablespoons chopped capers
              1 tablespoon lemon juice

M E T H O D: Use a saucepan or a double boiler. Blend the chopped capers and lemon juice with the white sauce. Serve with boiled or baked fish and boiled meats.

CHEESE SAUCE

1 cup medium white sauce	1 teaspoon dry mustard
½ cup grated cheese	Dash of paprika

M E T H O D: Add the cheese to the white sauce. Stir in a double boiler until the cheese is melted. Season with mustard and paprika. Moisten the mustard with 2 teaspoons of water before adding to the sauce. Serve this with cauliflower, broccoli, eggs, or fish.

CREAM SAUCE

A cream sauce is simply a white sauce made with cream instead of milk or other liquid.

P R E P A R A T I O N   T I M E: 5 to 10 minutes

C O O K I N G   T I M E: 12 to 20 minutes, depending on method

CRANBERRY SAUCE

4 cups cranberries   2 cups sugar
1 cup water

M E T H O D: Wash and pick over the cranberries. Put them in a saucepan, add the water, and cook gently until the berries begin to pop. They actually make a slight cracking noise as they swell and break. Add the sugar and cook gently from 10 to 15 minutes longer. Stir often to prevent burning. Cool before serving. This makes a thick sauce. Serve with turkey and other poultry.

STRAINED CRANBERRY JELLY OR SAUCE

Cook the cranberries as directed for Cranberry Sauce until the skins pop and break. Put the berries through a sieve or a food mill. Return the strained berries to the saucepan, add the sugar, and simmer about 10 minutes. This will make a stiff jelly. It may be put in individual molds or a fancy mold.

CRANBERRY RELISH

1 pound raw cranberries   1 large navel orange
2 cups sugar, white or brown

METHOD: Wash and pick over the berries. Grind them in a food chopper. Cut the orange into wedges and grind. Any orange will do; using the navel orange eliminates the necessity of taking out seeds. Mix the cranberry and orange together, add the sugar, and mix well. Allow to stand at room temperature for at least 1 hour, stirring occasionally. Chill before serving. This relish may be stored in jars in the refrigerator.

CURRY SAUCE

This is a sauce for eggs, fish, and meats. It is not a real curry, merely a sauce flavored with curry powder. A real curry is entirely different, as you will see when you make one.

1 cup medium white sauce	1 teaspoon minced onion
1 teaspoon curry powder	1 teaspoon lemon juice

METHOD: Mix the seasonings together and then add to the white sauce. Heat in a double boiler and serve over meat, fish, or eggs. Or mix them into the sauce and serve on boiled rice.

FITZSAUCE

1 cup mayonnaise	4 tablespoons minced onion or
2 tablespoons cucumber	chopped chives
pickles chopped fine	1 tablespoon very finely
1 pinch of mustard, dry	chopped parsley
1 teaspoon lemon juice	¼ teaspoon salt
A little freshly ground pepper	

METHOD: Mix all ingredients thoroughly. Serve with fried or boiled fish. There is no question about the onion flavor in this sauce. It is frankly there and serves the purpose for which it was intended.

EGG SAUCE

Add 1 chopped hard-boiled egg to 1 cup of medium white sauce.

HOLLANDAISE SAUCE

Hollandaise sauce may be made with margarine or a good commercial shortening in place of butter; but the substitution is not recommended. It is the butter which makes Hollandaise sauce a delight on fish, asparagus, broccoli, artichokes, and an important part of Eggs Benedictine.

This sauce should be cooked over hot water, which means that you put just enough water in the bottom of the double boiler to make steam but not enough to cover the bottom of the upper pot. Do not have the water in the lower container boiling; let it simmer. This is a dish for last-minute preparation.

⅓ cup butter	⅓ cup hot water
½ teaspoon salt	1 tablespoon lemon juice
2 egg yolks, beaten	Few grains cayenne

M E T H O D: Cream the butter and salt. Add the beaten yolks and mix well. Do not put over steam until 5 minutes before serving time; then add the hot water a little at a time, stirring constantly until the sauce thickens. Add the lemon juice and cayenne and cook for a minute as you keep stirring.

Serve hot with hot foods, cold with cold foods.

If the sauce should break or curdle, add 1 tablespoon of cream and mix thoroughly.

MOCK HOLLANDAISE SAUCE

This sauce is much easier to make and is a palatable substitute for the real sauce.

1 cup thick white sauce	¼ teaspoon salt
3 tablespoons butter	Few grains cayenne
3 tablespoons lemon juice	Dash paprika
2 egg yolks, beaten	

M E T H O D: Have the white sauce in the top of a double boiler. Add the butter, stirring constantly. When the butter is blended and melted, add the lemon juice, seasoning, and beaten egg yolks. Keep stirring until the ingredients are blended and the sauce thick. Serve hot with hot foods, cold with cold. Delicious on cold salmon.

HOT HORSE-RADISH SAUCE

Freshly grated horse-radish is preferred. If you grate your own, you will shed tears during the process, but it is worth it, and is perhaps good for your sinus. Freshly grated horse-radish needs either lemon juice or a mild white vinegar. If you use the prepared horse-radish, *omit* the lemon juice or vinegar.

1 cup medium white sauce	2 tablespoons lemon juice
½ cup white bread crumbs	or mild white vinegar
¼ cup freshly grated horse-radish	½ teaspoon salt

M E T H O D: Add the bread crumbs and horse-radish to the white sauce. Mix well and add the lemon juice or vinegar and salt gradually. Serve hot with ham, roast beef, and fried or broiled fish.

UNCOOKED HORSE-RADISH SAUCE

½ cup cream, whipped	3 tablespoons mild white vinegar or lemon juice
6 tablespoons freshly grated horse-radish	1 teaspoon sugar
1 teaspoon salt	

Beat the cream stiff. Mix the other ingredients in a bowl until well blended. Omit vinegar or lemon juice if you use prepared horse-radish. Fold in the whipped cream and serve cold with boiled fish, ham, and particularly with roast beef.

MINT SAUCE

¼ cup water	½ cup finely chopped mint leaves
3 tablespoons sugar	
¼ cup mild vinegar	⅛ teaspoon salt

METHOD: Put the water and sugar in a saucepan and mix. Add the mint leaves and simmer for about 10 minutes. Add the vinegar and salt and remove from the fire. Cool before serving. This is the handmaiden to roast lamb.

MUSHROOM SAUCE

¼ pound mushrooms
1½ tablespoons butter or fat
2 tablespoons flour
½ cup milk

½ cup mushroom stock made from stems and peelings
Salt and pepper

METHOD: Wash, peel, and remove the stems of the mushrooms. Put the peelings and tough stem ends in a saucepan. Cover with ¾ cup of water and stew for at least 15 minutes.

While the peelings and stems are stewing, cut the caps into thin slices and fry them in a skillet with the butter for about 5 minutes. Add the flour to the fried mushrooms and mix well. Add the milk slowly, mixing well to avoid lumps. Cook slowly, add the ½ cup of mushroom stock (strained), bring to the boiling point, and then season with salt and pepper.

MUSTARD SAUCE

Add 1 teaspoon of dry mustard to 1 cup of medium white sauce and serve with corned beef or fish. Mix mustard with 2 teaspoons water before adding to the sauce.

LOBSTER OR SHRIMP SAUCE

Add ½ cup of shredded lobster or chopped shrimp to 1 cup of white sauce. Taste for seasoning and add more if necessary. Serve with boiled, baked, or steamed fish.

OYSTER SAUCE

Cook 1 pint of small oysters in their own liquor until the edges curl, no longer. Drain and add the oysters to 1 cup white sauce. Taste for seasoning. Serve with boiled, baked, or steamed fish.

PARSLEY SAUCE

Add 3 tablespoons of finely chopped parsley to 1 cup of thin white sauce. Serve with boiled fish or over small boiled potatoes.

TARTAR SAUCE

1 cup mayonnaise   Pinch dry mustard
1 tablespoon chopped pickles   1 teaspoon onion juice
                1 tablespoon chopped capers

M E T H O D: Mix the ingredients with the mayonnaise until well blended and keep in the refrigerator until needed. Serve with fried or broiled fish.

CHAPTER XII

SOUPS

H O M E - M A D E soups have that certain something which canned soups lack. Nevertheless, when time is short or materials are not at hand, canned or packaged soups prove useful. Keep a generous supply on your emergency shelf at all times.

All through this book you have been urged to save most of the water in which food has been cooked. There are good reasons for saving that water. It contains many of the natural mineral elements of the food, which are health giving. In addition to being good for you, most broths have a fine flavor and therefore should please you when served in soup.

If ham water is not too salty, it is an excellent basis for split pea or Yankee bean soup. Corned beef water, if not too salty, is a good soup stock. Boiled beef water should be used for a vegetable soup. Pot liquors of all the greens may be used in vegetable soup.

Store your vegetable waters and pot liquors in jars in the refrigerator. Vegetable juices make good cream soups. Don't be afraid of combinations that will blend pleasingly. Pea water and carrot water is a tried combination. Onion and potato water will combine well together. Onion water will combine with most vegetable flavors.

Save the cooked vegetables also, even small amounts, because when they are put through a food mill or a sieve they will enhance the flavor of a cream soup.

It is flavor that makes a soup good.

You have a chance to be inventive in your soup making. Allow yourself to experiment with combinations. Use cooked foods, bones, celery tops, odd carrots, queer-shaped tomatoes. But before you do that, or feel you can do it, you will want to know how it is done.

Modern kitchens are not equipped for a stock pot, or *pot au feu*, as the French call it. A stock pot is a large kettle kept on the back of the stove at all times, into which is put—washed of course—all odd scraps, outside lettuce and cabbage leaves, good pea pods, peelings, cooked bones, fresh bones, scraps of meat and fat—anything at all. It is allowed to simmer and the broth is taken off for soups and sauces. But by saving vegetable water, gravy if not too fat, meat juices from the roast and cooked food, you give yourself the equivalent of the stock pot.

SOUP VEGETABLES

The following list is sometimes called "soup greens."

Beans, lima	Onions
Beans, string	Okra
Beans, wax	Parsnips
Cabbage	Parsley
Carrots	Peas
Cauliflower	Pepper, green (use sparingly)
Celery stalks and leaves	Potato
Leeks	Tomatoes
Lettuce leaves	Turnips, white or yellow

After the soup is made, the vegetables can be used in various ways. They are good in a cooked vegetable salad, mixed with other cooked vegetables. Or put them in a greased casserole, cover with 1 cup of cheese sauce, and heat in a slow oven (300°) for half an hour; or they may be eaten right in the soup.

SOUP CEREALS

Use 1 teaspoon of any of these cereals to each cup of soup:

Barley	Quick-cooking tapioca
Oatmeal	Rice

Chicken and turkey bones, chop bones, steak bones, and bones from a roast are all good soup material. Lamb and mutton bones because of their peculiar flavor are best cooked alone and combined with barley.

BONE SOUPS

CHICKEN-BONE SOUP

Break up the bones from roast, fried, or broiled chicken and place them in a kettle. Add about twice as much water as there are bones. Sprinkle with ¼ teaspoon of salt. Add 1 medium onion, sliced, 1 cup of celery, any leftover chicken gravy on hand, and ½ cup diced carrots. Simmer for about an hour—even longer will not hurt it. Strain and use as a clear soup, or add ½ cup of medium cream sauce to each 2 cups of broth.

TURKEY-BONE SOUP

Follow directions for Chicken-Bone soup.

BEEF-BONE SOUP

If possible break up beefsteak and roast bones. Put in a stewing kettle. Add twice as much water as bones and sprinkle with 1 teaspoon of salt. Add a few peppercorns. Bring slowly to the boil and simmer for 1 hour. Add any vegetables on hand—always onion, celery if possible, and carrot. Tomatoes are good in this soup. A tablespoon or 2 of rice or barley, depending on the amount of water, adds to the broth. After the vegetables have been added, simmer for 1 hour longer. Remove the bones and serve at once as a thick soup. Or strain and serve as a clear broth.

LAMB-BONE SOUP

Put lamb or mutton bones in a stewing kettle. Add twice as much water as bones and 1 teaspoon of salt, 1 or 2 tablespoons of barley, 1 medium onion, sliced or diced, 1 carrot, diced (at least ¼ cup), 1 white turnip, diced, ¼ teaspoon of paprika, and a few grains of cayenne. Simmer for 2 hours. Remove the bones and serve, but first remove the fat. Or allow soup to cool, remove the fat, and reheat before serving.

MEAT BROTHS

Soup stock is the clear liquid remaining after straining the soup.

Bouillon is a clear, strained soup made from lean beef, a beef bone, tomatoes, and other vegetables.

Consommé is also a clear soup made from lean beef, a veal bone, a chicken, and vegetables, but no tomatoes.

Leg or shinbone cuts are good soup meat. Any lean meat is good. Always get a bone.

SOUP STOCK OR BOUILLON

PREPARATION TIME: about 1 hour

COOKING TIME: 3–4 hours of simmering

To make 6 cups of soup you will need:

3 pounds lean meat and bone	½ green pepper
12 cups cold water	½ cup chopped onion
2½ cups diced vegetables	1 tablespoon salt
1 cup tomatoes	4 peppercorns

METHOD: Wash the meat and bone and place it in a large kettle. Sprinkle the salt over the meat and let it stand for a few minutes before measuring the cold water. Add the peppercorns and place the kettle over medium heat. When the water boils reduce the heat and simmer for about 3 hours.

The meat must simmer with the bone for about 3 hours before the vegetables are added, though the onion can be added when the meat is started. The combination of odors is tantalizing.

At the end of 3 hours remove the meat, add the diced vegetables, and simmer for 1 hour longer. Strain. Cool the liquid and remove the fat. Save the meat and the vegetables and use them as suggested on pages 240 and 241.

TO REMOVE FAT FROM HOT SOUPS OR LIQUIDS:
This may be done by dropping a few ice cubes into the soup. The fat will congeal about the cubes at once. Lift out the cubes, slip off the hardened fat, and return the cubes back to the liquid.
Or drop a few lettuce leaves in the soup. The leaves will absorb much of the fat.
Or blot the top of the soup with absorbent paper to take up the fat.
Or, best of all, let the soup cool and take off the congealed fat.

If you serve the soup as bouillon, it should be clarified.

TO CLARIFY SOUP STOCK: Remove the fat from cold stock and measure the stock. Use the white of 1 egg and the crushed egg shell for each quart of stock. Add 2 teaspoons of cold water to the egg white and beat lightly. Add the beaten egg white and crushed shell to the stock and bring to the boil. Boil at least 2 minutes, remove from the fire, and allow to stand for about 30 minutes. Put a double thickness of cheesecloth in a large strainer and strain the broth.

Reheat the strained stock. While it is heating, slice a lemon. Place the lemon slice in the soup plate. Put a whole clove on the lemon slice. Pour the soup into the plate, floating the lemon. A tablespoon of sherry added just before serving enhances the bouillon.

CONSOMMÉ

PREPARATION TIME: about 1 hour

COOKING TIME: 3–4 hours of simmering

For 6 cups of consommé you will need:

1½ pounds lean beef and 1½ pounds veal with a veal knuckle or

good veal bone, or ½ pound lean beef and ½ pound veal
and veal bone and 1 small stewing chicken, 2–3 pounds

4 peppercorns	1 cup diced onion
2 cloves	1 tablespoon salt
2 sprigs parsley	12 cups cold water (4 cups for
½ cup diced celery	each pound of meat and
½ cup diced carrots	bone)

Follow the directions for Soup Stock or Bouillon. Clarify as
described above and serve hot.

Because of the chicken and veal bone, this broth should form
a jelly when cold. It may be served as cold consommé, with a
wedge of lemon.

SOUP MEAT

The meat can be kept warm after removing from the kettle and
may be served with a horse-radish sauce or mustard sauce or any
condiment you fancy. Or prepare a Scotch Mold.

SCOTCH MOLD

Shred the soup meat or put it through a food grinder. Mix thoroughly with 1 cup of the soup vegetables, which should be mashed.
For soup meat cooked without a veal bone, ½ tablespoon of gelatin will be needed. Dissolve ½ tablespoon of gelatin in 2 tablespoons of cold water. Heat 1 cup of soup stock and add to the
dissolved gelatin. Mix well and allow to cool. No gelatin is needed
with veal-bone stock.

Season the meat and vegetable mixture with spices. Here is a
chance to let yourself go on seasonings. The mixture should be
spicy but not overloaded. Try one of these:

½ teaspoon poultry seasoning	Pinch powdered clove
¼ teaspoon pepper	Pinch powdered mace
Pinch powdered ginger	Salt as needed

After the spices and seasonings have been well incorporated in the meat and vegetable mixture, stir into it some of the stock prepared with gelatin. Have the mixture moist but not too wet. Place the mixture in a mold or a crockery bowl and even off the top. Cover with wax paper and place a small plate or saucer on the wax paper. Place a weight on the plate or saucer. Store in the refrigerator until thoroughly chilled and the gelatin is set. Unmold and serve cold, cut in slices.

CHICKEN SOUP

PREPARATION TIME: about 1 hour

COOKING TIME: about 3 hours

1 stewing hen, 3–5 pounds	½ cup diced onion
1 tablespoon salt	1 cup diced celery
4 cups of water per pound of chicken	4–5 sprigs parsley
	2–3 peppercorns

METHOD: Cut up the chicken and sprinkle with the salt. Add 4 cups of water for each pound of chicken. Add the onion and peppercorns. Bring the kettle to a boil over a medium fire, reduce the heat, and simmer for 2 hours. If the chicken is not tender, extend the time and add 1 or 2 cups of boiling water. When the chicken is tender, add the vegetables and simmer until the vegetables are tender. Remove the parsley sprigs. If the soup is to be served at once, remove some of the fat. If possible, allow the chicken to cool in the soup. When the liquid is cool remove the chicken and then the fat. This soup is excellent the second day when reheated. The cooked chicken may be removed from the bone and used in a salad or as creamed chicken.

CHICKEN BROTH

Prepare Chicken Soup. Strain and clarify as directed on p. 244.

CHICKEN LOAF

This delicious cold loaf may be made from the chicken and veal removed from Consommé or the chicken from Chicken Soup.

Remove all the chicken from the bones, keeping the white and dark meat separate. If you run short of chicken to fill up the loaf pan, hard-cook 3 eggs.

Chicken, or chicken and veal	1 tablespoon gelatin
3 hard-cooked eggs if necessary	Salt and pepper
2 cups strained chicken broth or consommé	

M E T H O D: Arrange the chicken in the loaf pan, a layer of white and a layer of dark meat. Place the shelled eggs on the chicken. Fill in around the eggs with small pieces of the chicken. Cover the eggs with layers of chicken.

Take ¼ cup of cold broth and soften the gelatin in it. Heat the balance of the broth to boiling and add to the cold broth and gelatin. Stir until well mixed. Season the broth, adding a little ginger and mace if you like them.

Pour the broth over the chicken in the mold a little at a time, making sure that the chicken is well covered with the broth. If you do not use all the broth, return it to your stock or save it to use in a sauce, or when it is cold eat it. It's good.

Cover the loaf pan with waxed paper and place a small board over the paper. Place a weight on the board and allow the broth to chill. When the loaf has been completely chilled in the refrigerator, unmold and serve in slices.

VEGETABLE SOUPS

A good thick soup is a heartening meal in itself. For family dinners and Sunday-night suppers serve plenty of soup, a salad, a dessert, and call it a meal.

MIXED VEGETABLE SOUP

Follow the directions for Soup Stock or Bouillon but do not strain. Rice or barley may be added with the vegetables, and any of the Soup Vegetables listed on p. 241 may be added to your soup. When the vegetables are done the soup may be served. It is advisable, however, to remove most of the fat.

BEAN, LENTIL, OR SPLIT-PEA SOUP

The collective name for leguminous plants and their edible seeds such as peas, beans, etc., is "pulse." The term covers all dried legumes when describing them collectively.

All dried pulse should be soaked overnight, whether they are black beans, navy beans, kidney beans, lima beans, peas, or lentils. If you have boiled a ham or have had a boiled dinner, by all means use that pot liquor.

Any of these soups are good with a hambone, usually the hock end. A turkey carcass is not bad, or ½ pound of fat and lean salt pork may be used or about a pound bacon square.

PREPARATION TIME: about 1 hour

COOKING TIME: about 3 hours of simmering

BASIC RECIPE:

Hambone, meat, or carcass	½ teaspoon poultry seasoning
12 cups water (use that pot-liquor you saved)	Piece bay leaf
1 large onion, diced	4 peppercorns
5–6 stalks celery, minced or grated, with leaves	2 tablespoons flour
2 medium carrots, grated	2 tablespoons fat from the soup
	Salt as needed

SPLIT or DRIED PEA SOUP: Add to the basic recipe 2 cups peas (soaked overnight)

LIMA BEAN SOUP or DRIED BEAN SOUP: Add to the basic recipe 2 cups limas (soaked overnight) or dried beans.

L E N T I L   S O U P: Add to the basic recipe 2 cups lentils (soaked overnight), 1 cup tomato juice, and just before serving 1 teaspoon lemon juice.

M E T H O D: Drain the soaked pulse. Place them in a large kettle with the meat or carcass. Add the water. Bring to a boil and simmer, covered, about 2 hours.

Add the onion and other ingredients and simmer another hour.

Remove the meat or carcass. Strain the soup through a sieve, pressing all the pulp through. It expedites the sieving process to run some of the liquid through the sieve a second time.

Remove as much of the fat as possible.

Take 2 tablespoons of the soup fat and combine with 2 teaspoons of flour. To this flour and fat add some soup, a little at a time, mixing to a smooth paste first and then a lumpless liquid. Put the soup back into the kettle, add the flour mixture, and bring to a boil, stirring often. Taste to see if salt is necessary.

Many people scout the idea of the flour. They think the peas or beans make the soup thick enough. They do. There is no question about that. The flour is used to bind the mixture and hold it together. If you eat pea or bean soup and find the pulp at the bottom of the plate, you can be sure no binder was used.

If you like, add 2 cups of cream or milk when you reheat after the flour has been added.

Serve with Croutons.

CROUTONS

One slice of bread will make enough croutons for 4 servings. Remove the crusts and dice the bread. Put 1 tablespoon or more of butter in a skillet. Put the bread in the butter and sauté or fry until the bread is nicely browned. Stir often to prevent burning. Or remove the crusts, spread the bread on both sides with butter, dice, place on a baking sheet, and brown in a hot oven (400°).

This soup business, like Tennyson's "Brook," could go on forever. There is no limit to what you can do.

CREAM SOUPS

There is no need to tell you how delicious cream soups can be. You know that. But do you know a good basic recipe for cream soup?

The basis is a good white sauce. You now know how to make white sauce. You simply add vegetable water and pulp to the sauce for delicious soup.

There are only a few things to remember:

Use 1 cup of white sauce to 1 to 2 cups of liquid and purée.

Use Thin White Sauce for thick purées of such vegetables as:

Asparagus	Cauliflower
Beans—any dried beans or	Corn
fresh limas	Peas
Carrot	Potato

Use Medium White Sauce for the more watery purées such as:

Celery	Onion
Leek	Spinach
Mushroom (use a food chopper)	Tomato

Always measure the amount of liquid and purée before making your white sauce. Decide whether or not the liquid and purée are thick or thin. If they are thin, use a medium white sauce. If thick, such as bean or potato, use a thin white sauce. The soup should be creamy and should not suggest flour in any way, so be sure your sauce is properly cooked.

BASIC METHOD FOR CREAM SOUPS WITH COOKED VEGETABLES: First purée your cooked vegetables through a food mill, a sieve, or a food chopper. Add the vegetable water and measure. Decide if it is thick or thin. Prepare your white sauce, remembering that you may use up to 2 cups of vegetable and water to 1 cup of white sauce. Mix the vegetable purée with the white sauce and season to taste. A little onion salt might be the thing that is needed, or a suggestion of parsley. Taste and decide. Remember, add the seasonings lightly until the flavor is right.

CHAPTER XIII

CEREAL PRODUCTS

CORN-MEAL DISHES

CORN-MEAL MUSH

C O R N - M E A L mush is a dish of reasonable variety. It substitutes nicely for potatoes, particularly if there is rich gravy. Sometime try a mound of hot mush covered with any good rich gravy.

Cold mush sliced about ¼ inch thick may be browned in bacon fat or cooking oil and served as a breakfast dish with lemon juice and powdered sugar, or with butter and syrup.

P R E P A R A T I O N   T I M E: about 10 minutes

C O O K I N G   T I M E: 1 hour or longer in the top of a double boiler

For 4 servings you will need:

1 cup corn meal, white or yellow	1 cup cold water
	2 teaspoons salt
4 cups boiling water	

M E T H O D: Mix the corn meal into the cup of water. Add the salt and mix well. Put the 4 cups of boiling water in the top of a double boiler and place the top over direct heat. Stir in the corn-meal mixture, adding it slowly to the boiling water. When the mixture has been added, place the top of the double boiler over hot water and cook for at least 1 hour. Stir the mixture frequently. Some cooks cook their mush for 3 hours. Serve hot if it is to be used as a substitute for potatoes. Delicious with lamb or veal stew gravy. If it is to be used as fried mush, cool in a small loaf pan.

FRIED MUSH

Prepare Corn-Meal Mush. Cool in a loaf pan and cut into ¼-inch slices. Brown in hot bacon fat and serve with lemon juice and powdered sugar or with butter and any breakfast syrup.

POLENTA

Polenta is the Italian version of corn-meal mush. It is served hot with meat sauces or gravies. Often it is served with grated cheese, and sometimes the cheese is cooked in the polenta. When cold it may be fried as mush and served with tomato sauce or a meat sauce, or it can be used as a base for a delicious casserole.

PREPARATION TIME: about 10 minutes

COOKING TIME: 1–3 hours

For 4 servings you will need:

1 cup white corn meal (some cooks use yellow)	1½ teaspoons salt
	⅛ teaspoon paprika
1 cup cold water	Pinch cayenne or red pepper
4 cups boiling water	

METHOD: Mix the corn meal and cold water in a bowl. Add the salt and seasoning. Put 4 cups of boiling water in the top of a double boiler and put it over direct heat. Stir in the corn-meal mixture a little at a time. When the mixture has been blended evenly with the boiling water, place the top of the double boiler over hot water and cook, stirring often. Cook for at least 1 hour, longer if possible.

Serve hot, sprinkled generously with grated cheese, or use it as a potato substitute and cover with a good rich gravy—lamb, beef, or veal.

You might like 1 cup of grated cheese mixed into the polenta for the last 15 minutes of cooking. Cheese or no cheese, polenta is a grand excuse for eating gravy.

FRIED POLENTA

Slice cold polenta, with or without cheese, and sauté in a small amount of fat until a golden brown. Serve with syrup. It is delicious. Never throw away any leftover mush or polenta.

CORN-MEAL PUDDING

This makes an excellent luncheon dish when served with a green salad, or it may be the main course for dinner.

PREPARATION TIME: about 30 minutes

COOKING TIME: about 75 minutes

For 4 servings you will need:

2½ cups scalded milk	¼ teaspoon paprika
½ cup corn meal, white or yellow	Pinch cayenne pepper
2 tablespoons butter	4 eggs, separated
½ cup grated cheese	1 cup cooked diced ham, chicken, turkey, shrimp, lobster, or fish
1 teaspoon salt	

METHOD: Heat the milk in the top of a double boiler. When it is bubbling at the edges, stir in the corn meal and add the butter. Add the grated cheese and seasonings and cook for about 30 minutes, stirring often. Beat the egg yolks. Add the well-beaten yolks to the mush and cook until the mixture thickens. Cool. Beat the egg whites until stiff. Add the cup of cooked meat or fish to the mush and mix well. Fold in the egg whites. Transfer to an ungreased casserole or baking dish and bake in a moderate oven (350°) for at least 30 minutes, or until the batter is rather crisp.

MACARONI, SPAGHETTI, AND PASTAS

The most common starchy foods are special forms of pastas— shells, elbows, etc.—noodles, macaroni, spaghetti. We recommend buying a good brand of any of these.

SPECIAL PASTAS

Pastas double their bulk when cooked.

COOKING TIME: 12 to 15 minutes
For 4 servings you will need:

8 cups boiling water
1 teaspoon salt
2 cups pasta

METHOD: Bring the water to a furious boil and add the salt, then the pasta slowly so as not to retard the boiling. Boil uncovered until tender. Drain in a colander and rinse with cold water. Reheat over boiling water. They may be left in the colander after rinsing. Place the colander in a pot in which a little water is boiling. Do not allow water to touch the pasta. Keep hot until ready to serve.

These may be used as a substitute for macaroni in combination dishes, or served with pot roast or rich stews instead of potatoes.

MACARONI, SPAGHETTI, AND NOODLES

Macaroni and spaghetti double in bulk when cooked; noodles increase ¼ in bulk.

COOKING TIME: 20–25 minutes

NOTE: Tenderized packaged goods require less cooking time. Check time on package.

For 4 servings you will need:
8 cups boiling water
1 teaspoon salt
2 cups any of the above, broken

METHOD: Follow the directions for Special Pastas, but cook for at least 20 minutes.

When we were very young we knew some Italian families who had a fascinating method of testing their spaghetti. The mother would take a few lengths of the spaghetti on a fork and hurl it at the wall over the sink. If the spaghetti stuck to the wall it was done!

Boiled spaghetti, macaroni, or noodles are good when served with butter and a sprinkling of cheese. They are delicious when served with a good Italian sauce.

If you have some Italian friends, ask them for their recipe for sauce and try it. It usually takes hours to make, but it is worth the trouble.

If you are using meat balls and sauce, remove the meat balls from the sauce, pour the sauce over the spaghetti, and then dot the surface with the meat balls. A few pieces of parsley about the edge of the dish give it color. Grated cheese is an essential accompaniment to this dish.

We usually make casserole dishes out of these pastas and use fresh ground meat or cooked meat in various combinations. Fish and all kinds of seafoods can be combined with pastas in a casserole.

MACARONI OR SPAGHETTI BAKED WITH CHEESE

PREPARATION TIME: about 40 minutes

COOKING TIME: 35 minutes

4 cups cooked pasta   1 cup thin cream sauce
½ cup grated cheese

METHOD: Place the cooked pasta in a greased baking dish. Mix the grated cheese in the cream sauce, pour over the pasta, and bake for 30 minutes in a moderate oven (325°). If the top has not browned, put the casserole under the broiler for a moment to give the top a rich golden brown. Remember it takes only a minute. Watch it.

You can vary this recipe by adding to the above:

1 cup shredded tuna, chopped cooked chicken, diced cooked
    shrimp, or flaked cooked fish
¼ cup milk
Salt and pepper to taste

Add the fish or chicken to the white sauce after the cheese. Taste
for seasoning, pour the mixture over the pasta, and bake as directed.

If you prefer to omit the cheese with fish or chicken, then add
the fish or chicken to the cream sauce and omit the extra ¼ cup
of milk. Bake as directed.

MACARONI OR SPAGHETTI WITH MEAT AND TOMATOES

This is a good one-dish meal when served with a green salad and
a light dessert. This recipe will serve 8, approximately 1 cup per
helping.

PREPARATION TIME: about 1 hour

COOKING TIME: at least 1 hour

½ pound ground meat or
    2 cups cooked meat, ground or diced
4 cups cooked pasta
4 slices of bacon, diced, or
    4 thin slices of salt pork
½ cup chopped onion
1 clove garlic
½ cup diced green pepper
½ cup diced celery or
    1 teaspoon celery salt
6-8 medium tomatoes or No. 2 can of tomatoes
½ pound sautéed fresh chopped mushrooms or No. 1 can with
    liquid
½ teaspoon poultry seasoning (optional)
1 tablespoon Worcestershire sauce

Salt
Few grains cayenne
Grated cheese

M E T H O D : Boil 2 cups of broken spaghetti or macaroni and rinse. This will give you 4 cups of cooked pasta. Rub the sides and bottom of the baking dish with the clove of garlic. Place the pasta in the greased baking dish.

Rub a large skillet with the clove of garlic, add the diced bacon or pork, and fry over a low flame. Add the onion and the ground meat. Break up the meat with a fork and mix well with the onion, bacon, and fat. Cook about 10 minutes. If cooked meat is used, it need not be cooked after it is well mixed with the bacon and onion. Add the diced celery and green pepper, the tomatoes, and the mushrooms. Season with the poultry seasoning and the Worcestershire sauce. Add salt and taste. Add the cayenne. Cook until the mixture begins to bubble. Pour over the pasta. Mix well and place in a moderate oven (325°) uncovered. If the mixture becomes dry while baking, add some hot stock or bouillon. After 30 minutes sprinkle the top with grated or powdered cheese and continue to bake for 30 minutes. Serve with French bread or hard rolls.

R I C E

B O I L E D   R I C E

P R E P A R A T I O N   T I M E : 5 minutes

C O O K I N G   T I M E : 20 minutes or longer

For 4 servings you will need:

1 cup rice
10 cups boiling water
1 tablespoon salt

M E T H O D : Wash the rice and pick out any imperfect grains. Have the water boiling and add the salt. Drop the rice slowly into the boiling salted water. Grease the upper inside surface of the kettle lightly with a cooking oil to prevent boiling over. Cook uncovered until the rice is tender, about 20 minutes. Test the rice by lifting a few kernels out with a fork. If they are soft when pressed between the fingers, the rice is done. Drain in a colander. The water may be used for soup. Wash the cooked rice with boiling water to remove the loose starch and separate the grains. Drain, shake the colander to get rid of extra moisture, place the colander on a pan, and place in a warm oven until ready to serve. Leave the oven door open.

WILD RICE

One cup of wild rice will make 3 cups of cooked wild rice.

Wild rice may be prepared overnight. Wash 1 cup of rice, put it in a bowl, add 1 teaspoon of salt, and cover the rice with boiling water and let it stand all night.

To serve it with poultry or game, drain the rice, put it in the top of a double boiler, add 4 tablespoons of butter, and cook about 1 hour, stirring often with a fork.

Or put the washed rice in the top of a double boiler. Add 1 teaspoon of salt and 4 cups of boiling bouillon or stock. A small amount of minced garlic or a slice of minced onion may be added. Cook the rice in the double boiler until tender, 45–60 minutes. When done, add 4 tablespoons butter and serve.

CHAPTER XIV

HOW TO USE COOKED FOODS

MANY of us are creatures of habit, oftentimes the victims of prejudices from an earlier day.

We knew a man who did not like cranberries. That's all right; but the point is that he had never tasted cranberries. He had simply made up his mind he would not like them. We know another man who will not eat fowl of any kind. Why, he has never said. We can understand a person's not liking rabbit, liver, heart, kidney, or tripe; but it is a little difficult to understand why a man who enjoys good roast beef refuses to eat it cold, or in any other guise, particularly in his own home. Those same men will eat hash in a restaurant. Is it because they think the meat is especially cooked for hash, and hash alone, in restaurants?

In fairness to man, let it be said that many women take the same attitude about the second appearance of any food at their table.

We form some of our own mental habits; others are formed for us. A child who hears his father or mother refuse to eat a good roast the second day is certainly justified if he also refuses to eat it. But that child will eventually grow up to be a nuisance to some man or woman, even as you and I.

Not so long ago milk was kept fresh in the springhouse, the hogs were not killed until the cold weather had set in, country people cut their own ice and put it down in salt hay, thunderstorms soured the milk and cream, soups and stews went sour. That was before refrigeration was common, before most people had refrigerators, long before artificial refrigeration was available for the home.

In those days it was not safe to keep food too long. Things had to be eaten or they would spoil. And now many of us have hang-

260

overs from those days, ideas handed on to us that are as out-
moded as the stagecoach. Once the term "cold storage" carried
with it contempt. Now we recommend frozen foods. Most of us
would be in a bad way for food if it were not for the once-despised
cold storage.

If you take proper care of your food, it will keep for a long
time in a modern refrigerator. There are certain things you should
do, however. You should not leave cooked meat out of the refrigerator any longer than it is necessary to slice and prepare it
for a meal. You should store soups, gravies, and vegetables as
soon as they are cool and keep them in the refrigerator until you
want to use them. You should thoroughly reheat all soups, gravies,
and sauces. Bring them to a boil and allow them to boil gently
for 10 minutes before serving. If soups and gravies are to be
stored for long periods before use, they should be reheated and
boiled once every 24–36 hours.

All refrigerators should be clean and in perfect working order. Don't clutter them with dabs of this and that. There is no
point in saving a tablespoon of some food if there is no possible
use for it in the immediate future.

There is never much of a diversified food problem with a large
family. It is the person who lives alone, and does or does not
like it, and the families of 2 or 3 who are faced with a problem
if they want good food with variety, not just a diet of steaks and
chops.

If you like roast beef you have probably discovered that a small
roast doesn't taste like much of anything. It really needs two ribs
to be good. If you are lucky, you may get the small end. Two
ribs will weigh about 5 pounds. (We have nothing against a rolled
roast except that a standing rib roast seems to taste better than
a rolled rib roast.)

If you are a small family, why not have roast beef when you
have guests? Perhaps you will find that you have enough of the
roast beef left for one meal of delicious cold roast beef. After

the cold meal there doesn't seem to be enough meat for any particular purpose. You can always make hash. This is what to do when you have some extra roast beef, pot roast, steak ends, or corned beef:

HASH

Try to plan to have 2 or 3 fairly large cold baked potatoes ready for the hash. If baked potatoes are not available, use cold boiled potatoes. Take your cold meat. Cut off most of the fat—all of it if you dislike fat—and put the meat through a food chopper. Measure the meat. You will need about 2 cups of diced cooked potatoes for each cup of ground meat. A medium potato makes about 1 cup of diced potatoes, so you can figure that you will need 2 medium boiled or baked potatoes for each cup of ground meat. One medium onion will flavor 2 cups of meat and 4 cups of diced potatoes. You can decrease the amount if you are not an onion lover. Do you have a little cold gravy in the refrigerator? The hash needs to be moistened. Don't, unless you can't help yourself, moisten good hash with plain water. If you have no gravy or stock, use boiling water and a bouillon cube. Mix the potatoes, meat, and onion, grated, in a bowl. Season with salt and pepper. Add, if you like, a little celery salt or a little smoked hickory salt. Moisten with gravy or stock, mixing well. The hash should be moist but not wet. Heat 2–3 tablespoons of fat or bacon drippings in a skillet. Put the hash in, press it down with a spatula, and allow it to cook slowly for 15 or 20 minutes over low heat. You may cover the skillet for a little while if you like. Loosen the edges with the spatula and lift to see if it is browning on the bottom. If it is not, increase the heat a little, not too much. Hash should be nicely crusted and browned but not burned. When the hash is brown, cut across the middle of the hash in the skillet and fold one half over the other. Slip onto a platter, garnish with parsley, and serve.

CHICKEN OR TURKEY HASH

Follow the preceding directions, with these differences: Cube the chicken or turkey instead of putting it through a food grinder. Add the grated onion and cold baked potato and moisten with milk or cream or chicken or turkey gravy, never anything else. Season to taste and cook in a skillet or brown in a shallow baking pan in the oven. If you oven-cook the hash, watch it and keep it moist by adding hot milk or cream while it is cooking.

CREAMED MEATS

There are any number of good and tasty dishes which can be prepared with cold meat.

Have you ever tried creamed lamb? Prepare 1 cup of thin white sauce for each 2 cups of cold diced meat. Put the meat in the sauce and heat it in a double boiler. Chopped parsley and chives or onion juice give it flavor. A teaspoon of Worcestershire sauce doesn't hurt it a bit. Serve on toast or boiled rice.

Chicken, veal, or turkey may be treated the same way. For those who like green peppers or pimento, a little of either or both may be added to the white meat sauces for flavor and color. Do not use more than 1 tablespoon, diced or minced, per cup of cream sauce.

HOT POTS

These ideas are variations of the old Lancashire Hot Pot. Make them with cooked meats, beef or lamb or veal. You should have a fairly deep baking dish or casserole with a cover.

PREPARATION TIME: about 45 minutes

COOKING TIME: about 2½ hours

For 4 servings you will need:

2 cups cubed cooked meat	Pepper (freshly ground is best)
4–5 medium raw potatoes, sliced	Salt
	Flour
2 medium onions, sliced	¼ teaspoon assorted ground herbs
2–3 good-sized carrots, sliced	
2 cups stock	1 tablespoon Worcestershire sauce

M E T H O D: Grease the casserole and put a layer of sliced potatoes on the bottom of it. The slices should not be more than ¼ inch thick. Add a layer of cubed meat, cover the meat with slices of onion, then slices of carrot ¼ inch thick. Sprinkle the carrots lightly with pepper and salt, then with flour. Start again with potatoes and proceed layer by layer until all the material is used. Sprinkle the aromatic herbs on the top layer, add the Worcestershire sauce, and then the stock. The stock should not float the top layer, but should be seen just under the surface. Cover the dish with a lid, put it in a moderate oven (325°), and cook for 2 hours. Remove the lid for the last 30 minutes of cooking. Test during cooking for moisture. The hot pot should not be allowed to dry out. It should be wet but not too juicy.

With a lettuce and tomato salad and a fruit dessert, it makes a good meal.

RICE AND MEAT CASSEROLES

When you make these dishes with cooked beef, lamb, or mutton, use tomatoes and almost anything at hand. But with chicken or veal be more restrained. Confine yourself to onion, celery, and a small amount of carrot.

Feel at liberty to vary the quantities given. After all, these dishes are an expression of your ability to use cooked meats and create palate-tempting dishes.

P R E P A R A T I O N   T I M E: about 45 minutes

C O O K I N G   T I M E: about 3 hours

For 4 servings you will need:

1 cup washed rice, white or brown

2 cups cooked beef, lamb or mutton

2½ cups tomatoes or a No. 2 can

2 medium onions, sliced or diced

½ cup diced carrots

½ cup diced celery

½ green pepper, diced

1 small clove garlic, minced

½ teaspoon chili powder

Salt

A few olives, sliced or cut from the stones

2 cups tomato juice or stock

M E T H O D: Wash the raw rice thoroughly and put it in a large mixing bowl. Add all the ingredients except the tomato juice or stock. Reserve that for later use. When the ingredients are well mixed, grease a casserole or large baking dish. Put the mixture in the casserole, cover, and put in a moderate oven (325°). Inspect the cooking every half hour. As the rice cooks it will expand and use up the moisture from the tomatoes and vegetables. Do not let the dish become dry. Keep it soggy or fairly wet. Heat the tomato juice or stock and add as needed. The longer the dish stays in the oven, the more stock you will need. Do not be alarmed if you find you must use more than the 2 cups suggested.

Toasted French bread, a green salad, fruit, and coffee make this a good busy-day meal. After the initial preparation, except for the occasional inspection for moisture, your dinner practically takes care of itself.

If you use chicken, turkey, or veal with raw rice, omit the tomatoes and tomato juice and substitute chicken broth or consommé for the stock. Use curry powder instead of the chili powder. If you or your family object to pale concoctions, use some kitchen bouquet to relieve the pallor.

COOKED VEGETABLES

Have you been plagued by a few odds and ends of this and that vegetable? This is a system we have found successful: Keep a covered dish in the refrigerator, and into it put small amounts of string beans, limas, peas, carrots, corn, broccoli, cauliflower, cabbage, turnips, or kohlrabi—drained, of course. (Cold asparagus you will probably use in salads or an omelet.) In a day or two you will probably have enough vegetables to use.

Combine them in a casserole and pour over them 1 cup of thin white sauce to which ½ cup of grated cheese has been added. Place the dish in a slow oven (300°) and heat for about 30 minutes.

Or take the combination of vegetables, pour over them 1 cup of bouillon, and heat for 30 minutes in a slow oven (300°). Drain before serving and save the liquid for future use.

Or use them for a cooked vegetable salad.

CHAPTER XV

SALADS AND SALAD DRESSINGS

IN THIS chapter you will find no radish roses, candlesticks made out of pineapple, bananas, and maraschino cherries, nor any other fantastic shape. Salads are good, not because they have been made to look like something which they are not, but because of what they are. Any salad when thoughtfully arranged can please the eye as well as tempt the appetite. It should be as beautiful as you can make it with the natural ingredients you are using.

In an effort to be different, too many cooks forget one of the most delicious salads, just plain greens, either alone or in combination, with the addition of a good French dressing. Don't be one of those cooks who ignore a good salad.

Salads can be generally classified this way:

Green salads—lettuce, escarole, endive, romaine, etc.
Fruit and nut salads
Raw vegetable salads
Cooked vegetable salads
Cooked meat salads, fish and fowl
Jellied salads or aspics

SALAD GREENS

All greens—lettuce, romaine, escarole, endive, spinach, etc., should be fresh and crisp when bought. Wash them carefully, shake free of moisture, and store in a cool or cold place to become crisp. A cheesecloth bag, a 10-pound sugar bag, or something similar, makes a very good storage bag for your greens.

Have you had difficulty removing the leaves from a tight head of lettuce? An easy way to separate the leaves is this: Cut the core or stem end, placing a sharp knife well into the head of lettuce.

Make a circular movement with the knife. The core should come out pointed at the end. Hold the lettuce under the cold-water spigot and allow the water to run gently into the hole. The water will begin to loosen the leaves so that with a little help from you they will come apart without being split or broken.

Wash all greens well, shake free of water, and store in a bag in your refrigerator, preferably in a covered pan.

All parts of a salad should be well chilled. Meat and vegetable mixtures should be marinated in French dressing in a cold place for at least 30 minutes before being used.

DRESSINGS

Clothes may not make a man, but a good dressing certainly makes a salad. Never use inferior salad dressings. Don't use oil that is even slightly rancid. If it doesn't smell sweet and good, don't use it.

There are almost as many French dressings as there are cooks, and most of them are excellent. They vary because of the ingredients which go into them.

OIL AND VINEGAR DRESSING

This is one of the oldest of dressings, and was and still is served from cruets. Have a cruet of good olive oil and one of a good mild or wine vinegar, salt, and pepper. A pepper mill which will give you freshly ground pepper adds to the salad.

The oil and vinegar are sprinkled over the salad and seasoned to the taste of the individual. On lettuce and tomatoes a light sprinkling of sugar added to the oil and vinegar is good.

FRENCH DRESSING

This is a basic recipe from which other dressings and variations are made. You will need a jar or bottle which can be tightly sealed for shaking. No French dressing is good unless it is well mixed. The mixing may be done in a bowl if you prefer.

1 small clove garlic	2 teaspoons sugar
1 cup olive oil or good salad oil	⅛ teaspoon pepper
	1 teaspoon salt
3 tablespoons cider vinegar or wine vinegar, or 2 tablespoons lemon juice	⅛ teaspoon paprika
	½ teaspoon powdered dry mustard if desired

N O T E: There are a number of herb vinegars on the market which may be used instead of the vinegars suggested above. Most of them have a wine-vinegar base. They give variety to salads and give you some prestige as a cook when you use them properly.

M E T H O D: Drop the clove of garlic into the bottle or jar. Add the remaining ingredients and shake until well and completely blended.

There are probably many people in the world who have never made their own French dressing. Most French dressings bought in the shops have a decided red color. You may achieve this result by adding to the basic recipe 3 tablespoons of tomato catsup or ½ can of condensed tomato soup.

Always taste your dressing, particularly after additions. It may need a little more vinegar, salt, or pepper. Always shake well before using and never allow the clove of garlic to escape from the bottle.

O T H E R A D D I T I O N S: You may add to your French dressing for variation any of the following:

1 tablespoon prepared horse-radish
1 tablespoon chopped parsley
1 tablespoon chopped green pepper
1 tablespoon chopped onion
2 tablespoons chopped chutney
2 tablespoons crumbled roquefort cheese for green salad
¼ teaspoon dried herbs
½ teaspoon fresh herbs

Confine your additions to 1 or 2 of the list at any one time. Too much of anything is too much.

CHIFFONADE FRENCH DRESSING

To the basic French dressing recipe add:

¼ cup chopped cooked beets
2 tablespoons chopped pars-
　　ley

1 chopped hard-cooked egg
1 tablespoon chopped chives or
　　2 teaspoons chopped onion

2 tablespoons chopped green pepper

THOUSAND-ISLAND DRESSING

To the basic French dressing add:

2 tablespoons chopped green
　　pepper

1 tablespoon chopped parsley
2 tablespoons chopped olives

2 tablespoons chopped onion

If you use plain olives, add 1 teaspoon chopped pimento. Stuffed olives usually have the pimento in them.

MAYONNAISE DRESSING

Good mayonnaise can be bought in the markets, and it is a task to make it at home. But it is worth trying once.

1 egg yolk
2 tablespoons vinegar
¼ teaspoon mustard
1 mixing bowl

1 egg beater
¾ teaspoon salt
⅛ teaspoon pepper
¼ teaspoon paprika

1 cup good salad oil

Most electric mixers have a special gadget for the making of mayonnaise. The real trick is the beating in of the oil, a little at a time.

M E T H O D: Beat the egg yolk well. Add 1 tablespoon of vinegar and beat again. Add the mustard, salt, pepper, and paprika and mix well. Now for the beating. Drop 1 teaspoonful of oil into the egg mixture and beat until it is well mixed. Add 1 teaspoonful at a time, beating constantly. When about half of the oil has been used in small quantities, the mixture should begin to be quite thick. You still have 1 tablespoon of vinegar which must be added. Add a little at a time as you beat in the remainder of the oil in slightly larger quantities. You must beat, beat, beat, if you want good mayonnaise. Store in a cool place.

The mayonnaise may be added to and varied for many purposes.

FITZSAUCE: See page 235

FRUIT SALAD DRESSING: Whip ⅓ cup of heavy cream until stiff. Fold it into 1 cup of mayonnaise.

RED MAYONNAISE: Add ¼ cup of catsup to 1 cup of mayonnaise.

RUSSIAN DRESSING: Mix ½ cup of chili sauce and 2 tablespoons of minced green pepper into 1 cup of mayonnaise. Serve on chunks of head lettuce or anything else you like.

TARTAR SAUCE: See page 239

OTHER ADDITIONS: Add to mayonnaise any of the following:

½ cup of grated and well-drained cucumber
3 tablespoons of chopped sour pickles and
2 tablespoons of chopped pickled onions
3 tablespoons of chopped parsley
3 tablespoons of chopped chives

BOILED OR COOKED SALAD DRESSING

This dressing has a piquancy all its own. It can be used generally in salads instead of mayonnaise, particularly with romaine and sliced tomatoes.

1 scant teaspoon mustard	2 drops Tabasco sauce or
1 teaspoon salt	few grains cayenne
1 or 2 tablespoons sugar	1 egg, beaten
2 tablespoons flour	1 cup milk
Pinch paprika	¼ cup vinegar

2 tablespoons butter or fat

A ROUNDED SPOONFUL means exactly what it says. When you dip a spoon into a powdered substance, it rounds up over the edges. A level spoonful has to be evened off. Do not level off for a rounded spoonful. If you are in doubt, use 2 level spoonfuls.

METHOD: Put hot water in the bottom of the double boiler and place over medium heat. In the top of your double boiler mix the mustard, salt, sugar, flour, paprika, and Tabasco sauce or cayenne. When well mixed, add the beaten egg and mix again. Add the milk and vinegar and place the top pan over the hot water. Cook, stirring constantly, until the mixture thickens and is smooth. Add the butter and stir it in until it is all melted and incorporated in the mixture. Cool and store in the refrigerator.

VARIATION: If the boiled dressing is to be served on fruit, ½ cup of whipped cream may be folded in for a cream dressing.

ADDITIONS: If you like you may add to the basic recipe one of the following combinations:

2 tablespoons of chopped onion or chives and 2 tablespoons of chopped parsley

3 tablespoons of chopped celery, 2 tablespoons of chopped green pepper, and 2 tablespoons of chopped pimento

SOUR-CREAM SALAD DRESSING

1 teaspoon salt	1 tablespoon lemon juice
1 tablespoon sugar	2 tablespoons good vinegar
Pinch cayenne or ⅛ tea-	1 cup sour cream
spoon white pepper	

M E T H O D: Mix the salt, sugar, and pepper in a bowl. Add the lemon juice and vinegar, then stir in the sour cream, mixing until smooth. Chill until needed.

If you like any color so long as it is red, you may add ½ cup tomato catsup to the above recipe.

HONEY SALAD DRESSING FOR FRUIT

½ cup salad oil
2 tablespoons lemon juice and
2 tablespoons lime juice (all lemon juice may be used)
½ teaspoon salt
½ cup liquid honey

M E T H O D: Combine the oil, citrus juice, and salt, mixing well with a fork. Add the honey a little at a time, beating it into the oil and juice with a fork until all the honey is well mixed with the other ingredients. Store in a tightly covered jar in the refrigerator until needed. Mix well before serving.

GREEN SALADS

Let us begin at the beginning and consider lettuce or green salads. Combination, or mixed, salads have their place, but they are quite often a meal in themselves. As an accompaniment to a good steak, chop, or roast dinner, there is nothing better than a plain green salad with a good French dressing. If you prefer Thousand-Island or Russian dressing, that is a matter of taste.

Have the greens crisp and cold. You may use broken pieces of lettuce pulled apart with your fingers, or you may cut a solid head into cubes or wedges. Drop the pieces lightly into a bowl rubbed with a clove of garlic.

T O   R U B   W I T H   G A R L I C means to peel and bruise a clove of garlic. Then, with the garlic held firmly in the fingers, rub the bruised clove over the surface of the bowl and discard the clove.

Pour the French dressing a little at a time over the leaves. Toss

lightly with a wooden or glass fork and spoon. Add more dressing and toss until the lettuce is coated with but not saturated by
the dressing.

T O   T O S S   A   S A L A D means to lift the leaves or combination of
vegetables from the bottom of the bowl and turn over lightly.
It is not a mixing movement. It is lifting from the bottom and
dropping gently back into the bowl.

Lettuce may be combined with all or any of the following for
a good green salad: chicory, dandelion, endive, escarole, young
nasturtium leaves, romaine, spinach, sorrel, and watercress.

VEGETABLE SALADS

RAW VEGETABLE SALAD

If you want to feature this salad at a buffet supper, use any
or all of the above greens in combination with any or all of the
following list of vegetables. A large mixing bowl of the raw
vegetables and greens will serve from 15–20 people generously.
Save some whole lettuce leaves to line the side of the mixing bowl,
also some of the sliced, diced, or slivered vegetables for decoration. Nothing looks more attractive than a well-presented vegetable
salad.

You will need 2 bowls, 1 for mixing the salad and 1 lined
with lettuce leaves for serving.

If you want to have a taste of garlic in the salad in addition
to the garlic in the dressing, rub the mixing bowl with a clove of
garlic. Or take a stale, hard roll (the harder the better). Rub the
surface of the roll with a bruised clove of garlic. Slice the roll
and cut into tiny cubes and add it to the vegetables when the salad
is mixed.

Now for vegetables in the salad which will delight you and your
guests. Use any or all. Limit yourself only by the amount you
want to serve.

Cabbage, chopped. In combination with several other vegetables. Not more than ½ cup.

Cauliflower. Break up the buds into fairly small pieces. ½ cup.

Carrots, cut into thin slices or slivers, or chopped. ½ cup.

Celery, diced. 1 cup.

Cucumbers, thin slices or cubes. ½ cup.

Leek, cut into thin slices (1 leek).

Onion, cut into thin slices or diced. 1 or 2 of medium size.

Onions, green. Cut into slices, use some of the green top. 1 bunch.

Peppers, sweet, red or green. ¼ to ½ cup.

Radishes, sliced thin. 1 bunch.

Turnip, white, small, thin slices or diced. ½ cup.

Tomato, sliced or preferably in wedges. 2–3 medium, peeled.

Zucchini, young and small, thin slices. 2–3.

Prepare your vegetables and keep them chilled until just before serving. Mix them with broken greens in a bowl. Add French dressing and toss. Pour the tossed vegetables into the bowl lined with lettuce leaves and garnish with pieces of the vegetables saved out for decorating purposes. The decoration is up to you.

Some people like thin slices of salami, bologna, cheese, or ham in this salad. Others like 1 tablespoon of anchovy paste in the French dressing.

TOMATO SALADS

The tomato is justly one of the most popular ingredients in a salad. Its uses are many. It may be used as part of a salad, as a garnish, or as the basis of a stuffed salad.

To prepare tomatoes for salads, it is advisable to skin them (p. 222).

If tomatoes are to be stuffed, they must be hollowed. Cut out the core and then with a sharp knife, being careful not to injure the outside layer of pulp, take out the inner sections containing the seeds. Salt the tomatoes and invert them, allowing them to drain for a few minutes. Chill them and then fill them with whatever mixture you have on hand. Almost anything will do, from avocado to tuna fish.

COLE SLAW

This is a very versatile cabbage salad. Have the cabbage fresh, crisp, and young if possible. Remove the outer leaves and cut out the core. If it is a large head, cut it in half before coring. Cut it into thin shreds. Some people chop it, but the thin shreds are preferable. Drop the cabbage in ice-cold water. (A bowl of cold water containing several ice cubes will do very nicely.) Allow the cabbage to remain in the water at least 15 minutes. Drain, shake free of moisture, and dry if necessary between two towels. Chill the cabbage to crisp it. Just before serving time place the chilled shredded cabbage in a salad bowl.

You have many choices from this point on. You may moisten it with French dressing or any of its variations. You may use mayonnaise and its variations. Or you may use a boiled dressing or a sour-cream dressing.

You may also add crushed pineapple, shredded carrot, shredded green pepper, some slivers of red cabbage.

A combination slaw of red and green cabbage is a nice variation.

COOKED VEGETABLE SALADS

Cooked vegetables may be marinated in French dressing, mixed with mayonnaise or salad dressing, and chilled. Serve on a lettuce leaf. Mound the vegetables carefully. A sloppy salad is not attractive to the eye.

POTATO SALAD

A good potato salad is hard to beat as part of a picnic lunch or a cold supper. Try this one for 4 people:

5 medium potatoes	1 teaspoon salt
2 cups diced celery if desired	⅛ teaspoon pepper
2 tablespoons minced parsley	Paprika
2 tablespoons chopped onion,	French dressing
or more if you prefer	Mayonnaise dressing
1 hard-cooked egg	

Wash the potatoes and boil them in their jackets. Cool before preparing the salad. It is well to plan ahead and cook the potatoes in the morning if the salad is to be used in the evening. Peel the cooled potatoes; marinate lightly with French dressing, and chill. Just before serving time combine the marinated potatoes with the celery, parsley, onion, salt, and pepper. Moisten the combined vegetables with mayonnaise. Arrange on lettuce leaves, decorate with slices of hard-cooked egg, and sprinkle with paprika.

SALAD COMBINATIONS

There is no limit to the combinations. For example, romaine covered with slices of orange and served with French dressing is good with lamb stew or lamb chops. (Add a little chopped mint to the dressing.)

Romaine, wedges of grapefruit, and slices of avocado are delicious with French dressing or a mixture of orange juice and wine vinegar and oil. Never use mayonnaise or cooked salad dressing with avocado.

Lettuce and thin slices of Bermuda or sweet Spanish onion with vinegar and oil or French dressing are hard to beat.

There's nothing the matter with slices of tomato on lettuce leaves with a good French dressing. Some people prefer a thin sprinkling of sugar and a few drops of vinegar.

Half an avocado filled with orange juice is delicious, or you may prefer French dressing in the pit cavity.

Any cooked vegetable may be put in a salad.

Leftover baked beans combined with diced onion and celery make a good salad.

Macaroni, spaghetti, or noodles may be successfully combined with cooked vegetables, marinated, and served mounded on lettuce leaves. Try it sometime.

GARNISHES FOR SALADS

When we talked about raw vegetable salads we spoke of decorating the salad so that it would have "eye appeal." A little gilding of the lily does not hurt any salad.

A colorless salad—that is, one made from any of the pastas, chicken salad, and all light salads—does not suffer a bit if a few wedges of tomato and a few slices of hard-cooked egg are used to liven it up and give it character.

Among the most popular garnishes are:

Hard-cooked eggs, chopped, sliced, or in wedges
Tomato, wedges or slices
Asparagus tips
Cooked beets, used with discrimination
Strips of sweet pepper, either green or red
Strips of pimento
Chives, chopped or minced
Parsley, chopped or minced
Sprinkling of paprika

MEAT AND FISH SALADS

The meat most often used for salads is chicken; but a combination of cold chicken, pork, and veal is very good. Cold diced rabbit may also be used in combination with other meats.

Any cooked fish may be used in a salad. Lobster, crab, and shrimp are prime favorites. Tuna and salmon are widely used. Smoked fish gives a salad a definite flavor.

The basic procedure for meat and fish salads is the same. You may vary the quantities in this recipe if you like.

2 cups meat or fish   Paprika
1 cup diced celery   French dressing
Seasoning   Mayonnaise
              Garnishes

Marinate the meat or fish in French dressing. (Marinate slightly; do not soak.) Chill. Combine with the celery and moisten with mayonnaise. Season. Heap or mound on lettuce leaves, garnish, sprinkle with paprika, and serve very cold with extra dressing.

FRUIT SALADS

If you are in a hurry, or are just plain lazy, you can buy canned fruit mix. It is good, but a fresh fruit salad is entirely different and is worth the time and trouble it takes to prepare the fruits. A combination of fruits is always good. The fresh fruits most often used (in season, of course) are:

Apples   Melons of all kinds, diced or in
Apricots   balls, add a delicious flavor
Bananas   Oranges
Cherries   Peaches
Figs   Pears
Grapes, seeded, worth the   Pineapple
   trouble   Strawberries
Grapefruit

Broken pieces of walnut meats and pecans or shredded almonds may be added to fruit combinations.

Prepare the fruit by peeling and either slicing or cubing. Put the fruit to be used in a bowl, dust lightly with powdered sugar, and sprinkle lightly with either lemon juice or lime juice. Allow the fruit to stand at room temperature for about 30 minutes. After 30 minutes place in the refrigerator and chill. Do not overdo the chilling. Fruits for salad should not be iced or too cold.

If you use fresh pineapple, cut the pineapple in half lengthwise, scoop out the fruit, and save the shells. Serve the salad in the pineapple shells. Try a tablespoon of Kirsch sprinkled over each serving, no other dressing.

If you want a dressing, use either mayonnaise or boiled dressing and fold in from ⅓ to ½ cup of whipped cream or try the honey dressing on page 273

Fruit salad may be served on lettuce leaves or on a bed of shredded lettuce and garnished with small lettuce leaves.

COTTAGE CHEESE AND FRUITS

When cottage cheese is used, it is generally the heart of the salad. Cottage cheese and pears or cottage cheese and pineapple slices are very popular served on lettuce with a little French dressing, and some of the fruit juice if canned fruit is being used.

ASPICS

There is a prepared packaged aspic on the market that is good and gives most satisfactory results. Follow the directions on the package. You may substitute tomato juice or stock for the liquid designated in the instructions. Always allow gelatin mixtures to thicken slightly before adding solids. Add about 1½ cups of diced cooked vegetables or a combination of vegetables and meat. Place in wet individual molds or a small wet ring mold and chill. Unmold before serving. One package serves 4–6, depending on the bulk of the additions.

TO UNMOLD: There are many ways to unmold jellied salads. Sometimes they can be contrary. Take molded jellies from the refrigerator and allow to stand at room temperature for 10 minutes before serving. Invert individual molds on lettuce leaves and lift off the mold. Invert ring molds on the plate from which they are to be served.

If at the required time the jelly has not dropped from the mold, you will have to take steps. Lift one edge of the mold just a little bit and peek under to see if the jelly has left the mold. No. Too bad. Wring out a towel in very hot water and place it on the mold for a few seconds, then take another peek. Be patient; it will come down. You may have to wet the towel several times. Be sure it is wrung fairly dry. You don't want water in your salad. You may have to apply the same treatment to the ring mold. Sometimes a gentle but determined tapping of the mold with the back of a knife will make it drop.

One sure way to unmold your jelly is to have a pan of very hot water ready when you take the molds from the refrigerator. Don't attempt to do anything else while you are doing this job, or you may melt your nicely molded salad. Hold the mold by the edges and insert the mold in the hot water for not more than 10 seconds. Lift from the hot water and turn onto the service plate. Sometimes molded jellies slip. They don't look good on the floor, so work quickly and carefully. Much of the unmolding difficulty may be circumvented by brushing inside of molds with a light coating of fine oil, peanut, sesame, or a French dressing if of suitable flavor.

GELATIN

If you don't have on hand, or can't get, a packaged aspic, but you do have some unflavored gelatin, here is a basic aspic recipe. But first, about unflavored gelatin: Buy it in packages or, if you will use a great deal, in bulk. Each envelope in a package contains 1 tablespoon of gelatin or enough to thicken and jell 2 cups (1 pint) of liquid.

Raw or unflavored gelatin must be softened in cold water, then dissolved in hot water.

A little acid in the liquid helps the jelling process.

If you intend to add bulk to your jelly and would like it to be stiff, use a little less than 2 cups of all liquids in your recipe.

If you are making a clear jelly from fruit juice or a jellied soup, use 2 full cups of liquid. Remember, a little acid always helps. You may use 1 tablespoon of lemon juice with fruit juices and either lemon juice or vinegar in aspics.

Remember, soften the gelatine in cold water or liquid before dissolving it in hot liquid. The cool liquid you use is part of your total 2 cups. Don't forget that!

BASIC ASPIC

1 tablespoon gelatin	Salt
¼ cup cold stock	Pepper
1¼ cups boiling stock	1 tablespoon sugar
2 tablespoons vinegar or lemon juice	1½ cups vegetables or meat may be inserted

M E T H O D: Dissolve the gelatin in ¼ cup of cold stock. Heat 1¼ cups of stock to the boiling point and pour over the melted gelatin in the cold stock. Mix well until the gelatin is melted. Add the acid and taste for seasoning. The stock has been salted and the vegetables or meat have been exposed to salt. You do not want too much. Add a little if you think it is needed. The same precaution is necessary with pepper, although meat and vegetable aspics can be a little "hot." Add the sugar and stir well. Chill.

Add the meat and vegetables after the jelly is well chilled but before it begins to set (thicken or jell).

With all jellies to be used in molds there is this trick to learn: Vegetables and meats will either float to the top or sink to the bottom of the mold. If you want your mold to look attractive, remove the jelly from the refrigerator after it has been well chilled. Perhaps you would like to put some slices of egg and some squares, circles, or diamonds of green pepper or pimento so they will be on the top of the mold when it is unmolded and will make it look attractive.

Slice your eggs and whatever you want to use in a decorative way. Place them in the bottom of the mold. Take a little of the jelly and pour over the arranged pieces. Use just enough jelly to cover them. Put the mold in the refrigerator and let it set. Keep the main bowl of jelly at room temperature. You may fill your mold little by little following this method, arrange layers of fruit or vegetables, using just a little jelly, and return the mold to the refrigerator after each addition. This may seem like a lot of bother, but it pays dividends in appearance.

TOMATO ASPIC

Use the recipe for Basic Aspic. Substitute tomato juice for the stock and add 1 tablespoon of onion juice.

NATURAL ASPIC

Remember when we were talking about soups that would jell because of the materials used in their preparation, veal and chicken bones, etc? That is a natural aspic jelly. If you have some on hand, by all means use it.

JELLIED FRUIT SALADS

There is always the packaged fruit gelatin to be used as a base. Lemon and lime can be used with almost anything, but use other flavors with discrimination, according to the fruit you are using with it.

Follow the directions on the package, then add your fruit just before the jelly mixture is ready to set.

CAUTION: Fresh pineapple won't work. If you have fresh pineapple, scald it before adding it to a jelly salad or a jelly dessert. Canned pineapple is all right to use.

If you have some fruit juice left over from canning, from cans of fruit or stewed fruit, make a gelatin from the liquid and use it for a salad or a dessert.

1 tablespoon unflavored gelatin	1¾ cups hot fruit juice
¼ cup cold fruit juice	1 tablespoon lemon juice
	Pinch of salt

Sugar if needed

M E T H O D: Soak the gelatin in the cold fruit juice. Add the hot fruit juice, the salt, the lemon juice, and the sugar if necessary. Chill.

Serve plain as a fruit jelly or use with fruits.

Save the juices from sweet pickled peaches and spiced fruits. They make an excellent base for a different jellied salad. Follow the above directions and then add either fruits or chopped raw cabbage and celery.

For a different flavor, add 2 tablespoons of sherry to amber-colored jellies; 2 tablespoons of burgundy to red ones.

CHAPTER XVI

BREADS, ROLLS, AND BISCUITS

H A V E you been tantalized by the smell of baking home-made bread? Have you known the delight of the crust of hot bread, golden brown, oozing with butter? If you haven't, it is worth a try.

Many new cooks are unnecessarily terrified at the thought of making bread. It does take time, but not nearly as much time as it did in Grandma's day. Perhaps you can remember the little stand which stood behind the kitchen stove and held the rising dough. We don't have to do it that way now. Life has been speeded up, and bread making along with it.

If you follow directions you will have good bread. The recipe below makes 4 large loaves. That may seem a lot of bread, but you will find it vanishes.

BREAD

P R E P A R A T I O N   T I M E: 4–5 hours

C O O K I N G   T I M E: about 45 minutes of baking time, 15 minutes in a hot oven (425°–450°), and 30 minutes more in a moderate oven (350°–375°)

2 cakes compressed yeast ⎫
¼ cup lukewarm water ⎬ First operation
1 teaspoon sugar ⎭
2 cups scalded milk
2 tablespoons vegetable shortening and 2 tablespoons butter
    (all vegetable shortening may be used)
1 tablespoon salt
2 tablespoons sugar
12 cups sifted enriched flour

1¾ cups water

Extra grease and flour

M E T H O D: First assemble all the things you are going to need —ingredients, 2 large bowls and 1 small, and a double boiler.

The first operation is to prepare the yeast. Put 1 teaspoon of sugar in a small bowl. Crumble the yeast over the sugar and then add ¼ cup of lukewarm water. Do not mix this. Set it aside while you work.

Put the 2 cups of milk in the double boiler and let that scald while you are preparing other ingredients.

Put the 4 tablespoons of shortening into a large bowl and add the salt and sugar.

Measure and sift 12 cups of flour into the other large bowl. Measure again after sifting.

When the milk is scalded, pour it over the shortening in the bowl and stir until the shortening is all melted. Then add the water and allow this mixture to stand until it has cooled to lukewarm. Do not be in a hurry to use the mixture when it is too hot. It will spoil the yeast if you do.

When the milk and water mixture is really lukewarm, add the yeast mixture and stir for a minute or two.

Now add the flour, about a cup at a time, and mix very thoroughly. If you measure the 12 cups into a container at one time and then use it until it is all gone, you won't lose count and make mistakes. When the flour is all incorporated into the liquid, you will have a stiff dough.

Sprinkle the surface of a pastry board or canvas lightly with flour. Transfer the stiff dough to the floured board and knead.

T O K N E A D D O U G H means to work or press dough with the hands until it is a smooth, pliable mass.

When kneading dough press it down with the palms of the hands. Fold it over and punch it down with the knuckles of your clenched fists. Push away from you as you press, then fold over, roll into a ball, flatten out, punch again, and repeat. Work at it until the dough is smooth and elastic—about 10 minutes. Extra flour is needed for the kneading process so that the dough does not stick to the board or the hands, but use as little extra flour as possible. When the dough is smooth, roll it into a ball and drop it into a large bowl which has been greased with shortening. Melt some extra shortening and brush the top of the ball of dough after it has been placed in the bowl. Cover the bowl with a folded tea towel and set it somewhere so that it will be out of a draft. A warm corner of the kitchen is best. The dough must now rise. It will take about 2 hours to double in bulk. Those 2 hours can be filled with other household chores.

When the dough has doubled in bulk, it is ready for the next step. It may take longer than 2 hours. If the kitchen is really warm it may not take the 2 hours.

Grease your bread pans before you begin the second operation.

Flour your board and place the raised dough onto the board. Sprinkle it lightly with flour and punch it down to remove all the air bubbles. Divide the dough into 4 equal parts. Knead each piece lightly this time, shape into loaf of a size to fit your pans, and then place it in a pan. Place the filled pans in a warm corner and cover them with a tea towel. The dough must double in bulk again while it is in the pan. This second rising takes about an hour.

Preheat your oven for baking to about 425°.

When the dough has doubled in bulk in the pans, prick the top of the loaves with the tines of a fork in about 7 places. Place the pans in the oven and bake at 425° for 15 minutes. Don't peek during this period. Don't peek at all if you can control your curiosity. The bread really will be better if you stay away from it while it is in the oven.

At the end of the first 15 minutes reduce the oven heat to 375° and bake for 30 minutes longer.

At the end of the total 45 minutes the bread should be a rich golden brown and smell like something dreamed about. Test with a cake tester or a stiff splint. If the splint or the tester comes out dry, the bread is done.

Remove from the pans at once. If you like a softer crust, brush the top of the loaves with melted butter when you take them out of the oven. Cool the bread on its side on a rack.

If you can control yourself allow the bread to cool at least 10 minutes before you cut off that crust to sample it.

SWEET OR COFFEE BREAD

If you can make plain bread, you can also make this coffee bread. And when you have tried this recipe, you will be able to make any coffee bread.

PREPARATION TIME: 4–5 hours

COOKING TIME: about 30 minutes

1 cup scalded milk	4½ cups sifted flour
1 cake compressed yeast	2 teaspoons cinnamon
¼ cup lukewarm milk	2 eggs, lightly beaten
¼ cup sugar	1½ cups seedless raisins
1 teaspoon salt	¼ cup chopped nuts
4 tablespoons butter or vege- table shortening	¼ cup honey
	Powdered sugar

METHOD: Scald the milk after all the ingredients have been assembled.

While the cup of milk is scalding, crumble the yeast cake into a small bowl, add ½ teaspoon of sugar taken from the ¼ cup, and the lukewarm milk. Let it stand.

Put the sugar, salt, and shortening into a large bowl and cover with the scalded milk. Mix this until the shortening is melted. Allow the mixture to cool to lukewarm.

While the mixture is cooling, measure 4½ cups of sifted flour. Add the 2 teaspoons of cinnamon and sift into a bowl. Beat the 2 eggs lightly.

When the milk and shortening mixture is lukewarm, add the

yeast mixture and mix. Add the beaten eggs. Add the sifted flour and cinnamon mixture, about a cup at a time, mixing thoroughly. Add the raisins and chopped nuts. Dust the raisins with flour before adding them to the dough.

When all ingredients have been incorporated, turn the dough on a floured board or canvas and knead lightly (see Bread). Grease a bowl and place the kneaded dough in the greased bowl. Grease the top of the dough. Cover bowl with a tea towel and allow the dough to rise in a warm place until double in bulk, about 2 hours. Do not remove from the bowl, but at the end of the first 2 hours, punch down or press out the air bubbles and allow the dough to rise again until double in bulk. This will take about 1 hour.

At the end of the second rising remove the dough from bowl and cut it into 2 equal parts.

Dust each part with flour and roll or press out with the palms of the hands until it forms a rectangle about 3 inches wide, 10 inches long, and ½ inch thick.

Cut each rectangle into 3 strips. Braid the three strips into a loaf, pinching the ends together. Place on a greased cookie sheet, cover with a tea towel, and allow to rise until about double in bulk.

Preheat your oven to 375°.

Bake the braids for 30 minutes.

When the braids are done, transfer them to a rack on a board and spread them with honey and dust them with powdered sugar. This bread is delicious when freshly baked. It also keeps well— if you can keep it.

ROLLS

This roll recipe is very versatile. The dough may be kept in the refrigerator and used as needed. It is flexible and may be used for plain rolls, or may be made into shapes, or the dough may be rolled to ½ inch thickness and cut into biscuit-size rolls. It makes good bread no matter how you use it.

PREPARATION TIME: about 2 hours

COOKING TIME: 12–15 minutes

1 cake compressed yeast	4 tablespoons shortening
½ teaspoon sugar	2 tablespoons butter
2 tablespoons lukewarm water	3 tablespoons sugar
1 cup hot water	1 egg, well beaten
1 teaspoon salt	4 cups sifted enriched flour

METHOD: Crumble the yeast cake in a small bowl, add the ½ teaspoon of sugar and the 2 tablespoons of lukewarm water.

Put the hot water, salt, shortening, butter, and the 3 tablespoons of sugar in a large bowl. Mix well until the shortening is dissolved. Allow to cool until it is lukewarm. Add the yeast mixture and stir. Add the beaten egg. Add about ⅔ of the sifted flour, mix well, and then beat. Add more flour, using the full amount to make a stiff dough.

If the dough is to be used at once, transfer to a floured board and knead lightly. Shape into small rolls, or roll out to ¼ inch thickness and cut with a biscuit cutter. Place on a greased baking or cookie sheet to rise until doubled in bulk. It usually takes about 1½ hours. Or shape in any of the following ways:

PARKER HOUSE ROLLS: Roll or pat the dough until it is ½ inch thick. Cut with a large round biscuit cutter. Butter half of the round, fold over, and press lightly. Place on greased cookie sheet to rise until doubled in bulk, about 1½ hours.

BOWKNOTS: Roll about ⅜ inch thick, cut into 6-inch strips ½ inch wide. Tie the strips into bowknots. Place on greased sheet and allow to double in bulk, about 1½ hours.

CRESCENTS: Roll about ⅜ inch thick and cut into 3-inch squares. Cut each square into 2 triangles and roll each triangle into crescents, beginning with the long side and rolling toward the point. Place on a greased cookie sheet and let rise until double in bulk.

When the dough has doubled in bulk, brush the tops with milk, melted butter, or diluted egg yolk. Place in an oven preheated to 400° and bake from 12 to 15 minutes.

If the dough is not to be used at once, cover after mixing and keep in the refrigerator until wanted. Remember, it will take about 1½ hours for the dough to rise to double its bulk and be ready for baking.

BAKING POWDER BISCUITS

First it is important to know something about baking powder. There are 3 common types:

1. Cream of tartar and tartaric acid
2. Calcium acid phosphate (double-action)
3. Sodium aluminum phosphate and calcium acid phosphate (double-action)

It is always wise to check the labels and see what you are buying. The cream of tartar type is the one used in the recipes in this book. If you have or must buy the phosphate type, numbers 2 and 3, use half the amounts specified in the recipes because all but the cream of tartar type are known as double-acting.

Biscuits seem to be the stumbling block for many a good cook. If you use good ingredients and follow directions you should be able to make good biscuits. Have a try at it.

PREPARATION TIME: about 20 minutes

COOKING TIME: about 12 minutes

2 cups sifted all-purpose flour   1 teaspoon salt
4 teaspoons baking powder   4 tablespoons shortening
¾ cup milk and water, mixed

METHOD: Put your flour sifter in a mixing bowl. Measure the 2 cups of sifted flour into the sifter, add the baking powder and salt, and sift. Transfer the sifted flour to a clean piece of waxed paper or a plate. Sift again into the mixing bowl. Put the shortening in the flour and cut in or blend. Remember, to cut in is to cut shortening into flour with a knife or a blender. Some cooks like to work the flour in with the tips of their fingers. (Not recommended if you use nail polish.) The fat should be cut into the flour until the fat is reduced to small particles.

Add the liquid a little at a time, mixing with a broad knife or a fork. Mix until all the flour is taken up and the dough is soft but not runny. Owing to differences in flour, a little more or a little less liquid may be needed. You want a dough that is soft and moist, that lumps about the spoon or knife as you mix it, a dough that has taken up all the flour. It must not be wet and runny because you want to be able to handle it. When the dough is mixed, take some flour and sprinkle it over your pastry board. Rub your hands with flour and pat the dough lightly, shaping it until it is about ½ inch thick and large enough to fit over the top of a filled baking dish, or is ready to be cut into biscuits.

If you are going to use the dough to cover the contents of a filled baking dish, lift it with both hands and put it in place. Press it lightly along the edges of the dish and put the dish in a pre-heated oven (450°) and bake from 12–15 minutes.

If you are making biscuits, cut them with a cutter, place on a greased baking sheet, and put in a hot oven (450°) and bake about 12 minutes. Never look at the biscuits during the first 12 minutes of baking time. Remember, no fair peeking. Leave them alone and they will probably be very good biscuits.

DROP BISCUITS

PREPARATION TIME: about 15 minutes

COOKING TIME: about 12 minutes

2 cups sifted all-purpose flour   1 teaspoon salt
4 teaspoons baking powder   4 tablespoons shortening
¾ cup milk and water, about half of each

M E T H O D: Follow directions for mixing Baking Powder Biscuits. Use all the liquid. The dough should be soft enough to drop from the spoon, but it must not be runny. It may be necessary to add a little extra liquid. Drop the dough by spoonfuls onto a greased cookie sheet and bake in a hot oven (450°) for 12 minutes, or a little longer if necessary.

SHORT OR RICH DOUGH

This is for crusts for meat pies and casserole dishes, extra tender biscuits, or for shortcakes.

P R E P A R A T I O N   T I M E: about 20 minutes

C O O K I N G   T I M E: about 12 minutes

2 cups sifted all-purpose flour   1 teaspoon salt
4 teaspoons baking powder   6 tablespoons shortening
¾ cup milk and water, about half of each

M E T H O D: Follow directions for Baking Powder Biscuits. For meat pie covering, roll or pat the dough to the size of dish to be covered. For shortcakes cut or shape to the desired size.

PREPARED MIXTURES

Now in case you do not feel up to making your own biscuit dough, buy a package of prepared biscuit flour, follow the directions carefully and you will have good biscuits.

CORN BREAD

Some people like thick corn bread. We like it thin and crunchy. We use a fairly large pan for this recipe to be sure to have thin bread. It may be baked in a cake tin or an 8-inch baking pan. It will be a little thicker than we like it but perhaps you like your corn bread fairly thick.

PREPARATION TIME: about 30 minutes

COOKING TIME: 25–30 minutes

1½ cups scalded milk	2 teaspoons sugar
1 cup corn meal	2 eggs, beaten
1½ tablespoons shortening	1½ teaspoons baking powder

½ teaspoon salt

METHOD: Scald the milk. Put the corn meal and shortening in a bowl. Pour the scalded milk over the corn meal and shortening, mix, and allow to cool. When the mixture is cool add the beaten eggs, baking powder, sugar, and salt. Mix well. Have your baking pan ready and greased. Pour the mixture into the pan and put it in a preheated hot oven (400°). Bake from 25 to 30 minutes until it is golden brown and crusty. Serve hot with butter.

MUFFINS

Muffins are easy to make. They offer a variety of choice of flours and ingredients. They are all equally good.

PREPARATION TIME: about 20 minutes

COOKING TIME: 20 to 25 minutes in a hot oven (400°)

See the Muffin Chart for the ingredients you will need for about 14 muffins.

METHOD: Combine and sift together the flour ingredients, sugar, baking powder, and salt. Add the beaten egg and milk. Mix well. Add the melted shortening. Dredge in flour all dry or well-drained berries, nuts, and raisins and add to the mixed batter. Stir them in, incorporating them in the batter. Fill well-greased muffin tins about ⅔ full. Bake in a hot oven (400°) for 20–25 minutes. After 20 minutes test with a cake tester. If no dough adheres to the tester, the muffins are done. Serve hot.

MUFFIN CHART

INGREDIENTS	Plain	Corn Meal	Bran	Whole-wheat	Berry	Nut or Raisin
Flour						
White	2 cups	1 cup	1 cup	1 cup	2 cups	2 cups
Corn meal		1 cup				
Bran			1 cup			
Whole-wheat				1 cup		
Sugar	2 tbsp.	2 tbsp.	2 tbsp.	2 tbsp.	2 tbsp.	2 tbsp.
Baking powder	4 tsp.	4 tsp.	4 tsp.	5 tsp.	4 tsp.	4 tsp.
Salt	1 tsp.	1 tsp.	1 tsp.	1 tsp.	1 tsp.	1 tsp.
Egg, beaten	1	1	1	1	1	1
Milk	1 cup	1 cup	1 cup	¾ cup	1 cup	1 cup
Shortening, melted	3 tbsp.	3 tbsp.	3 tbsp.	3 tbsp.	3 tbsp.	3 tbsp.
Berries					1 cup	
Nuts or raisins						¾ cup

CHAPTER XVII

DESSERTS

T H E word "dessert" covers a tremendous amount of territory—too large a territory for this book to cover. Here you will find only a few simple, reliable, "old-fashioned" desserts. If you have reached this point, you are now in a fair way to become a good cook. It is true that you have had no experience with desserts, but you have become familiar with cooking terms.

Some people like desserts very much, other people fear them because of their caloric content.

Dessert is a matter of personal choice and taste. With some meals a good sharp cheese, a few crackers, and coffee are more than adequate for dessert.

Fruit after a heavy starchy meal is a good choice for dessert.

If the meal has been light, then a rich dessert has its place.

CUSTARD DESSERTS

BAKED CUSTARD

P R E P A R A T I O N   T I M E: about 15 minutes

C O O K I N G   T I M E: about 45 minutes

For 6 servings you will need:

2 eggs, well beaten	½ teaspoon vanilla (or lemon
2 tablespoons sugar	extract or maple flavoring)
Pinch salt	Pinch nutmeg
2 cups rich milk	

M E T H O D: Beat the eggs. Add the sugar, salt, milk, flavoring, and nutmeg. Mix well. Pour into individual custard cups or a small baking dish. Place the custard cups or baking dish in a pan of hot water and put the pan in a slow oven (300°) and cook until done.

That sounds indefinite, but the time varies. Because the milk is not scalded in this recipe, it takes the custard longer to bake. But it makes a custard which is always firm, never waters, and keeps for days in the refrigerator.

Custard may be tested by piercing with a silver knife. If the knife comes out clean with no custard sticking to it, it is done. Another test is to place the bowl of a teaspoon on the custard. If the spoon sinks into the custard it is not done. If the custard will hold the weight of the spoon it is done and may be taken from the oven and cooled. It will take at least 45 minutes to bake.

CUSTARD PIE

The Baked Custard above makes a delicious filling for pie. When the mixture is ready pour it into a pie pan lined with pie crust and brushed with beaten egg, and baked in a hot oven for 10 minutes.

For Pie Crust see page 299.

Bake in a hot oven (425°) for 10 minutes, reduce heat to 300°, and cook until the custard sets, probably 30 minutes or longer.

COCONUT CUSTARD PIE

Add ¼ cup of shredded coconut to the recipe for Baked Custard. Bake as for Custard Pie.

BREAD PUDDING

This is an old stand-by and has been for years.

PREPARATION TIME: 20 minutes

COOKING TIME: about 45 minutes

For 4–6 servings you will need:

2 eggs

1½ cups bread crumbs—any kind, white, brown or raisin. Stale coffee cake or sweet buns may be diced and used

3 cups hot milk

¾ cup sugar

¼ teaspoon salt

½ teaspoon vanilla

2 tablespoons butter

½ cup nut meats, broken

½ cup raisins or currants

¼ teaspoon grated nutmeg

M E T H O D: Beat the eggs well. Add the crumbs, hot milk, sugar, salt, and vanilla, and mix well. Add the nut meats and the raisins and mix again. Put into a greased baking dish, dot with pieces of butter, sprinkle with nutmeg, and bake in a moderate oven (325°) for about 45 minutes, or until the pudding is firm. This may be served hot or cold without or with a sauce. Lemon sauce or boiled custard is good. Some people like whipped cream.

CHOCOLATE BREAD PUDDING

Follow the recipe for Bread Pudding. Add 3 squares of melted cooking chocolate to the mixture and omit the raisins and nutmeg.

RICE PUDDING

Please, no traffic with rice pudding made from cooked rice! This really is nothing but sweetened boiled rice with milk. Nor do you want rice pudding that needs to be cut with an ax. If you like a rich creamy rice pudding, try this one. This is frequently called "poor man's rice pudding."

P R E P A R A T I O N   T I M E: about 10 minutes

C O O K I N G   T I M E: about 2 hours

4 cups milk

3 tablespoons uncooked rice

3 tablespoons sugar

2 tablespoons butter

½ teaspoon vanilla

½ teaspoon salt

Sprinkling of nutmeg, light

M E T H O D: Put the milk in a baking pan. Wash and drain the raw rice. Either white or brown rice may be used. Add the rice to the milk, then the sugar, butter, vanilla, salt, and nutmeg. Mix well. Place the pan in a slow oven (250°–275°) and bake for at least 2 hours. The trick with this pudding is to stir it often. The milk will form a skin over the top of the pudding. Stir the mixture, turning in the skin. Do this as often as you think of it, the oftener the better. For the last 15 minutes allow the skin to form and cover the pudding. The pudding will be rich and creamy and really delicious.

If you like raisins, add ¼ cup to the other ingredients. It changes the flavor of the pudding somewhat but is still good.

T I P: Put the raisins in just after the last stirring. In 15 minutes they will be hot and plump and the pudding looks better than if raisins are cooked the whole 2 hours.

PIES

Pie crust is not difficult to make, but it does need some practice. If possible, buy yourself a pastry outfit, as described on page 37.

PIE CRUST

Don't make pie crust by the guess method. Measure carefully, use cold ingredients, work rapidly, roll lightly, and be sure to preheat your oven. Remember, pies should bake at a fairly high temperature for the first 10 or 15 minutes and then cook at a reduced heat.

P R E P A R A T I O N T I M E: about 30 minutes, including chilling

For a single crust you will need:

1½ cups sifted flour, either pastry or all-purpose	½ cup shortening 3 tablespoons cold water
1 teaspoon salt	

M E T H O D: Use a large mixing bowl. Sift the flour before measuring. All measurements are level.

Put the cold water, salt, and shortening in a bowl. Take a fork and cream the shortening in the water.

You may think this recipe sounds silly. The salt melts in the water, and all you seem to be doing is softening the shortening in a water bath. Just keep at it until the shortening is soft and pretty generally plastered over the bottom of the bowl. Add all the flour at once. Just dump it into the water and shortening mixture. Take a mixing spoon and start stirring. Stir around and around. It seems like a hopeless task at first, but as you persist with your stirring the ingredients blend and finally hold together in a rather compact ball, or at least the mass is now lumped together. Under no circumstances add more water. Put into the refrigerator for at least 15 minutes.

Take out of the refrigerator and place the wad of dough on a floured board or canvas. Start to roll. Roll from the center and roll lightly but firmly. Always roll out, away from the center; do not roll back. Shape your crust. If you find it has a tendency to run to points, cut off the long points and lay over the gaps. Do not try to stretch the crust. Roll until it is large enough to fit over your pie pan or plate.

Are you wondering how to get it into the pan? Roll it around the rolling pin. With the crust rolled about the pin, lay the pin over the pan and unroll. When you become expert you will be able to pick it up and drop it over the pan. Fit the crust into the pan. Trim off the edge at the edge of the pan. Your bottom crust is now ready for the filling, whatever it may be.

For a double crust you will need:

2 cups sifted flour	4 tablespoons cold water
⅔ cup shortening	1½ teaspoons salt

Follow the instructions given for single crust. When rolling, divide the dough into 2 sections, one slightly larger than the other. Use the larger piece for the bottom or shell.

After the filling is in, wet the edges of the shell with milk or water. Roll out the top crust and fit it on the pie. Press down along the edges. Cut some slits in the crust to allow the steam to escape.

For baking a pie, check the heat required for the particular filling you are using and preheat your oven. Many pie failures are due to not preheating the oven. Cook at high heat for 10 or 15 minutes, then reduce the heat and continue cooking.

When pies are filled with uncooked "timber," or filling, they should be placed on the bottom rack of the oven so that the bottom crust will be well baked.

KINDS OF PIE

Pie is probably our national dessert, with apple pie the prime favorite. There are 3 general classes of pie:

1. The double-crust pie
2. The deep-dish pie
3. The one-crust or open-face pie

You have two methods of making pastry (pages 293 and 299). Use the one that seems simpler and easier for you. Also, it is possible to buy a good pie mix. Follow directions on the package and you will get good results.

APPLE PIE

PREPARATION TIME: about 1 hour, including pastry

COOKING TIME: 10 minutes in a hot oven (450°) and then 25 to 30 minutes longer in a moderate oven (350°)

5 or 6 tart cooking apples	¼ teaspoon ground nutmeg
1 cup sugar	¼ teaspoon powdered cinna-
1 tablespoon butter	mon
2 tablespoons flour	2 tablespoons water

Pastry for double crust

Preheat your oven to 450°. Wash, peel, core, and slice the apples.

Line a 9-inch pie pan with plain pastry. Put the apples in the pastry shell and pour the sugar over the apples. Dot the surface with pieces of the butter, sprinkle with 2 tablespoons flour, and add the water. Sprinkle the nutmeg and cinnamon over the top. Moisten the edge of the crust. Place the top crust in place and press down firmly along the edge, using either your thumb or a fork. Pierce the top crust in several places with the tines of a fork to allow the steam to escape.

Place the pie on the bottom shelf of your hot oven and bake at 450° for ten minutes. Reduce the heat to 350° and bake from 25 to 30 minutes longer.

BERRY PIES

Boysenberry	Gooseberry
Blackberry	Huckleberry
Blueberry	Loganberry
Cherry *	Raspberry
Currant *	Strawberry

Youngberry

These pies may be made with a double crust or with a lattice top.

LATTICE-TOP PIES: To make a lattice top, prepare the crust and cut into long strips. Lay the strips over the top of the filling, leaving about a half inch between each strip. When one row of strips has been applied and fastened to the moist edge of the undercrust, put on a second row of strips at right angles to the first row.

PREPARATION TIME: about 1 hour

COOKING TIME: 10 minutes in a hot oven (450°) and about 30 minutes longer in a moderate oven (350°)

Pastry for double crust	2 teaspoons instant tapioca if
2 cups berries	desired
1 cup (or more) sugar	1½ tablespoons lemon juice
4 tablespoons flour	1 tablespoon butter

* Cherry and currant pies are included with berry pies because they are made the same way.

METHOD: Preheat your oven to 450°. Wash, hull, and clean the berries. Pit the cherries if you are using them. Put the berries or cherries in a bowl. Mix the flour and sugar. Sprinkle the flour and sugar over the berries. Sprinkle the tapioca over the mixture. Add the lemon juice. Mix gently with a spoon until well mixed. Let stand while you roll out and fit the bottom crust into the pie pan. You may roll the top crust and have it ready. Cut your top crust at least ½ inch larger than the pan so that it may be folded under bottom crust edge to keep the juices in the pan. Fill the pie pan with the fruit mixture. Dot with pieces of butter. Place the top crust or lattice on the fruit. Prick a full crust with the tines of a fork and bake for 10 minutes on the bottom shelf of a hot oven (450°). Reduce the heat to 350° and bake for another 30 minutes until top crust is a rich golden brown.

Berry and fruit pies are likely to boil over, so put a baking sheet in the bottom of the oven to catch any overflow.

FRUIT PIES

Apricot	Plum
Peach	Nectarine

Follow the instructions for Apple Pie. Use about 5 cups of sliced fruit. Increase the sugar if the fruit is particularly sour.

RHUBARB PIE

Follow the instructions for Apple Pie (p. 301). Use 4 cups of diced, unpeeled rhubarb, 2 cups of sugar, and about 2 tablespoons of water.

DEEP-DISH PIES

People who object to a wet and sometimes soggy bottom crust prefer the deep-dish pie. Any of the berry or fruit pies may be made as deep-dish pies. Follow the instructions for fruit or berry pie. Use either a deep pie pan or a baking dish. Just fill your baking dish with fruit and sugar mixture. A pinch of salt and about 1 teaspoon of lemon juice may be added to fruit pies.

Cover with a top crust—no bottom crust—slightly thicker than ordinary pie crust. About ¼ inch in thickness.

Preheat your oven to 450°. Bake for 10 minutes, then reduce the heat to 350° and bake about 30 minutes longer. Serve with ice cream, whipped cream, or a custard sauce.

COBBLERS

P R E P A R A T I O N   T I M E: about 45 minutes

C O O K I N G   T I M E: about 30 minutes

A cobbler is practically a deep-dish pie, using a rich biscuit dough instead of a pie crust. Serve with hard sauce, ice cream, whipped cream, or custard sauce.

Follow the instructions for fruit or berry pies.

For the biscuit dough to serve 4–6, you will need:

1 cup sifted all-purpose flour	3 tablespoons butter or short-
2 teaspoons baking powder	ening
½ teaspoon salt	6 tablespoons milk or cold
1½ teaspoons sugar	water

M E T H O D: Add the baking powder and salt to the sifted flour and sift again into a bowl. Add the sugar and cut in the shortening. Add the milk and stir rapidly until the dough lumps and is free from the edge of the bowl. This should not take more than part of a minute. Don't stir too much or too long. Place the dough on a floured board or the pastry canvas. Roll gently until about ¼ inch thick and large enough to cover the baking dish. Place over the fruit. Press down the edges and trim excess dough with a sharp knife.

Place in a hot oven (425°) and bake for about 30 minutes.

ONE-CRUST OR OPEN PIES

Any of the fruit pies may be baked without a top crust, although it is not a common practice. The usual one-crust pies are:

Butterscotch   Chocolate
Custard   Lemon
           Vanilla Cream

A very suitable filling for butterscotch, chocolate, lemon, or vanilla cream pie may be made from the packaged puddings sold in the markets. The package usually has instructions for the use of the pudding as a pie filling. Add a little more chocolate (1 melted square) to the chocolate pudding and grate the rind of 1 lemon into the prepared lemon pudding.

A favorite lemon filling is made from sweetened condensed milk.

CONDENSED-MILK LEMON PIE

1 large can sweetened condensed milk (about 1⅓
 cups)
Grated rind of 1 lemon

½ cup lemon juice
2 eggs, separated
2 tablespoons granulated
 sugar

M E T H O D: Empty the condensed milk into a bowl. Add the lemon juice and grated rind and the lightly beaten egg yolks. Mix. The mixture thickens as you work with it. The egg whites may be used for a meringue (p. 307) or incorporated into the filling, as follows:

Beat the egg whites until stiff, adding the granulated sugar about a teaspoon at a time and whipping after each addition until the sugar is all incorporated and the whites stiff. Fold the whites into the milk and lemon mixture. Pour into a graham cracker crust. Put the filled crust into a slow oven (300°) for 15 minutes, or simply put it in the refrigerator until ready to serve.

GRAHAM-CRACKER PIE CRUST

This simple crust should hold no terrors for the beginner. You will need 1½ cups of graham cracker crumbs (about 22 crackers).

Roll the crackers on a board with a rolling pin until they are fine crumbs. If you put a sheet of waxed paper on the board before rolling, it will enable you to lift and pour the crumbs easily. Measure the crumbs into a bowl and mix them with ⅓ cup of powdered sugar. Cream ½ cup of butter or margarine before adding to the crumbs and sugar. Mix well. Take a little of the mixture at a time and pat it into position around the edges of a pie plate. Use the back of a tablespoon or your fingers. When the sides are covered, cover the bottom of the dish. Place in a refrigerator and allow to stand for several hours before adding the pie filling.

When preparing the graham cracker crust for a chocolate filling, add ½ teaspoon of cinnamon or nutmeg to the cracker-sugar mixture.

For a butterscotch filling, add 3 drops of almond extract to the cracker-sugar mixture.

For a vanilla filling, add ½ teaspoon of powdered ginger to the crust mixture.

COLD PIES

Make a graham-cracker shell and then fill it with:

Thick applesauce, topped with meringue or whipped cream.

Fresh or frozen sugared strawberries topped with meringue or whipped cream.

Fresh or frozen sugared peaches topped with meringue or whipped cream.

You can realize the possibilities and variations of this dessert.

If you plan on baking a meringue on your filling, remember that glass is susceptible to heat. Take the glass pie plate out of the refrigerator and allow it to come to room temperature before placing it in the oven.

PIE SHELLS

Some pie filling does not need any baking. The graham-cracker crust is generally used for such pies, but some people prefer a baked pastry shell.

You may have a special pie plate for baking shells—a perforated double pie plate. In that case you simply drape your pie crust over the back of the smaller half and clamp the larger one in place. But if you have only ordinary pie plates, do this:

Line the pie plate with your pastry. Prick the shell all over to let the air escape. Bake on the top shelf of a very hot oven (500°) to set the edges quickly and prevent shrinking. If the edges seem in danger of browning too much, transfer to the lower shelf for the rest of the time, 10–12 minutes in all.

If the shell starts to bulge during the first few minutes, prick it again with a fork and it will lie flat. Another way to prevent bulging is to set another pie plate the same size inside the first one with the crust between them—or a double layer of dried beans will hold it flat. The pie plate or the beans must be removed before the shell is done so the bottom can crisp.

MERINGUES

MERINGUE FOR PIE

One-crust pies are often topped with meringue. There is no particular secret to making a good meringue. The trick is a lot of beating. To cover 1 pie you will need:

> 2 egg whites
> 4 tablespoons sugar, granulated or powdered
> ¼ teaspoon cream of tartar
> Pinch salt

Beat the egg whites until foamy.

TO BEAT EGG WHITES FOAMY: Beat only slightly, until large bubbles are formed on the surface.

Add the salt and the cream of tartar. Beat again until the whites are stiff but not dry. Now add the sugar, ½ teaspoonful at a time, beating well after each addition. Beat until all the sugar has been absorbed and the whites will form peaks when the beater is lifted up and out of them. To cover a pie, pour the meringue over the pie and shape with a spatula. Spread lightly. You want to keep all that air that you have beaten into it. Make sure it touches the sides or the meringue is likely to contract. Bake in a slow oven (300°) for 15 to 20 minutes. Cool slowly.

MERINGUE SHELLS

Filled meringue shells make a good dessert. They may be filled with ice cream, creamed puddings, or fruits and topped with whipped cream. They are not desserts for people who want to stay slim but they can be delightful.

Use these proportions:

1 egg white	⅛ teaspoon cream of tartar
4 tablespoons sugar	Few grains salt

Follow the beating instructions under Meringue for Pie. Drop by large spoonfuls onto a cookie sheet. Bake in a slow oven (250°) 45–60 minutes. When the meringues are done and while they are still warm, prepare them for the filling. If they are to be used singly, press a hole in the top by gently pressing with the thumb. If two meringues are to be used together, puncture the bottom with the thumb. After filling, press 2 together. They must be handled lightly, for they are very delicate.

COOKIES

A well-filled cookie jar is a versatile adjunct to a busy house-wife. Cookies make a good snack at any time. They add a touch to stewed fruit or ice cream, and they buck you up no end when someone drops in unexpectedly for tea.

DROP COOKIES

These cookies are good but not particularly rich. They are easy to make and keep well in a jar—if you can keep the family away from them.

PREPARATION TIME: about 30 minutes

COOKING TIME: 12–15 minutes for 1 cookie sheetful

For 5 dozen cookies you will need:

1 cup butter or margarine	1 teaspoon salt
¼ cup white sugar	4 cups sifted flour
1 cup brown sugar	2 eggs, lightly beaten
2 teaspoons baking powder	½ cup milk
¼ teaspoon soda	1 teaspoon vanilla
1 cup chopped raisins	

METHOD: Cream the shortening and sugars until well blended. Add the eggs and the vanilla and cream to the sugar and shortening. Add the baking powder, soda, and salt to the sifted flour and sift again. Add some of the flour to the egg and shortening mixture and mix well. Add a little of the milk and mix well. Add alternately the balance of the flour and milk a little at a time until all are well blended. Mix in chopped raisins. Lightly grease the cookie sheet and drop the dough by spoonfuls onto it. Bake in a moderate oven (350°) 12–15 minutes. Remove from the sheet with a spatula and cool on a platter.

RAISIN AND NUT COOKIES

Follow the basic recipe for Drop Cookies. Add:

¼ teaspoon powdered clove
¼ teaspoon powdered cinnamon
1 cup chopped nut meats

CANDY COOKIES

Follow the basic recipe for Drop Cookies. Omit the raisins and substitute:

1½ cups diced gum drops or
1½ cups diced candied orange peel or 1½ cups diced candied
cherries

DATE AND NUT COOKIES I

Follow the basic recipe for Drop Cookies. Omit the raisins and substitute:

1 cup chopped pitted dates
1 cup chopped nut meats

Or you may try some combinations of your own. Any dried fruit may be chopped and added. Figs are good. Mixed candied fruit may be used. Any jellied candy may be used.

DATE AND NUT COOKIES II

PREPARATION TIME: about 30 minutes

COOKING TIME: 12–15 minutes for 1 cookie sheetful

For 3 dozen cookies you will need:

2½ cups sifted flour	1 teaspoon cinnamon
1 cup butter or margarine	½ teaspoon nutmeg
1½ cups brown sugar	3 eggs, lightly beaten
½ teaspoon soda	1 cup chopped or cut-up dates
¼ teaspoon salt	1 cup chopped walnuts

METHOD: Put the flour in a large mixing bowl and cut in the shortening until well blended. Add the sugar, salt, and soda. Cream with the flour and shortening. Add the cinnamon and nutmeg. Add dissolved soda to the lightly beaten eggs and mix. Blend with the mixture. Add the dates and nuts. Mix very well and drop from a spoon onto a lightly greased cookie sheet. Bake in a moderate oven (350°) 12–15 minutes. The cookies should be a light brown.

RAISIN BARS

PREPARATION TIME: about 30 minutes

COOKING TIME: 30 minutes

For 3 dozen cookies you will need:

½ cup butter or margarine	2 eggs, well beaten
1 cup granulated sugar	¾ cup sifted cake flour
2 squares unsweetened cooking chocolate, melted	¼ teaspoon baking powder
	¼ teaspoon salt

¾ cup seedless raisins

M E T H O D: Cream the shortening. Add the sugar and cream with the shortening. Add the beaten eggs and the melted chocolate.

N O T E: To melt chocolate you may appreciate this method: Put a large piece of waxed paper in the top of the double boiler. Put the chocolate in the waxed paper. When it has melted, lift out the paper, use the chocolate, and have no messy pot to clean.

Blend the eggs and chocolate into the creamed sugar and short-ening. Sift the flour, baking powder, and salt into the mixture. Add the raisins and mix well. Lightly grease a shallow 8-by-10 pan. Put the mixture in the pan and even it with a spatula. Bake in a moderate oven (350°) for 30 minutes. Cut into squares or bars.

CHOCOLATE COOKIES

Perhaps the most famous of all chocolate cookies today is the Toll House Chocolate Chip Cookie. In fairness to Ruth Wakefield, who originated the vogue for this cookie, and the many manufac-turers of chocolate chips, you should get the recipe first from her good book, "Toll House Recipes," or from one of the packages of chocolate chips.

Here is another chocolate cookie which is easy to make:

P R E P A R A T I O N   T I M E: about 20 minutes

C O O K I N G   T I M E: 15 minutes for 1 cookie sheetful

For 2 dozen cookies you will need:

1 cup toasted bread crumbs   1 cup chopped nut meats
2 squares unsweetened choco- ½ teaspoon vanilla
    late, melted   ⅛ teaspoon salt
            1 15-oz. can sweetened condensed milk

M E T H O D: Toast 3 or 4 slices of bread until golden brown. Dry thoroughly in the oven. Melt the chocolate in the top of a double boiler. Roll the dry toasted bread with a rolling pin on a sheet of waxed paper. Add the condensed milk to the melted chocolate. Mix well. Add the vanilla and salt and mix. Add the nut meats to the bread crumbs. Add the combination to the condensed milk mixture and mix well. Use a teaspoon to drop the cookies on a lightly greased cookie sheet. Bake in a moderate oven (350°) for 15 minutes. Remove to a platter at once to cool.

MERINGUE NUT DROPS

We usually make these when we have used egg yolks for Hollandaise sauce. They are delicious.

PREPARATION TIME: about 30 minutes

COOKING TIME: about 1 hour

For 25–30 cookies you will need:

2 egg whites   1 teaspoon vanilla
½ cup confectioners' sugar   ¾ cup finely chopped nut meats

M E T H O D: Beat the egg whites. Add the confectioners' sugar a tablespoonful at a time and continue beating until the sugar has been used and the mixture is dry and foamy. Add the vanilla and chopped nuts, folding them into the mixture. Dip a piece of unglazed wrapping paper into water, then lay it over your cookie sheet. Drop the cookie dough by teaspoonfuls onto the paper. Bake in a slow oven (250°) for about 1 hour. Remove from the paper at once to cool.

These cookies are brittle, so handle them gently. If they stick to the paper, dampen the underside of the paper and they will come off easily.

FRUIT-PULP COOKIES

PREPARATION TIME: about 30 minutes

COOKING TIME: 15 minutes

For 50 cookies you will need:

1 cup sugar	1 cup unsweetened fruit pulp
½ cup shortening	(applesauce, persimmon,
1 egg	peach, apricot, or nectar-
1 cup chopped nuts	ine pulp may be used)
1 cup chopped raisins	½ teaspoon powdered clove
½ teaspoon soda	½ teaspoon powdered nutmeg
	½ teaspoon powdered cinnamon
	½ teaspoon salt

2 cups sifted flour

METHOD: Cream the sugar and shortening. When well blended add the unbeaten egg, nuts, and raisins and mix well. Add the soda to the fruit pulp. Sift the spices and salt with the flour. Add some of the fruit pulp to the shortening mixture. Add some flour and mix well. Alternate the fruit pulp and flour until all has been incorporated and is well blended. After mixing, put the batter in the refrigerator for several hours. When ready to bake, drop by teaspoonfuls on a lightly greased cookie sheet and bake in a moderate oven (350°) for 15 minutes.

OATMEAL COOKIES

This cookie may be made at any time, shaped into long rolls wrapped in waxed paper, and placed in the refrigerator to chill thoroughly. It may be kept in the refrigerator for days or weeks.

PREPARATION TIME: about 30 minutes

COOKING TIME: 10 minutes for 1 cookie sheetful

For 5 dozen cookies you will need:

1 cup butter or margarine	1½ cups sifted flour
1 cup brown sugar	1 teaspoon salt
1 cup granulated sugar	1 teaspoon soda
2 eggs, beaten	3 cups quick-cooking oatmeal
1 teaspoon vanilla	½ cup chopped walnuts

M E T H O D: Cream the shortening and the sugars until completely blended. Add the beaten eggs and the vanilla. Beat this into the creamed shortening and sugar. Your arm will tire, but the results will be worth it. Sift the salt and soda with the flour and add to the mixture. Mix well. Add the oatmeal and the nut meats. Stir until well incorporated. Take a handful of the dough and form into a long roll. Make several. Wrap the rolls in waxed paper and place in the refrigerator. Chill thoroughly before baking.

When ready to bake, cut in ¼-inch slices and bake on an ungreased cookie sheet in a moderate oven (350°) for 10 minutes. These cookies are crisp and crunchy. The nice thing about refrigerator cookies is that you don't have to bake them all at once.

CAKE

Layer cake, like pie, is a popular American dessert. And you can now make a cake. There are several things you should know, however, before you begin.

CAKE POINTERS:

1. Never experiment with the recipe you are using. Follow it carefully.

2. Use exact and level measurements.

3. Sift the flour before measuring.

4. Do not use damp flour.

5. Have the butter or shortening and other ingredients at room temperature.

6. Read your recipe carefully. Assemble all the things you are going to need.

7. Do not melt the butter unless the recipe calls for melted butter or shortening.

8. Grease your cake pans before you start your cake batter.

9. Preheat your oven to the required temperature.

10. As soon as your cake batter is mixed, fill your pans and bake at once.

11. If you use commercial unsalted shortening instead of butter, you must add double the specified amount of salt. Or if no salt is specified, add ¼ teaspoon per cup of flour.

12. Test your cake with a wire cake tester or a straw. Grandma used a splint from the broom, which may not have been sanitary, but it works.

13. When a cake is done it shrinks away from the sides of the pan.

14. When a cake is done it will spring back when pressed lightly with the fingers.

15. When a cake is cool put filling between layers and frost or ice.

STANDARD BUTTER CAKE

This recipe is known by several names—Foundation or Plain Cake, Standard Cake, or Layer Cake. Its uses are many. After mixing, it may be baked in a greased and slightly floured loaf tin for 50–60 minutes in a moderate oven (350°). Or it may be baked in muffin or cupcake tins, lightly greased, for about 20 minutes in a moderate oven (375°). Or it will make 2 9-inch layers baked in 2 lightly greased cake pans in a moderate oven (375°) 25–30 minutes.

PREPARATION TIME: about 30 minutes

COOKING TIME: depending on how cooked (see above)

⅓ cup butter or other shortening

1 cup granulated sugar

2 eggs, separated

2 cups sifted cake flour

3 teaspoons baking powder

¼ teaspoon salt

⅔ cup milk

1 teaspoon vanilla

METHOD: Sift your sugar at least twice. Place the shortening or butter in a bowl and cream. Add the sugar, a tablespoon at a time. Cream and beat well until all the sugar has been added. Beat until your tired arm can take no more. Now add the well-beaten egg yolks and beat again. Your arm should be able to take it. When the egg and mixture are well blended, add the vanilla and mix well.

You sifted the flour before measuring. Now sift all the dry ingredients with the flour. Add a little flour to the first mixture, mix, add a little milk and mix again. Alternate the flour and milk until both have been well mixed with the first mixture, but don't overdo the mixing. Beat the egg whites until stiff and pour into the mixture, mixing lightly until well blended.

The batter is now ready for a greased loaf pan, the muffin tins, or layer tins. This amount will make 3 8-inch layers or 2 9-inch ones.

Place the cake in a preheated oven and bake according to times listed above.

NOTE: Not all cake batters are beaten, so read your recipes carefully. If the instructions tell you to separate the eggs, to beat the whites until stiff and "fold in," do it and do not beat. Remember that. Never beat a mixture into which you have folded stiffened egg whites unless the instructions say "beat."

When the cake is done, cool. When cool, fill the layers and frost, or frost the loaf or cupcakes.

When making a loaf cake you may add to the batter ¾ cup of lightly floured raisins, nut meats, currants, or unflavored coconut. Use a pan about 3 by 5 by 9 inches.

TO FLOUR RAISINS OR NUT MEATS FOR A CAKE
means to sprinkle the nuts or raisins with a light coating of flour. This helps to distribute them evenly through the batter.

Also with any one of the above additions, you may add spices to the flour just before the final sifting, as follows:

1 teaspoon cinnamon
½ teaspoon powdered clove
¼ teaspoon nutmeg

This one cake recipe will make you a truly versatile cake maker.
You can vary your frostings and fillings. You can vary your loaf cakes. You can vary your layer cakes and the family need never know, unless you let them read this book, that you start with just one recipe.

EFFECT OF ALTITUDE. If you live in high places at an altitude from 3000 to 5000 feet, you have a problem with cakes. The higher you go, the less sugar and baking powder you will need. At this altitude take out 1 tablespoon of sugar and ½ teaspoon of baking powder.

From 5000 to 7500 feet, take out 2 tablespoons of sugar and ½ teaspoon of baking powder. Increase your baking temperature about 10 degrees.

From 7500 to 10,000 feet, take out ¼ cup of sugar, 1 teaspoon of baking powder, and 1 tablespoon of shortening. Increase your baking temperature about 15 degrees.

You may have to experiment a little to find just the right amounts for your particular altitude.

CAKE FILLINGS AND FROSTINGS

If you have made a layer cake you will want a filling between the layers. A favorite cake filling and frosting is a pint of cream, beaten until very stiff. Stop before the butter stage. Sweeten lightly with powdered sugar, about 2 tablespoons, and mix in ½ teaspoon of vanilla. If there should be any cake left, store it in the refrigerator.

BANANA FILLING

PREPARATION TIME: about 30 minutes

1 cup whipping cream
6 tablespoons confectioners' sugar
Pinch salt
1 cup banana pulp or thin slices
½ teaspoon vanilla

METHOD: Beat the cream until stiff. Add the sugar, vanilla, and salt. Fold in the banana. Spread between the layers and over the sides and top of the cake. Bananas darken rapidly. This cake should be eaten up and not saved.

CREAM FILLING

PREPARATION TIME: about 10 minutes

COOKING TIME: about 15 minutes

5 tablespoons sugar
3 tablespoons flour
Pinch salt
1 egg, beaten
1 cup milk
1 teaspoon vanilla

METHOD: Mix the sugar, flour, and salt in the top of a double boiler. Add the beaten egg and mix well. Place over boiling water in the double boiler. Add the milk gradually and cook until the mixture thickens. Stir or it will be lumpy. When the mixture cools, add the vanilla. Spread between the layers of a cake or use for Boston Cream Pie.

COFFEE CREAM FILLING: Take out 3 tablespoons of milk and add 3 tablespoons double-strength coffee.

CHOCOLATE CREAM FILLING: Add 4 tablespoons of sugar and 1 square of melted chocolate.

BOSTON CREAM PIE

After a layer of cake has cooled, cut the layer in half horizontally. Use a bread knife or a cake knife—either will work better than an ordinary knife. Pile Cream Filling on the lower half of the cut layer. Replace the top and powder with confectioners' sugar.

UNCOOKED FROSTING OR ICING

This is often called "confectioners' icing or frosting."

    1½ tablespoons butter or 1 egg yolk, beaten
    1½ cups sifted confectioners' sugar
    3 tablespoons milk or cream
    1 teaspoon vanilla
    ⅛ teaspoon salt

M E T H O D: Cream the butter and add the sifted sugar, creaming together. Or beat the yolk well, add the sifted sugar, and cream together until well blended. Add the milk or cream, a tablespoon at a time, until the frosting is the right consistency to spread. You may not need all the milk. Add the salt and vanilla. Mix well and spread on the cake.

C H O C O L A T E F R O S T I N G: Add 3 tablespoons of cocoa to the sugar and sift.

M O C H A F R O S T I N G: Add 2 tablespoons of cocoa to the sugar and use 3 tablespoons of double-strength coffee instead of milk.

M A P L E F R O S T I N G: Use 3 tablespoons of maple syrup instead of the milk.

F R U I T F R O S T I N G: Crushed drained berries or fruit make a different and satisfying frosting. Add the fruit or berries to the sugar and cream. Do not add all the liquid at once. Add it gradually to keep the frosting the right spreading consistency. It must not be runny.

SEVEN-MINUTE FROSTING

PREPARATION TIME: about 5 minutes

COOKING TIME: 7–10 minutes

1 cup sugar

4 tablespoons water

1 egg white

½ teaspoon vanilla

METHOD: Have hot water in the lower section of a double boiler. Put the sugar, water, and unbeaten egg white in the top section. Put over the hot water. Start beating and beat constantly until the frosting is thick enough to spread. It takes from 7 to 10 minutes. When it has reached spreading consistency, add the vanilla and frost the cake, using a spatula or a broad knife.

FRUIT-PULP PUDDING

PREPARATION TIME: about 30 minutes

COOKING TIME: 1½ hours

For 6 to 8 servings you will need:

Persimmon pulp

Peach pulp

Apricot pulp, or

Plum pulp

1 cup sugar

1 cup fruit pulp

1 teaspoon soda

2 tablespoons melted butter

¼ teaspoon cinnamon

½ teaspoon salt

1 egg, well beaten

1 cup sifted flour

½ cup chopped nut meats

½ cup chopped raisins

METHOD: Mix the sugar and fruit pulp. Add the soda and mix well. Add the melted butter. Sift the cinnamon and salt with the flour. Add the egg to the pulp mixture, then the flour. Mix well. Add the chopped nuts and raisins. Mix well. Turn into a loaf pan. Place the loaf pan in a large baking pan with hot water and bake in a moderate oven (350°) for 1½ hours. Test with a cake tester or splint. If the tester is dry, the pudding is done.

A pint of soft vanilla ice cream makes a good sauce. If desired add some sherry or brandy, about a tablespoon, to the sauce.

LAST ADVICE

If you have tried the cake recipe and are familiar with the method, if you now know how to cream shortening, if you understand the difference between mix, beat, and fold in, you will be able to attack any cake or cookie recipe. Be sure to follow the directions carefully. When it says "cream," then cream. Don't expect to have good cake by makeshift methods.

For the beginner there are several good cake mixes on the market. There is one for gold cake, white cake, spice cake, devil's food, and there is always a gingerbread mix. Follow directions. They have been carefully tested to give best results. You won't have many failures if you do as you are told.

CHAPTER XVIII

SOME JAMS AND JELLIES

T H E making of jams and jellies need not be a difficult task. It is important to follow directions, to measure carefully, and to cook no longer than necessary.

Good jam or jelly requires 3 things: acid, pectin, and sugar. You can't make jelly or jam without them.

Most fruits contain enough acid, although there are some exceptions. Very ripe apples lose much of their acid. Solid-meated grapes contain very little acid. Mulberries seem to have no acid at all when they are ripe enough for use. Our old ally the lemon comes to our aid with its juice. Lemon juice can be added to the non-acid fruits, and a small amount of lemon juice to any ripe fruit helps in the jam and jelly making.

Pectin is found in most fruits, but there are some fruits which are lacking in this natural substance. Strawberries and pineapple contain very little pectin. Very ripe fruits seem to lose much of their natural pectin. That is one of the reasons why jelly recipes suggest the use of partially ripened fruit.

If fruit lacks pectin, then pectin must be added, either by combining the fruit which lacks pectin with a fruit rich in pectin or by the use of commercial pectin.

Many cooks dislike commercial pectin. Others believe that it gives more and better flavored jellies or jams, and certainly it saves time. If you have never used it, try it. Follow directions and see for yourself how good the jam or jelly will be.

JELLY MAKING

In order to make jelly it is necessary to have juice. Small amounts of juice cooked in a wide-open kettle give best results.

PREPARING JUICES I

Hard fruits such as apples, crabapples, guavas, pears, and quinces should be well washed. After washing, do not peel or core. Cut the fruit into eighths or sixteenths. Do not remove the seeds. About 8 pounds of fruit should make enough juice for 1 batch of jelly.

After cutting the fruit, measure into a wide kettle. Do not use an iron one. Aluminum or agate pans are best. Add enough water barely to cover the prepared fruit. Place the kettle over the heat and bring to a boil slowly. Simmer until the fruit becomes mushy.

The fruit is now ready for a jelly bag, which can be a 10-pound sugar bag, bleached. Scald the jelly bag with boiling water before adding the fruit pulp. You can buy jelly making outfits in hardware stores, which are composed of a stand to hold the bag so that it will drip into a bowl or kettle. A nail over the sink somewhere or even the spigot will do if you have nothing else to fasten the bag to.

Fill the bag with the pulp and allow it to drip. You can prepare the fruit and allow it to drip overnight. For clear fine jelly, do not squeeze the bag at all, but use only the juice which drips through by gravity.

For a second batch, squeeze the bag. This jelly, however, will be cloudy.

PREPARING JUICES II

Soft fruits such as apricots, peaches, plums, and berries should be washed, then cut into small pieces and measured into a kettle, using ¼ cup of water for each 4 cups of fruit.

Mash the fruit and bring to a boil slowly. Cook for a few minutes. Transfer the pulp and juice to a jelly bag and allow to drip.

If you use commercial pectin, you can crush the berries and allow them to drip without any cooking at all.

OTHER PREPARATIONS IN JELLY MAKING

The glasses in which jelly is to be kept should be sterile. Wash in hot soapy water, rinse well, scald with boiling water, and then place on a cookie sheet and put them in a 200° oven. Keep them hot until ready to fill.

Have your paraffin ready to float on the jelly as soon as it is put into the glasses. Use an old teapot for the paraffin. Put the unmelted wax in the teapot, place the teapot in a pan of water, and place the pan on an asbestos mat over a low flame. Paraffin can be dangerous. Never melt it over an open flame.

APPLE JELLY

Prepare the juice according to instructions. Measure it into a large open kettle. If you have used fully ripe apples, add 2 tablespoons of lemon juice for every 4 cups of juice. If you use tart, underripe fruit, no lemon juice is needed. Measure ¾ cup of sugar for each cup of juice into a separate bowl.

Bring the juice to a boil, then add the sugar, stirring well.

After the sugar is added, keep stirring. Cook over a hot fire until the jelly is boiling fully. It will take about 15 minutes or longer. Keep testing. The spoon test is used by most experienced cooks. When the jelly is about ready, the liquid will run from the tilted spoon in two streams. As most of the liquid leaves the spoon, the last few drops will run together and form a triangular sheet.

The saucer test is another method for testing jelly. Put a small amount of the jelly on a saucer and cool quickly. If you use the saucer test you should remove the kettle from the fire while the sample is cooling, or you may overcook the jelly. If the cooled sample is definitely jelly, you are ready to fill your glasses.

Or you can test with a candy thermometer. At sea level the jelly is done at 220°. At high altitudes the temperature is lower.

First remove any scum which may float on the surface of the liquid.

Fill your glasses within ¼ inch of the top. Coat at once with a thin layer of melted paraffin.

When cool, label, cover, and store in a cool, dark place.

CRABAPPLE JELLY

Follow directions for Apple Jelly, using 1 cup of sugar for each cup of juice.

GUAVA JELLY

Follow directions for Apple Jelly. Add 1 tablespoon of lemon juice for each cup of juice. Use 1 cup of sugar for each cup of juice.

STRAWBERRY JELLY

Follow directions for Apple Jelly or use commercial pectin and follow the directions that come with it. Add ¼ cup of lemon juice for 4–6 cups of juice. Use ¾ cup of sugar for each cup of juice.

BERRY JELLIES

Follow the directions for Apple Jelly. If all fully ripe fruit is used for the juice, then lemon juice must be added. Use 2 to 4 tablespoons for 4–6 cups of juice. Use ¾–1 cup of sugar for each cup of juice.

GRAPE JELLY

Follow directions for Apple Jelly. If fully ripe fruit is used for juice, add 2–4 tablespoons of lemon juice for 4–6 cups of juice. Use ¾–1 cup of sugar.

QUINCE JELLY

Follow directions for Apple Jelly. Use ¾ cup sugar for each cup of juice.

COMBINATION JELLIES

CURRANT AND RED RASPBERRY: use 1 cup of sugar for each cup of juice.

APPLE AND PINEAPPLE: use ¾ cup sugar for each cup of juice.

PLUM AND APPLE: use 1 cup of sugar to each cup of juice.

JAMS

Jam is made from a combination of juice and pulp. When preparing fruit for jam, wash, core, and pit it.

Hard fruits must be softened by cooking before being mashed. Soft fruits and berries may be mashed before cooking. A good jam has the fruit evenly distributed throughout.

The old-fashioned method of making jam, and it is good, requires pound for pound or cup for cup of sugar and fruit pulp.

Apricots, peaches, berries, plums, and other soft fruits may be prepared, crushed, and measured in a kettle. Add an equal amount of sugar to the fruit and allow to stand overnight.

The fruit and sugar must be thoroughly mixed and heated slowly until the sugar is dissolved. Once the sugar is dissolved, the heat should be increased and the mixture boiled rapidly, stirring often to prevent scorching or burning.

It takes 20 minutes or more of rapid boiling for jam to be cooked. Test by either the spoon or saucer method (see Apple Jelly). When the jam is done, skim it and put it into sterilized jars. Paraffin at once. When cool, label and store.

JAM AND JELLY WITH COMMERCIAL PECTIN

Our mothers and grandmothers made jelly without the aid of commercial pectin. They made good jelly, too; but that is no argument against the use of commercial pectin.

Pectin may be had in two forms, powder or liquid. All commercial pectins have a book of directions with them. The directions are carefully prepared for your benefit. Do exactly as directed. Do not experiment. Do not be a prima donna. If you don't like to follow directions, buy your jam or jelly at the market. When the directions say to boil at full rolling boil for 30 seconds, they mean just that and nothing else.

There is a great deal of satisfaction in having a well-stocked larder, particularly if you have made most of the things yourself.

A FEW RELISHES

One of the best reasons for making relishes is the enchanting smell which fills the house for at least one day.

Making relishes is not hard, but it takes up a great deal of time. The preparation time is long, and the cooking time is unusually long. But the results are more than worth the time and effort involved.

CHILI SAUCE

For 5 pints you will need:

28 ripe medium tomatoes, peeled and chopped to make 8 cups	1 green sweet pepper, chopped
2 pounds white onions, finely chopped or ground	2 cups sugar
1 red sweet pepper, chopped	3 tablespoons salt
	¼ teaspoon cayenne pepper
	3 cups cider vinegar

To be put in a bag:

1 tablespoon whole cloves	3 cinnamon sticks or 5 tablespoons powdered cinnamon
1 tablespoon mustard seed	

M E T H O D: Wash and chop the tomatoes. After they have been chopped, allow them to drain in a colander, keeping the liquid.

Peel the onions. Remove the white pith and seeds from the peppers. Grind the onions and the peppers.

Measure 8 cups of tomatoes into a large kettle. If there isn't a full 8 cups, make up the balance with the juice from the draining. Add the onion, peppers, sugar, salt, and cayenne.

Start over low heat, stirring until the sugar is dissolved. Cook for 1 hour. Add the vinegar and the bag with the spices.

C A U T I O N: Use cinnamon sticks if possible. Powdered cinnamon will make a dark chili sauce.

Continue the cooking, stirring often, until the mixture becomes thick.

When done, put the chili sauce in hot sterilized jars and seal immediately.

TOMATO CATSUP

For 4 pints you will need:

10 pounds ripe tomatoes	2 tablespoons paprika
3 pounds onions	¼ teaspoon cayenne pepper
3 red sweet peppers	¼ teaspoon black pepper
1 cup cider vinegar	1 teaspoon ground mustard
1 cup sugar	3 tablespoons salt

2 tablespoons flour

To be put in a bag:

1 teaspoon whole allspice	3 cinnamon sticks or 3 table-
1 teaspoon whole cloves	spoons powdered cinnamon

1 teaspoon celery seed

M E T H O D: Wash and chop the onions, tomatoes, and peppers. Combine the vegetables and cook until tender. Put the vegetables through a sieve. Use the pulp and the liquid. Place in a large open kettle and boil until the pulp begins to thicken. Drain off about ¼ cup of liquid.

Add the sugar, vinegar, paprika, red and black pepper, and the ground mustard. Add the other spices in a bag.

C A U T I O N: Use cinnamon sticks if possible, as the powdered cinnamon will darken the catsup.

Continue cooking, stirring often, until quite thick.

Make a paste of the 2 tablespoons of flour and the ¼ cup of liquid. Add this paste to the cooking catsup and be sure to mix well. Continue to cook for 10 minutes to cook the flour, which will act as a binder.

When done, fill sterilized jars and seal. It is best to have the jars hot. Store in a cool place.

PICCALILLI

This is an overnight job. If you prefer, prepare the vegetables in the morning and allow them to stand all day, then do the cooking at night.

For 4 pints you will need:

5 pounds solid green tomatoes	½ cup salt
2 green sweet peppers	4 cups cider vinegar
1 red sweet pepper	2 cups sugar
2 pounds onions, chopped	1 tablespoon horse-radish
¼ teaspoon cayenne pepper	

To be put in a bag:

1 tablespoon celery seed	2 tablespoons mustard seed
1 tablespoon whole cloves	

M E T H O D : Wash the tomatoes and peppers. Take out seeds and pith from the peppers and peel the onions. Put all the vegetables through a grinder, using the coarse blade, or chop fine. Put the prepared vegetables in a bowl and cover with the salt. Cover and let stand overnight. Drain in the morning.

When ready to cook, combine the vinegar, sugar, horse-radish, and pepper. Mix well and drop the spice bag in the liquid. Bring to a boil and add the drained vegetables.

Have hot sterilized jars ready.

After the drained vegetables have been added to the boiling liquid, heat to the boiling point but do not boil.

Pack in the hot jars and seal immediately.

CHAPTER XIX

HINTS FOR SMALL FAMILIES

COOKING FOR ONE

So many people say, "I'm not interested in cooking for myself." One easy answer to that problem is to invite people in for dinner quite often.

The buying problem for a person living alone is difficult. There is always more than one person needs. No one likes to waste food so what can be done about it?

A person living alone should take interest in his or her food. Be on the lookout for interesting recipes and vary your meals by trying new foods, not just any old makeshift but a good meal. Perhaps a few of these suggestions will be helpful.

First, meats. A single chop, either veal, lamb, or pork, can be purchased; so can a single slice of filet mignon.

Small chickens may also be bought. Now what would you do with a small chicken? You could have the butcher cut it in 4 sections. That would give 2 pieces of white or breast meat and 2 pieces of dark or leg meat. You could fry half of the chicken. Cold chicken is good. The other half you could stew with some celery and onion, make a thickened gravy, and have some boiled rice. Or the gravy is equally good over a baked potato.

If you did not eat all of the fried or stewed chicken, you could take the meat from the bone and make creamed chicken or chicken salad by using some celery.

If you bought a half-pound of ground meat you could make one hamburger patty with half of it and fry or broil it for 1 meal.

You could combine some bread crumbs with the other half, add a little chopped onion, make some meat balls, fry them in hot fat, add water or bouillon, and simmer slowly until done. Serve these with potato, boiled rice, or a portion of cooked noodles.

When living alone you need only cook as much rice, noodles, or spaghetti as you can consume.

You can buy a pound of stewing beef and have a stew for 1 dinner. For your next meal you can make yourself a small meat pie. All you will need to do is to make about ¼ of the recipe for biscuits and cover your baking dish with it.

If you like liver you can buy a single slice from the butcher and have it with bacon or with fried onions, whichever you prefer.

If you are fond of fish, you can buy a slice or a filet at the market and prepare it for yourself.

Lettuce keeps for several days. Most salad vegetables keep well in the refrigerator. You can always have a salad and vary it for several meals. Remember, a good dressing helps.

A can of peas may be used plain the first night with a little chopped fresh mint or even a little dried mint cooked in the liquid drained from the peas. You can make a hearty cream of pea soup by pressing the balance through a sieve and using a cup of cream or white sauce.

A can of string beans may be used plain, only adding seasoning and butter. The next time, to give them variety, mince a small onion and add to the balance of the beans and cook them slowly until the onion is tender.

You can save odd bits of vegetables until you have enough to make an individual casserole. Make ½ cup of white sauce, add about 4 tablespoons of cheese, stir until cheese melts, and pour over the vegetables for an appetizing dish.

Potatoes are no problem. If you are fond of potatoes, vary your program. Cook 2 or 3 at a time, either boiled or baked. Cold potatoes can be used in many ways—sliced and fried plain, or hashed brown, or mixed with a little onion and fried, or creamed.

Raw-fried potatoes are hard to beat in any man's language.

There are a lot of tricks to be done with a can of corn, either the cream style or the niblets. Gauge the contents of a can of corn in relation to your appetite. Use about ⅓ of a can as plain stewed corn.

Use ⅓ for a tasty corn pudding. Beat an egg. Add salt and pepper. Remember, you are seasoning for yourself. Add 2 tablespoons of bread crumbs or a half of a slice of bread crumbled. Mix with the corn and bake in a slow oven (300°) for about 30 minutes. Perhaps add some onion and celery salt. Try different seasonings.

Make corn oysters out of the remaining corn. It is very simple. Beat an egg. Mix 1 tablespoon of flour with the corn and add to the egg. Drop the mixture by tablespoonfuls into hot shallow fat and fry until golden brown.

With a can of tomatoes you can have stewed tomatoes and use the balance for a soup, or you can put the pulp through a sieve and have tomato paste for a small casserole. Rice, tomatoes, and onion baked slowly in the oven make a good dish.

There are so many things to do with eggs. Just plain bacon and eggs is a good meal any time.

A half pound of mushrooms will give you 2 meals. Pan-broil or sauté half the mushrooms and serve them on toast. Cream the other half. Stew the stems and peelings in 1 cup of water and use the liquid for a soup or stock.

Canned soups may be made to do double duty. One half can of condensed soup may be used as soup, the other half the next night as the liquid for a casserole dish.

A small flat can of salmon can be used for a salad with mayonnaise, or combined with an egg and a few bread crumbs and fried as salmon cakes.

Desserts are not quite so simple. If you care for pastry, you can make up some pastry dough and keep it in your refrigerator. You can make yourself an apple tart or a berry tart. You can also use the same type of pastry to cover a small meat pie.

Stewed fruits can do double duty as desserts and breakfast fruit.

When your oven is on, make some cup custards. One egg to 1 cup of milk, a little sugar, a few grains of salt, a little vanilla, and a pinch of nutmeg. Cup custards will keep for days in the refrigerator.

You owe it to yourself to have a variety of food, well served and thoroughly enjoyable.

COOKING FOR TWO

The main problem again is buying and variety. Good cooking for 2 requires careful thought and planning.

It is no fun to have a roast and then eat it for days and days. Plan to have a couple in for dinner the night you are having a roast. The second night eat cold roast beef or lamb or pork. On the third night, if you have cold roast beef, cut 2 fairly thick slices and put them in the broiler just long enough for them to be thoroughly heated. This is a nice variation from the cold-meat diet.

Cold lamb can be sliced and heated in 1 cup lamb gravy to which has been added 1 teaspoon of vinegar, ½ teaspoon of dry mustard, and 4 tablespoons of tart jelly. This is very good served on toast.

Cold pork may be diced, combined with diced celery and some bits of onion, and used as a salad.

Make an imitation chop suey with cold pork. Cut the pork into cubes. Slice 3 medium onions and use about 6 stalks of celery cut into ½-inch pieces. Cook this in a covered skillet with a little water for about 15 minutes. Season to taste, add pork gravy if there's any on hand, then the pork, and simmer in the skillet until the pork is hot. Serve on boiled rice.

Use cooked meat in hot pots and stews and casseroles. Grind cold meat, mix it with chopped parsley and chives, combine it with 1 cup of very thick white sauce, and have croquettes.

There is always hash, either canned or your own manufacture.

Many of the suggestions listed in Cooking for One may be used when catering for 2 people.

If you have leftover cooked vegetables they may be used in a casserole with a cream or cheese sauce, or they may be chopped, marinated, and used in a salad.

The main problem is not to waste the food you buy.

HOW TO HAVE A JOB AND COOK TOO

Are you living alone and hating restaurants or are there two of you—working and wishing you could eat at home more often? It is not simple to work all day and cook a good dinner at night. It can, however, be done if you are willing to plan ahead and devote at least Saturday afternoon or Sunday to your cooking problem. A good plan is to have your Sunday dinner Saturday night, which gives you a chance to entertain and leaves Sunday free.

A working person is interested in fairly quick meals after a day at a job. Here are some suggestions:

1. Have a week-end roast.

2. Frozen vegetables are all ready for the pot and take no time to prepare.

3. Cook tomorrow night's dinner while you are relaxed and enjoying tonight's fare.

Suppose you have a roast of lamb, either a leg or a rolled shoulder or a part of the forequarter. You will enjoy it as a hot roast the first day. It will be palatable as cold sliced meat for the second dinner. Slices warmed in gravy and served on toast or over boiled rice will be good the third day.

There is probably enough lamb left to make a stew. Cube the meat, add small onions or onions cut in chunks, a few carrots, some small turnips if you like them, and a small can of tomatoes. Add 2 cups of water or bouillon. While you are having dinner, put the stew over to simmer. Stews seem to taste better the second day anyhow. By the time you have finished dinner and have washed the dishes, the stew will be ready to transfer to a bowl to cool before putting it away in the refrigerator.

The next night, peel and quarter some potatoes, add them to the stew, and cook until the potatoes are tender. If the gravy is pale, add a little Kitchen Bouquet. Make a paste of 2 tablespoons of flour and some water. Add this paste to the stew for thickening unless you prefer thin gravy.

Perhaps there will be some stew left over. If there is, save it. Skip a night. Have a chop or a piece of steak or something quick, perhaps an omelet and some grilled bacon. Or you might like some fried sausage with fried apple slices or grilled or fried tomatoes.

For the next evening's dinner take the remainder of the stew. Add to it any suitable vegetables that may be left—peas, carrots, or celery. Put the stew in a casserole, cover it with some baking powder biscuit dough, and you will have a nice hot meat pie.

When fresh vegetables are available and you have the time, cook enough to last several meals. Have them plain boiled for the first meal. Peas and carrots may be combined and creamed later. Cooked potatoes can be fried, hashed brown, or creamed.

Salad material will keep several days. You can use cooked vegetables for salads. There is a definite loss of vitamin content in reheating cooked vegetables. Keep fresh tomatoes and a green pepper with your salad greens.

Remember that a grilled half of a grapefruit makes a good dessert if it has been covered with honey or sugar. A little sherry in a grapefruit before it is placed under the broiler is a more than palatable addition.

A busy woman can make tomorrow's dessert tonight. If you like and use prepared gelatins, they can be made right after dinner for the next night. Gelatin may be whipped and combined with egg whites or fresh fruit. Applesauce folded into whipped lime jelly is delicious.

Creamed chipped beef served with a baked potato and a green vegetable makes a good meal.

A potato will bake in an hour in a 400° oven. If you plan to have baked potatoes tomorrow night, wash them tonight. When you get home, turn the oven on and put the potatoes in. They can be cooking while you do some of your chores.

Creamed chipped beef doesn't take very long to fix. Frizzle the beef in a skillet with 2 tablespoons of butter. When the beef is frizzled, sprinkle about 2 tablespoons of flour over the beef and butter and mix well. Then add 2 cups of milk, adding slowly and stirring constantly until the flour and butter have combined with the milk. It doesn't take more than 15 minutes to prepare the frizzled beef. Plan it so the creamed beef will be ready when the potatoes are to be taken from the oven.

Canned soups are a boon to the cook who works all day. Canned tomato and canned mushroom soup can do double duty. A can of mushroom soup, a small package of potato chips, and a small can of tuna fish combined and baked as a casserole dish is surprisingly good. It is better for the addition of some onion juice and 1 or 2 tablespoons of chopped parsley.

A can of tomato soup, 2 cups of cooked rice, and a small can of shrimp baked for ½ hour in a casserole is a good meal when served with a vegetable and a salad.

Boil rice while you dine. Drain it and have it ready for the next night's casserole. If you want to have a stew tomorrow night, cook it while you prepare tonight's dinner, and it will be an effortless meal the next evening.

Cooked vegetables may be reheated most satisfactorily in the top of a double boiler.

If you plan to have creamed eggs and mushrooms on toast, hard-cook your eggs tonight. You will find it much more satisfying than to take the time to hard cook them the night you want to use them.

You can have fun planning meals for a week at a time and doing the necessary shopping all at one time.

If you like fish, do not buy it until the day you intend to use it unless you have adequate means of storing frozen foods, or frozen fish may be bought and used at once. It is very good.

If you like hamburger steak, buy enough chopped meat for two meals. Use half of the meat as hamburger steak. Store the balance in the refrigerator in the freezing tray or ice compartment. Boil some rice or spaghetti and drain it.

The next night you can fry the remaining meat with some sliced onion, season it well, combine it with the cooked rice or spaghetti, add a small can of tomato paste, and bake it in the oven for about ½ hour.

If you are having fish one night and you are going to have some left over, boil and wash some potatoes. The next night combine the fish and mashed potatoes, shape into cakes, and fry until golden brown. Stewed tomatoes are good with fish cakes.

If you don't have to begin from scratch every night, your cooking problem after a day's work will not seem so difficult. The only way to make it simple is to prepare some of tomorrow's menu tonight.

Of course, it is still a lot of work; but it is work that you can do while you are waiting for your dinner to cook, and the cooking can be done while you dine. It's worth a try.

CHAPTER XX

POST-GRADUATE RECIPES

SOUFFLES

M A N Y cooks fear a soufflé. But it is not a difficult dish to make. It will puff up nicely, and it will fall just as fast. It must be served when taken from the oven. The easiest way to make a good soufflé is to start with a thick white sauce.

CHEESE SOUFFLÉ

PREPARATION TIME: about 30 minutes

COOKING TIME: about 30 minutes

For 4 servings you will need:

1 cup of thick white sauce	1 teaspoon Worcestershire sauce
1 cup grated cheese	Pepper
½ teaspoon salt	3 eggs, separated

METHOD: Add the seasoning to the white sauce. Beat the egg yolks, add to the white sauce, add the grated cheese, and cook gently, stirring until the cheese has melted and the egg yolks are well incorporated and set. Remove from the heat and cool. Fold in the stiffly beaten egg whites. Pour the mixture into a 6–9-inch baking dish or in individual baking dishes. Place the dishes or dish in a pan of hot water and bake in a moderate oven (375°) until the center is firm. Serve at once or the soufflé will fall; and when a soufflé falls it is a "flop."

CORN SOUFFLÉ

Substitute 1 cup of corn pulp for the cheese in the Cheese Soufflé recipe.

FISH SOUFFLÉ

Substitute 1 cup of flaked fish for the cheese in the Cheese Soufflé recipe.

MEAT AND VEGETABLE SOUFFLÉS

Substitute 1 cup of minced meat or 1 cup of vegetable pulp for the cheese in the Cheese Soufflé recipe.

FRUIT SOUFFLÉS

A soufflé can serve as a dessert as well as an entree. Fruit soufflés are delicious and simple to make. They too must be served at once, or great is the fall.

Either fresh or canned fruit may be used for a soufflé. All fruit should be well drained and rubbed through a sieve. You want fruit pulp and not liquid. Save the liquid for a gelatin dessert. If there is still some liquid in the pulp after pressing through a sieve, drain the pulp in a cheesecloth to be rid of the juice. Since some fruits take more sugar than others, sweeten to taste.

PREPARATION TIME: about 30 minutes

COOKING TIME: 20–30 minutes

For 4 servings you will need:

1 cup of fruit pulp	3 egg whites
Sugar	Pinch salt

METHOD: Drain the fruit. Rub through a sieve and drain again if necessary. Sweeten to taste and add a pinch of salt. Put the fruit pulp in the top of a double boiler and heat until it is hot. While the fruit is heating, beat the egg whites until stiff. When the pulp is hot, fold in the egg whites. Fill a 6–9-inch baking dish with the combined fruit and egg white. Place the baking dish in a pan of hot water and bake in a moderate oven (375°) until the

egg white is set and the mixture firm. It will take 20–30 minutes.
Serve with whipped cream or a custard sauce.

VANILLA SOUFFLÉ

PREPARATION TIME: about 30 minutes

COOKING TIME: 20–30 minutes
For 4 servings you will need:

1 cup milk	⅓ cup sugar
4 tablespoons flour	3 eggs, separated
2 tablespoons butter	½ teaspoon vanilla

METHOD: Make a white sauce of the milk, flour, and butter. Add the sugar and stir until it is melted. Beat the egg yolks well and add to the white sauce. Keep stirring. Add the vanilla and remove the white sauce from the heat. Beat the egg whites until they are stiff and fold into the sauce mixture. Put the mixture in a 6–9-inch baking dish. Place the baking dish in a pan of hot water and bake in a moderate oven (375°) until the egg white is set—20–30 minutes.

Serve with cream, a lemon sauce, or plain.

BISQUES

A bisque is a rich thick soup, made by combining 2 separate liquids at the end of the cooking periods. One liquid contains the solid or meat ingredients, the other the milk or cream and flour.

BASIC RECIPE FOR BISQUE

PREPARATION AND COOKING TIME: about 1 hour

For 5–6 cups of soup you will need:
1 cup ground cooked chicken, fish, clams, lobster, or shrimp

1st Mixture	*2nd Mixture*
3 cups stock	2 tablespoons flour
2 tablespoons grated onion	2 cups milk or cream
Salt and pepper	2 tablespoons butter

M E T H O D: Put the meat, stock, and grated onion in a saucepan and simmer gently. While this is cooking, put the butter in the top of a double boiler. Mix the flour and milk in a glass jar by putting in ½ cup of the milk, adding the flour, then adding the balance of the milk and shaking until the milk and flour are completely blended. Pour the milk and flour mixture into the top of the double boiler and cook until the mixture thickens, about 20 minutes.

The success of bisque depends upon the almost equal temperature of the 2 liquids. When the flour mixture is done, combine the 2 liquids and add, if you like:

2 tablespoons sherry	1 tablespoon chopped chives
1 tablespoon chopped parsley	Some freshly ground pepper

Serve at once.

If you use a tureen you may pour the 2 liquids directly into the tureen, which has been preheated with hot water.

Bisque made in this way does not curdle or separate.

TOMATO BISQUE

Tomato bisque may be made by following the basic recipe, substituting 2 cups of strained tomatoes for the meat. Add a piece of bay leaf, 3 peppercorns, and 1 teaspoon of celery salt to the tomato and stock mixture and simmer for 30 minutes. Before combining the tomato mixture with the milk, add a pinch of baking soda. Strain the tomato mixture into the milk mixture. Serve at once after combining.

PARTY DESSERTS

MERINGUE SHORTCAKE

This is a dessert to remember and make for your grandchildren.

Prepare the meringue as instructed on p. 307, but use 4 egg whites. Put it into cake pans which have been lined with brown paper, spreading lightly with a spatula. The layers need not be too thick, but thick enough to stand up after baking.

You should have 3 or 4 layers.

Bake them in a slow oven (250°) for 45–60 minutes. Cool. Since they are very fragile, do not remove them from baking pan until you are ready to assemble the ingredients.

Prepare and sugar strawberries, raspberries, or sliced peaches. Allow the fruit to stand at room temperature for about an hour before putting in the refrigerator.

Place a layer of meringue on a serving plate. Cover the layer with prepared fruit, then cover the fruit with custard or whipped cream. Add the next layer and cover with fruit and sauce. Do this until the layers have been used. Cover the top layer with the balance of the fruit and the remaining custard or cream. Place in the refrigerator until ready to serve. Cut in wedges. This is a rich dessert.

CUSTARD SAUCE

Custard sauce must be cooked carefully. It is often called "boiled custard," but that is a misnomer. It should never boil. It must be cooked in a double boiler for best results.

2 cups rich milk	3 tablespoons sugar
3 egg yolks	Pinch salt

1 teaspoon vanilla, sherry, rum, or ¼ teaspoon grated lemon rind

METHOD: Scald the milk. While the milk is heating, beat the egg yolks lightly, then add the salt and sugar. Pour the hot milk over the yolk mixture. Stir well. Put the mixture in the top of a double boiler and cook over hot water until it begins to thicken. It won't be as thick as a white sauce, but it mustn't be watery. The mixture should coat the spoon.

TO COAT A SPOON means that the liquid has reached a consistency thick enough to adhere to the spoon in a glaze instead of running off and leaving the spoon clear when the contents are poured back into the saucepan.

Be careful not to overcook your custard sauce. When it has thickened, add the flavoring. If it is at all lumpy, strain. If it is smooth, straining is not necessary. Sprinkle the top of the custard with sugar to prevent crusting. Chill.

LEMON DESSERT

This and the Fruit Dessert which follows are good. Both may be made the day before, which is a godsend to a busy, harassed, or inexperienced cook. Both are light and both serve 10 or 12 people easily.

1 package lemon jelly
1½ cups hot water
½ cup sugar
Juice of 1½ lemons
Grated rind of 1 lemon

1 pint whipped cream or
    1 large can evaporated
    milk chilled in refrigerator for at least 24 hours
24 sweet crackers, any kind

M E T H O D: Put a medium bowl and a rotary egg beater in the refrigerator to chill. It will help when you whip the evaporated milk. Roll the crackers until they are fine crumbs. Dissolve the lemon jelly in the hot water. When dissolved, add the sugar, lemon juice, and grated lemon rind. Place in a large bowl and after allowing to cool, place in the refrigerator.

Do not let the gelatin mixture set. When it begins to be thick and syrupy and clings to the side of the bowl, remove it from the refrigerator and beat or whip it until it becomes light and frothy. It will fluff up and partially fill the large bowl.

Line your dish with the sweet cracker crumbs. The bottom should be well covered and some crumbs pushed up against the sides. Reserve about ½ cup of the crumbs for the top of the dessert.

Take the evaporated milk, chilled bowl, and beater from the

refrigerator. Open the can and pour the milk into the chilled bowl. Beat, not too fast, with the rotary beater. Keep at it. The milk will thicken to about the consistency of whipped cream. Fold the whipped milk into the jelly mixture. Pour your combined mixtures into an oblong baking dish, at least 8 by 12 inches. Smooth out, cover the top with the reserved half cup of crumbs, and put the dish in the refrigerator. It should chill for several hours. It is good to make it the night before it is to be used.

This dessert may be made with orange jelly, orange juice, and orange rind, adding the grated rind of 1 lemon for zip.

FRUIT DESSERT

    1 cup milk
    1 cup sugar
    Pinch salt
    1 egg, beaten
    1 teaspoon vanilla
    1 tablespoon plain gelatin
    ¼ cup cold water
    1 pint whipped cream or 1 can whipped evaporated milk
    1 cup drained crushed pineapple or 1 cup any sweetened drained
       fruit
1½ cups graham-cracker crumbs
    ⅓ cup powdered sugar
    3 tablespoons melted butter

If you use evaporated milk instead of whipping cream, the milk must be chilled for at least 24 hours. Chill the bowl and rotary beater you intend to use.

METHOD: Put the milk, sugar, salt, and egg in the top of a double boiler. Cook over hot water until the mixture coats the spoon. When thickened, add the vanilla.

Soften the gelatin in the ¼ cup of cold water. Heat over hot water until dissolved, add to the custard mixture, and allow the mixture to cool and thicken. Add the crushed fruit.

Whip your cream or your evaporated milk and fold into the first mixture. Line an 8 by 12 dish with the cracker crumbs. Save ¼ cup of crumbs to sprinkle over the top. If you have never used graham-cracker crumbs this way see Graham Cracker Crust for method and instructions.

Pour your custard-cream mixture into the crumb-lined dish, smooth with a spatula, sprinkle with the remaining crumbs, and place in the refrigerator until serving time.

Cut the dessert in squares or oblong pieces.

MAIN-COURSE DISHES FOR PARTIES

PARSLEY RICE

This dish is different, and very nice for a large party. The quantities given will serve from 15 to 20 people. It is a simple matter of arithmetic to double this recipe for 40 people or to cut it in half for a group of 8 or 10. It can be prepared in the morning and used any time later on when needed.

PREPARATION TIME: about an hour or longer if you are a slow worker

COOKING TIME: after combining, 50 to 60 minutes

5 quarts boiling salt water in a large kettle	½ teaspoon salt
5 teaspoons salt	2 cups milk
1 cup grated sharp cheese	1 cup minced or chopped parsley
2 cups rice	2 eggs, beaten
½ teaspoon celery salt	½ cup melted butter or margarine
¼ teaspoon pepper	
1 large onion, grated	

METHOD: Add the salt to the boiling water. Wash the rice and add it gradually to the boiling water and cook uncovered about 20 minutes until the rice is tender but not mushy. Drain the rice. Wash the parsley and shake it free of moisture, then chop or mince. It takes about 20 minutes to prepare a cupful. Grate the cheese. Melt the butter or margarine. Put the cheese in a large mixing bowl, add the milk, and mix well with the cheese. Add the beaten eggs and melted butter and mix well. Add the seasoning and the grated onion. Add the parsley and mix well. Combine the drained rice with the other mixture. Place the mixture in 2 greased casseroles (bacon drippings are good for this). Bake in a moderate oven (350°) for about 50 minutes. The mixture should be set and the top faintly browned.

MANITOBA STEW

This is another party dish, a 1-dish meal. It will serve about 15 people. It can be prepared and cooked in the morning and reheated at dinner or supper time. All stews taste better after they have had a chance to blend. Serve it in soup plates with a green salad and French bread rubbed with garlic and toasted.

PREPARATION TIME: about 90 minutes

COOKING TIME: about 2½ hours

1 large slice ham 2 inches thick	18 small new potatoes, scraped
	2 pounds peas, shelled
2 pounds cold roast lamb	18 small white onions
12 cups water	1 pound small carrots, sliced
4 vegetable bouillon cubes	½ teaspoon salt
1 pound string beans	½ teaspoon pepper
1 pound wax beans	2 tablespoons flour

METHOD: Cube the ham and cold lamb. Put them in a large kettle, cover with the water, and add the salt and pepper. Bring to a boil slowly. When the simmering stage has been reached, add the bouillon cubes and stir until cubes have melted. Cover the kettle and simmer for about an hour.

At the end of the hour of simmering, add the beans and cook for 30 minutes. Add the potatoes, onions, carrots, and peas in the order named and simmer for another 45 minutes.

It may be necessary to add more water. If you do, have the water hot. The stew should be rather thick. It is best not to add water unless it seems to be boiling dry. If the stew seems too thin, make a paste of the two tablespoons of flour with some water and add to the stew to bind it. Cook another 5 minutes if it is necessary to add the flour for thickening.

INDEX

INDEX

A CATALOG OF SELECTED
DOVER BOOKS
IN ALL FIELDS OF INTEREST

A CATALOG OF SELECTED DOVER
BOOKS IN ALL FIELDS OF INTEREST

DRAWINGS OF REMBRANDT, edited by Seymour Slive. Updated Lippmann, Hofstede de Groot edition, with definitive scholarly apparatus. All portraits, biblical sketches, landscapes, nudes. Oriental figures, classical studies, together with selection of work by followers. 550 illustrations. Total of 630pp. 9⅛ × 12¼.
21485-0, 21486-9 Pa., Two-vol. set $25.00

GHOST AND HORROR STORIES OF AMBROSE BIERCE, Ambrose Bierce. 24 tales vividly imagined, strangely prophetic, and decades ahead of their time in technical skill: "The Damned Thing," "An Inhabitant of Carcosa," "The Eyes of the Panther," "Moxon's Master," and 20 more. 199pp. 5⅜ × 8½. 20767-6 Pa. $3.95

ETHICAL WRITINGS OF MAIMONIDES, Maimonides. Most significant ethical works of great medieval sage, newly translated for utmost precision, readability. Laws Concerning Character Traits, Eight Chapters, more. 192pp. 5⅜ × 8½.
24522-5 Pa. $4.50

THE EXPLORATION OF THE COLORADO RIVER AND ITS CANYONS, J. W. Powell. Full text of Powell's 1,000-mile expedition down the fabled Colorado in 1869. Superb account of terrain, geology, vegetation, Indians, famine, mutiny, treacherous rapids, mighty canyons, during exploration of last unknown part of continental U.S. 400pp. 5⅜ × 8½. 20094-9 Pa. $6.95

HISTORY OF PHILOSOPHY, Julián Marías. Clearest one-volume history on the market. Every major philosopher and dozens of others, to Existentialism and later. 505pp. 5⅜ × 8½. 21739-6 Pa. $8.50

ALL ABOUT LIGHTNING, Martin A. Uman. Highly readable non-technical survey of nature and causes of lightning, thunderstorms, ball lightning, St. Elmo's Fire, much more. Illustrated. 192pp. 5⅜ × 8½. 25237-X Pa. $5.95

SAILING ALONE AROUND THE WORLD, Captain Joshua Slocum. First man to sail around the world, alone, in small boat. One of great feats of seamanship told in delightful manner. 67 illustrations. 294pp. 5⅜ × 8½. 20326-3 Pa. $4.50

LETTERS AND NOTES ON THE MANNERS, CUSTOMS AND CONDITIONS OF THE NORTH AMERICAN INDIANS, George Catlin. Classic account of life among Plains Indians: ceremonies, hunt, warfare, etc. 312 plates. 572pp. of text. 6⅛ × 9¼. 22118-0, 22119-9 Pa. Two-vol. set $15.90

ALASKA: The Harriman Expedition, 1899, John Burroughs, John Muir, et al. Informative, engrossing accounts of two-month, 9,000-mile expedition. Native peoples, wildlife, forests, geography, salmon industry, glaciers, more. Profusely illustrated. 240 black-and-white line drawings. 124 black-and-white photographs. 3 maps. Index. 576pp. 5⅜ × 8½. 25109-8 Pa. $11.95

THE BOOK OF BEASTS: Being a Translation from a Latin Bestiary of the Twelfth Century, T. H. White. Wonderful catalog real and fanciful beasts: manticore, griffin, phoenix, amphivius, jaculus, many more. White's witty erudite commentary on scientific, historical aspects. Fascinating glimpse of medieval mind. Illustrated. 296pp. 5⅜ × 8¼. (Available in U.S. only) 24609-4 Pa. $5.95

FRANK LLOYD WRIGHT: ARCHITECTURE AND NATURE With 160 Illustrations, Donald Hoffmann. Profusely illustrated study of influence of nature—especially prairie—on Wright's designs for Fallingwater, Robie House, Guggenheim Museum, other masterpieces. 96pp. 9¼ × 10¾. 25098-9 Pa. $7.95

FRANK LLOYD WRIGHT'S FALLINGWATER, Donald Hoffmann. Wright's famous waterfall house: planning and construction of organic idea. History of site, owners, Wright's personal involvement. Photographs of various stages of building. Preface by Edgar Kaufmann, Jr. 100 illustrations. 112pp. 9¼ × 10. 23671-4 Pa. $7.95

YEARS WITH FRANK LLOYD WRIGHT: Apprentice to Genius, Edgar Tafel. Insightful memoir by a former apprentice presents a revealing portrait of Wright the man, the inspired teacher, the greatest American architect. 372 black-and-white illustrations. Preface. Index. vi + 228pp. 8¼ × 11. 24801-1 Pa. $9.95

THE STORY OF KING ARTHUR AND HIS KNIGHTS, Howard Pyle. Enchanting version of King Arthur fable has delighted generations with imaginative narratives of exciting adventures and unforgettable illustrations by the author. 41 illustrations. xviii + 313pp. 6⅛ × 9¼. 21445-1 Pa. $5.95

THE GODS OF THE EGYPTIANS, E. A. Wallis Budge. Thorough coverage of numerous gods of ancient Egypt by foremost Egyptologist. Information on evolution of cults, rites and gods; the cult of Osiris; the Book of the Dead and its rites; the sacred animals and birds; Heaven and Hell; and more. 956pp. 6⅛ × 9¼. 22055-9, 22056-7 Pa., Two-vol. set $20.00

A THEOLOGICO-POLITICAL TREATISE, Benedict Spinoza. Also contains unfinished *Political Treatise*. Great classic on religious liberty, theory of government on common consent. R. Elwes translation. Total of 421pp. 5⅜ × 8½. 20249-6 Pa. $6.95

INCIDENTS OF TRAVEL IN CENTRAL AMERICA, CHIAPAS, AND YUCATAN, John L. Stephens. Almost single-handed discovery of Maya culture; exploration of ruined cities, monuments, temples; customs of Indians. 115 drawings. 892pp. 5⅜ × 8½. 22404-X, 22405-8 Pa., Two-vol. set $15.90

LOS CAPRICHOS, Francisco Goya. 80 plates of wild, grotesque monsters and caricatures. Prado manuscript included. 183pp. 6⅜ × 9⅜. 22384-1 Pa. $4.95

AUTOBIOGRAPHY: The Story of My Experiments with Truth, Mohandas K. Gandhi. Not hagiography, but Gandhi in his own words. Boyhood, legal studies, purification, the growth of the Satyagraha (nonviolent protest) movement. Critical, inspiring work of the man who freed India. 480pp. 5⅜ × 8½. (Available in U.S. only) 24593-4 Pa. $6.95

ILLUSTRATED DICTIONARY OF HISTORIC ARCHITECTURE, edited by Cyril M. Harris. Extraordinary compendium of clear, concise definitions for over 5,000 important architectural terms complemented by over 2,000 line drawings. Covers full spectrum of architecture from ancient ruins to 20th-century Modernism. Preface. 592pp. 7½ × 9⅝. 24444-X Pa. $14.95

THE NIGHT BEFORE CHRISTMAS, Clement Moore. Full text, and woodcuts from original 1848 book. Also critical, historical material. 19 illustrations. 40pp. 4⅝ × 6. 22797-9 Pa. $2.25

THE LESSON OF JAPANESE ARCHITECTURE: 165 Photographs, Jiro Harada. Memorable gallery of 165 photographs taken in the 1930's of exquisite Japanese homes of the well-to-do and historic buildings. 13 line diagrams. 192pp. 8⅜ × 11¼. 24778-3 Pa. $8.95

THE AUTOBIOGRAPHY OF CHARLES DARWIN AND SELECTED LETTERS, edited by Francis Darwin. The fascinating life of eccentric genius composed of an intimate memoir by Darwin (intended for his children); commentary by his son, Francis; hundreds of fragments from notebooks, journals, papers; and letters to and from Lyell, Hooker, Huxley, Wallace and Henslow. xi + 365pp. 5⅜ × 8. 20479-0 Pa. $5.95

WONDERS OF THE SKY: Observing Rainbows, Comets, Eclipses, the Stars and Other Phenomena, Fred Schaaf. Charming, easy-to-read poetic guide to all manner of celestial events visible to the naked eye. Mock suns, glories, Belt of Venus, more. Illustrated. 299pp. 5¼ × 8¼. 24402-4 Pa. $7.95

BURNHAM'S CELESTIAL HANDBOOK, Robert Burnham, Jr. Thorough guide to the stars beyond our solar system. Exhaustive treatment. Alphabetical by constellation: Andromeda to Cetus in Vol. 1; Chamaeleon to Orion in Vol. 2; and Pavo to Vulpecula in Vol. 3. Hundreds of illustrations. Index in Vol. 3. 2,000pp. 6⅛ × 9¼. 23567-X, 23568-8, 23673-0 Pa., Three-vol. set $36.85

STAR NAMES: Their Lore and Meaning, Richard Hinckley Allen. Fascinating history of names various cultures have given to constellations and literary and folkloristic uses that have been made of stars. Indexes to subjects. Arabic and Greek names. Biblical references. Bibliography. 563pp. 5⅜ × 8½. 21079-0 Pa. $7.95

THIRTY YEARS THAT SHOOK PHYSICS: The Story of Quantum Theory, George Gamow. Lucid, accessible introduction to influential theory of energy and matter. Careful explanations of Dirac's anti-particles, Bohr's model of the atom, much more. 12 plates. Numerous drawings. 240pp. 5⅜ × 8½. 24895-X Pa. $4.95

CHINESE DOMESTIC FURNITURE IN PHOTOGRAPHS AND MEASURED DRAWINGS, Gustav Ecke. A rare volume, now affordably priced for antique collectors, furniture buffs and art historians. Detailed review of styles ranging from early Shang to late Ming. Unabridged republication. 161 black-and-white drawings, photos. Total of 224pp. 8⅜ × 11¼. (Available in U.S. only) 25171-3 Pa. $12.95

VINCENT VAN GOGH: A Biography, Julius Meier-Graefe. Dynamic, penetrating study of artist's life, relationship with brother, Theo, painting techniques, travels, more. Readable, engrossing. 160pp. 5⅜ × 8½. (Available in U.S. only) 25253-1 Pa. $3.95

ILLUSTRATED GUIDE TO SHAKER FURNITURE, Robert Meader. All furniture and appurtenances, with much on unknown local styles. 235 photos. 146pp. 9 × 12. 22819-3 Pa. $7.95

WHALE SHIPS AND WHALING: A Pictorial Survey, George Francis Dow. Over 200 vintage engravings, drawings, photographs of barks, brigs, cutters, other vessels. Also harpoons, lances, whaling guns, many other artifacts. Comprehensive text by foremost authority. 207 black-and-white illustrations. 288pp. 6 × 9. 24808-9 Pa. $8.95

THE BERTRAMS, Anthony Trollope. Powerful portrayal of blind self-will and thwarted ambition includes one of Trollope's most heartrending love stories. 497pp. 5⅜ × 8½. 25119-5 Pa. $8.95

ADVENTURES WITH A HAND LENS, Richard Headstrom. Clearly written guide to observing and studying flowers and grasses, fish scales, moth and insect wings, egg cases, buds, feathers, seeds, leaf scars, moss, molds, ferns, common crystals, etc.—all with an ordinary, inexpensive magnifying glass. 209 exact line drawings aid in your discoveries. 220pp. 5⅜ × 8½. 23330-8 Pa. $3.95

RODIN ON ART AND ARTISTS, Auguste Rodin. Great sculptor's candid, wide-ranging comments on meaning of art; great artists; relation of sculpture to poetry, painting, music; philosophy of life, more. 76 superb black-and-white illustrations of Rodin's sculpture, drawings and prints. 119pp. 8⅜ × 11¼. 24487-3 Pa. $6.95

FIFTY CLASSIC FRENCH FILMS, 1912-1982: A Pictorial Record, Anthony Slide. Memorable stills from Grand Illusion, Beauty and the Beast, Hiroshima, Mon Amour, many more. Credits, plot synopses, reviews, etc. 160pp. 8¼ × 11. 25256-6 Pa. $11.95

THE PRINCIPLES OF PSYCHOLOGY, William James. Famous long course complete, unabridged. Stream of thought, time perception, memory, experimental methods; great work decades ahead of its time. 94 figures. 1,391pp. 5⅜ × 8½. 20381-6, 20382-4 Pa., Two-vol. set $19.90

BODIES IN A BOOKSHOP, R. T. Campbell. Challenging mystery of blackmail and murder with ingenious plot and superbly drawn characters. In the best tradition of British suspense fiction. 192pp. 5⅜ × 8½. 24720-1 Pa. $3.95

CALLAS: PORTRAIT OF A PRIMA DONNA, George Jellinek. Renowned commentator on the musical scene chronicles incredible career and life of the most controversial, fascinating, influential operatic personality of our time. 64 black-and-white photographs. 416pp. 5⅜ × 8¼. 25047-4 Pa. $7.95

GEOMETRY, RELATIVITY AND THE FOURTH DIMENSION, Rudolph Rucker. Exposition of fourth dimension, concepts of relativity as Flatland characters continue adventures. Popular, easily followed yet accurate, profound. 141 illustrations. 133pp. 5⅜ × 8½. 23400-2 Pa. $3.50

HOUSEHOLD STORIES BY THE BROTHERS GRIMM, with pictures by Walter Crane. 53 classic stories—Rumpelstiltskin, Rapunzel, Hansel and Gretel, the Fisherman and his Wife, Snow White, Tom Thumb, Sleeping Beauty, Cinderella, and so much more—lavishly illustrated with original 19th century drawings. 114 illustrations. x + 269pp. 5⅜ × 8½. 21080-4 Pa. $4.50

SUNDIALS, Albert Waugh. Far and away the best, most thorough coverage of ideas, mathematics concerned, types, construction, adjusting anywhere. Over 100 illustrations. 230pp. 5⅜ × 8½. 22947-5 Pa. $4.00

PICTURE HISTORY OF THE NORMANDIE: With 190 Illustrations, Frank O. Braynard. Full story of legendary French ocean liner: Art Deco interiors, design innovations, furnishings, celebrities, maiden voyage, tragic fire, much more. Extensive text. 144pp. 8⅞ × 11¾. 25257-4 Pa. $9.95

THE FIRST AMERICAN COOKBOOK: A Facsimile of "American Cookery," 1796, Amelia Simmons. Facsimile of the first American-written cookbook published in the United States contains authentic recipes for colonial favorites—pumpkin pudding, winter squash pudding, spruce beer, Indian slapjacks, and more. Introductory Essay and Glossary of colonial cooking terms. 80pp. 5⅜ × 8½. 24710-4 Pa. $3.50

101 PUZZLES IN THOUGHT AND LOGIC, C. R. Wylie, Jr. Solve murders and robberies, find out which fishermen are liars, how a blind man could possibly identify a color—purely by your own reasoning! 107pp. 5⅜ × 8½. 20367-0 Pa. $2.00

THE BOOK OF WORLD-FAMOUS MUSIC—CLASSICAL, POPULAR AND FOLK, James J. Fuld. Revised and enlarged republication of landmark work in musico-bibliography. Full information about nearly 1,000 songs and compositions including first lines of music and lyrics. New supplement. Index. 800pp. 5⅜ × 8¼. 24857-7 Pa. $14.95

ANTHROPOLOGY AND MODERN LIFE, Franz Boas. Great anthropologist's classic treatise on race and culture. Introduction by Ruth Bunzel. Only inexpensive paperback edition. 255pp. 5⅜ × 8½. 25245-0 Pa. $5.95

THE TALE OF PETER RABBIT, Beatrix Potter. The inimitable Peter's terrifying adventure in Mr. McGregor's garden, with all 27 wonderful, full-color Potter illustrations. 55pp. 4¼ × 5½. (Available in U.S. only) 22827-4 Pa. $1.75

THREE PROPHETIC SCIENCE FICTION NOVELS, H. G. Wells. *When the Sleeper Wakes, A Story of the Days to Come* and *The Time Machine* (full version). 335pp. 5⅜ × 8½. (Available in U.S. only) 20605-X Pa. $5.95

APICIUS COOKERY AND DINING IN IMPERIAL ROME, edited and translated by Joseph Dommers Vehling. Oldest known cookbook in existence offers readers a clear picture of what foods Romans ate, how they prepared them, etc. 49 illustrations. 301pp. 6⅛ × 9¼. 23563-7 Pa. $6.00

SHAKESPEARE LEXICON AND QUOTATION DICTIONARY, Alexander Schmidt. Full definitions, locations, shades of meaning of every word in plays and poems. More than 50,000 exact quotations. 1,485pp. 6½ × 9¼. 22726-X, 22727-8 Pa., Two-vol. set $27.90

THE WORLD'S GREAT SPEECHES, edited by Lewis Copeland and Lawrence W. Lamm. Vast collection of 278 speeches from Greeks to 1970. Powerful and effective models; unique look at history. 842pp. 5⅜ × 8½. 20468-5 Pa. $10.95

AMERICAN CLIPPER SHIPS: 1833–1858, Octavius T. Howe & Frederick C. Matthews. Fully-illustrated, encyclopedic review of 352 clipper ships from the period of America's greatest maritime supremacy. Introduction. 109 halftones. 5 black-and-white line illustrations. Index. Total of 928pp. 5⅜ × 8½.
25115-2, 25116-0 Pa., Two-vol. set $17.90

TOWARDS A NEW ARCHITECTURE, Le Corbusier. Pioneering manifesto by great architect, near legendary founder of "International School." Technical and aesthetic theories, views on industry, economics, relation of form to function, "mass-production spirit," much more. Profusely illustrated. Unabridged translation of 13th French edition. Introduction by Frederick Etchells. 320pp. 6⅛ × 9¼. (Available in U.S. only)
25023-7 Pa. $8.95

THE BOOK OF KELLS, edited by Blanche Cirker. Inexpensive collection of 32 full-color, full-page plates from the greatest illuminated manuscript of the Middle Ages, painstakingly reproduced from rare facsimile edition. Publisher's Note. Captions. 32pp. 9⅜ × 12¼.
24345-1 Pa. $4.50

BEST SCIENCE FICTION STORIES OF H. G. WELLS, H. G. Wells. Full novel *The Invisible Man*, plus 17 short stories: "The Crystal Egg," "Aepyornis Island," "The Strange Orchid," etc. 303pp. 5⅜ × 8½. (Available in U.S. only)
21531-8 Pa. $4.95

AMERICAN SAILING SHIPS: Their Plans and History, Charles G. Davis. Photos, construction details of schooners, frigates, clippers, other sailcraft of 18th to early 20th centuries—plus entertaining discourse on design, rigging, nautical lore, much more. 137 black-and-white illustrations. 240pp. 6⅛ × 9¼.
24658-2 Pa. $5.95

ENTERTAINING MATHEMATICAL PUZZLES, Martin Gardner. Selection of author's favorite conundrums involving arithmetic, money, speed, etc., with lively commentary. Complete solutions. 112pp. 5⅜ × 8½.   25211-6 Pa. $2.95

THE WILL TO BELIEVE, HUMAN IMMORTALITY, William James. Two books bound together. Effect of irrational on logical, and arguments for human immortality. 402pp. 5⅜ × 8½.   20291-7 Pa. $7.50

THE HAUNTED MONASTERY and THE CHINESE MAZE MURDERS, Robert Van Gulik. 2 full novels by Van Gulik continue adventures of Judge Dee and his companions. An evil Taoist monastery, seemingly supernatural events; overgrown topiary maze that hides strange crimes. Set in 7th-century China. 27 illustrations. 328pp. 5⅜ × 8½.   23502-5 Pa. $5.00

CELEBRATED CASES OF JUDGE DEE (DEE GOONG AN), translated by Robert Van Gulik. Authentic 18th-century Chinese detective novel; Dee and associates solve three interlocked cases. Led to Van Gulik's own stories with same characters. Extensive introduction. 9 illustrations. 237pp. 5⅜ × 8½.
23337-5 Pa. $4.95

Prices subject to change without notice.

Available at your book dealer or write for free catalog to Dept. GI, Dover Publications, Inc., 31 East 2nd St., Mineola, N.Y. 11501. Dover publishes more than 175 books each year on science, elementary and advanced mathematics, biology, music, art, literary history, social sciences and other areas.